D1602575

Re-Envisioning Peacekeeping

BORDERLINES

For more books in the series, see p. vi.

Re-Envisioning Peacekeeping

The United Nations and the Mobilization of Ideology

FRANÇOIS DEBRIX

BORDERLINES, VOLUME 13

University of Minnesota Press

Minneapolis

London

Published by the University of Minnesota Press
111 Third Avenue South, Suite 290
Minneapolis, MN 55401-2520
http://www.upress.umn.edu

Library of Congress Cataloging-in-Publication Data

Debrix, François
    Re-envisioning peacekeeping : the United Nations and the
mobilization of ideology / François Debrix.
        p.   cm. — (Borderlines ; v. 13)
    Includes index.
    ISBN 0-8166-3236-7 (hc : acid-free paper). — ISBN 0-8166-3237-5
(pb. : acid-free paper)
        1. United Nations—Peacekeeping forces.   I. Title.   II. Series:
Borderlines (Minneapolis, Minn.) ; v. 13.
JZ6374.D43   1999
341.5'84—dc21   99-40977

Printed in the United States of America on acid-free paper

11 10 09 08 07 06 05 04 03 02 01 00 99   10 9 8 7 6 5 4 3 2 1

Contents

BORDERLINES

Acknowledgments

There are several people whom I would like to thank for their contribution and support. Cynthia Weber, Diane Rubenstein, Aparajita Sagar, and Michael Weinstein have offered me constant encouragement and invaluable suggestions since I began this project at Purdue University. I owe my greatest intellectual debts to their generosity, lucidity, and friendship. I am indebted to Tim Luke for his careful readings of most of the chapters before they came to form a book and for his path-breaking writing, which indirectly influenced my critical perspective on international relations, political theory, and culture.

I would also like to thank David Campbell and Michael Shapiro, the editors of the Borderlines series, and Carrie Mullen, who supported the project from the beginning and provided sage advice throughout the review process. My gratitude also goes to James Der Derian, whose review of the manuscript helped make the book theoretically and empirically stronger, and to Siba Grovogui and Rob Walker, who provided critical comments on individual chapters. An earlier, shorter version of chapter 2 appeared in *Alternatives: Social Transformation and Humane Governance* 24, no. 2 (1999). This book is dedicated to my wife and colleague, Clair Apodaca, for her loving support and cheerful intellectual inspiration over the years.

Abbreviations

DHA	Department of Humanitarian Affairs (United Nations)
IAEA	International Atomic Energy Agency
ICRC	International Committee of the Red Cross
IFOR	Interposition Force (NATO)
MDM	Médecins du Monde
MSF	Médecins sans Frontières
NPT	(Nuclear) Non-Proliferation Treaty
OCHA	Office for the Coordination of Humanitarian Affairs (United Nations)
UNAMIR	United Nations Assistance Mission for Rwanda
UNDP	United Nations Development Programme
UNHCR	(Office of the) United Nations High Commissioner for Refugees
UNICEF	United Nations Children's Fund
UNOSOM	United Nations Operation in Somalia
UNPROFOR	United Nations Protection Force (Bosnia)
UNREO	United Nations Rwanda Emergency Office
UNSCOM	United Nations Special Commission (on Iraq)
WHO	World Health Organization

Introduction:
Re-Envisioning the United Nations

In a recent volume entitled *International Territory: The United Nations, 1945–95*,[1] photographer Adam Bartos provides a collection of snapshots that he took inside the United Nations building in New York. Bartos's arresting pictures, juxtaposed to one of Christopher Hitchens's short essays, represent different rooms, architectural designs, and still-life forms that seek to convey the "spirit of the UN." The photos are a realist overview of empty rooms and inert objects that appear to be deprived of any signification. Through Bartos's photographic eye, the UN (as a modernist architectural and structural design) looks as if it had been frozen in time.

THE TERRITORY OF THE "FIRST UNIVERSAL SOCIAL CONTRACT"

What is the meaning of this frozen structure? What is the political and symbolic relevance of this so-called international territory, confined inside a stern mid-twentieth century architectural framework, which claims to be the place where the general will of humankind is represented? Three of Bartos's photographs give us an insight into the meaning, role, and importance of the UN today. The first picture is labeled "security desk, visitors' lobby" (figure 1).[2] It depicts the front desk of the information and security office in the UN building. Nobody is working at the desk. In fact, apart from the exuberant modernist pattern (circular and curved wood desk, green walls, light grey ceiling with sharp lamps lighting the entire room), the signs and

1

Figure 1. Security desk, visitors' lobby, United Nations. Photograph courtesy of Adam Bartos.

arrows attached to the desk are the only potential indicators of meaning. One sign suggests that tours need to go left. Information signs indicate that, if visitors need to ask any question, it is probably at this desk that they can address their queries—except that, of

Figure 2. Delegates' dining room, United Nations. Photograph courtesy of Adam Bartos.

course, nobody is physically present to assist them. Finally, next to a red "security" sign, one reads: "no meeting tickets available at this time." The place has obviously been deserted. "At this time," the UN is not functional. It is not possible to obtain information or even gain security. At another time, in another era perhaps, it may have been possible to get information or security, but not today.

The second image is a photographic still life from the delegates' dining room (figure 2).[3] The photo focuses on the geometric design of a wooden bookcase, which once again is contrasted to the green background of the wall. A few items have been placed on the book- case: a neatly folded newspaper, two empty glasses, and, finally, a dark blue hat with yellow lining. The hat is, I believe, the central ob- ject in the picture. It resembles a U.S. Air Force or an old Soviet Navy cap, except that, upon closer inspection, one notices that it has the light blue emblem of the UN on the front. The hat is lying flat on what appears to be a large yellow envelope. On top of the bookcase, there are also two empty ashtrays and a fresh, although already fading, pink rose. Finally, on the wall, there are two signs, one in French, the other in English (their meaning is exactly the same), which read: "United Nations not responsible for property deposited

Figure 3. Security Council, mural by Per Krogh, United Nations. Photograph courtesy of Adam Bartos.

here." Is the United Nations no longer responsible for what happens inside its building or for what its delegates do in it? Is the UN always already beyond responsibility, as if there were no such thing as a United Nations Organization that could be held accountable for or be legally bound by the activities of its officers and civil servants? This is perhaps nothing more than a simple legal disclaimer, protecting the UN from a lawsuit by one of its employees in case of loss or theft (after all, this is New York!), or is it?

The third arresting snapshot is a view of the Security Council, the alleged center of power at the UN, with a corner of the Per Krohg mural in the background (figure 3).[4] Norwegian artist Per Krohg designed the mural in the late 1940s as a way of symbolizing "the promise of future peace and individual freedom."[5] Although it mostly employs modern forms, the mural is reminiscent of Italian Renaissance frescoes, depicting multiple scenes of human struggle with life and death. In the center of the mural, life, freedom, and humanity are evoked. But Bartos's photo is not focused on the mural. It is, once again, in the corner of the picture. Rather, the empty, light blue chairs of the Security Council occupy the center stage. The chairs come in pairs. They are connected to each other by means of audio-links (for translation presumably), electric devices, and an ashtray. It is as if there were a complex web of interconnectedness between the chairs only. Regardless of whether anyone actually sits in them, the chairs are able to communicate with each other. They have a (still) life of their own. They are the only actors inside the UN Security Council.

Instead of approaching the UN from the perspective of normative representation,[6] Bartos's look at the UN is a matter of realist visual rendition. For Bartos, the foundation that is relevant to understand the UN and its policies today is the building itself, its empty rooms, its inert structural life, and its colorful objects. There is nothing more to this "system of objects" at the UN than the objects themselves. Bartos's photos introduce the viewer into the postmodern world of the UN, a world where the international organization is now dominated by objects and plays of appearances. Bartos's brutally formalist display meets postmodern civilization as Jean Baudrillard understands it, a civilization in which "everyday objects . . . proliferate, needs multiply, production speeds up the life-span of such objects, [and] yet we lack the vocabulary to name them all."[7] Bartos intimates that one is compelled to understand/experience today's (post)modernity as a "system of objects" rather than as an ideological system where objects and representations derive their meaning from the way they are used, symbolized, produced, or abjected by the thinking human subject, the modern self. For Bartos (as for Baudrillard), the formalism of objects now takes precedence over logocentrism, the rationalism of subjects. In the absence of an appropriate vocabulary or system of signification produced by man to make sense of objects, we can only look at them, their organization, forms, and appearances, without necessarily being able to inscribe a sure meaning onto them.

This is the (visual) perspective that Bartos applies to the UN. In a postmodern age (which conveniently corresponds to the post–cold war era of international relations discourses), the UN is best understood as a postmodern construct, as a structure without depth. There is nothing more to (Bartos's) United Nations than the objects themselves, the architectural eeriness of the building, and the proliferation of signs, symbols, arrows inside the edifice which are nonetheless devoid of meaning and direction.

Bartos's photographic depiction of the UN is a postapocalyptic scene, a testimony of what may happen after the catastrophe, when only the buildings remain and the objects take over. In the offices of the Secretariat General, the Security Council, the General Assembly, the Economic and Social Council, and the hundreds of corridors and hallways, the global policies representative of the "first universal social contract," as former UN civil servant Erskine Childers once put it,[8] are a ghostly presence. They may remain as "spirits" but these are not visible to the (hyper)realist photographer's eye. As a postmodern visual rendition, Bartos's display is more than a contemporary look at the UN. Through the formalism of the image, Bartos takes us back to what, originally, the UN always already was: "a *formal* arrangement transcending national boundaries that provides for the establishment of an institutional machinery to facilitate cooperation among members."[9] At its inception, the UN was nothing more than a framework, a *form* of international life that would have to be ideologically filled in order to obtain signification and a sense of purpose. Bartos's postmodern (visual) reading of the UN is an ironic revisiting of what the international organization, in its basic formalism, always already was: an empty form or framework that, as J. Martin Rochester suggests, would require "faith to be taken seriously."[10]

Postmodern times are ironic times. The post–cold war condition of the United Nations is an ironic context too. At a time when the UN, freed from cold war ideologies and state rivalries, is primed to take the lead and direct humankind toward peace and harmony, its basic (empty) formalism is revealed even more blatantly. At a time when peacekeeping is given yet another chance to fulfill the promise of collective security, its exercise becomes less assured than ever, and peacekeeping missions, far from "empowering the UN,"[11] leave the image of the international organization as an impotent peace and security enforcer. The more the UN tries, the less it achieves. Or, rather, the more it intervenes, the more it shows its formal emptiness. Following once again Bartos's visual intimation, I would suggest there is no subject position, no acting subjectivity, no (international) agency at the UN: beyond logocentrism, the UN is merely a system of objects. There is really no autonomous agent or actor behind the façade, behind the walls of the UN building. The post–cold war age of the UN and peacekeeping, an era of renewed hope as some have claimed, is a time of ruthless irony. It is a time when meaning and intent no longer matter since appearance and pretense (always already) prevail.

FILLING IN THE SPACE OF GLOBAL POLITICS

The ironic context of post–cold war international relations is one marked by absence rather than presence, and by desperate attempts at covering such an absence. Agency at the UN is apparently lacking, but this is not a new phenomenon. More importantly, in a postrealist landscape of international affairs (more thoroughly detailed in chapter 1), the crucial absence is the perceived lack of a coherent and cohesive landscape of international politics, solidified by a clear vision of the international system and by precisely defined theories. As former UN Secretary General Boutros Boutros-Ghali indicated, post–cold war international politics is a field of disruption, destruction, disillusion, and uncertainty. It is what some have started to call a new world disorder rather than a New World Order, the prospect of a "coming anarchy" rather than the promise of collective security.[12] The international environment of the 1990s in which the UN is suddenly resurrected is replete with "inaccessible leaders, unknown entities, shadowy chains of command, disowned soldiers, nonexistent discipline, [and an] uncontrolled proliferation of arms."[13] The visions of international anarchy during the cold war period (to which realist and neorealist discourses claimed to have found the response) have not completely disappeared. They simply have been remobilized, put to new and different uses. Similarly, the state is still a privileged and sovereign entity that must be protected from threats coming from outside.[14] But other dimensions of international life can now be considered too. Indeed, today's international threats are different. States no longer need to base their foreign policy attitudes on matters of security, defense, or territorial integrity. At least in the former "First World," threats coming from enemy states with antagonistic ideologies have been reduced. Sovereign states can now be free to engage in other international quests such as economic development and growth, democratic welfare and stability, population control, environmental protection, and human rights recognition. The new international program offered to mostly Western liberal states at the onset of the 1990s is full of good promises. Yet, as Boutros-Ghali reminds us, it is also full of risks. New dangers to national security and to the satisfactory fulfillment of the new international projects emerge as well. Unlike the old cold war threats, however, the new regime of international insecurity is depicted as a vague and imprecise danger that affects not only states individually, but, more importantly, the entire global landscape of post–cold war politics. Phenomena like blind terrorism from "rogue" nations or regional groups, refugee movements, environmental spillovers, parallel economies, and international drug trafficking come to mind. International strategies of containment are thus still required. But they are no longer directed at a clearly identifiable target. Rather, international containment in the 1990s faces global challenges that can never be clearly recognized.

Strategies of international containment had already been reshuffled before the end of the cold war with the advent of what Timothy Luke had called "post-warring" regimes.[15] The notion of "postwar" or "post-warring" was used to designate the changes in foreign policy attitudes caused by the threat of nuclear destruction. In a nuclear age (late–cold war period), the imagery of total global annihilation had pushed states to design strategies of containment based on deterrence and simulation rather than on direct coercion or armed intervention. "Post-warring" practices had led states, and particularly the United States and the Soviet Union, to devise models of "warmaking" whose sole objective was *not* to be implemented in the real landscape of international politics. "Post-warring" strategies were meant to remain at a level of rhetorical or symbolic exchange (between superpowers) or simulated operationalization (by means of nuclear military drills or computer programs). Such policies were simply a matter of organizing "contradictory preparations for a 'war' that never should be fought."[16]

With the end of the cold war, strategic containment of international dangers once again needs to be reassessed. The threat of total nuclear destruction is no longer at the forefront of international preoccupations. The disappearance of the Soviet Union has ushered in an era of relative military stability marked by the collaborative diplomatic and military efforts against Iraq in the Gulf War. And yet containment is still necessary, in the name of state security and, more important perhaps, on behalf of liberal-capitalism, now left by itself to (re)organize societies and markets worldwide. To deter the polymorphous international threats mentioned above, new "post-warring" strategies need to be invented. "Post-warring" strategies indeed denote the absence of real threats and the presence of a simulated danger. In such a mode of missing reality, yet another regime of containment by means of deterrence and simulation must be created.

"Post-warring" strategies in a post–cold war era turn to the UN and its peacekeeping as a favorite mode of simulation of international politics. This (post) postwar scenario seeks to "fill the promised space" of global security by turning to the (empty) formalism of the UN.[17] As an empty form, the UN can be virtually anything. A virtual agent, the UN is remobilized in the 1990s to fulfill not only security but also (and more importantly) ideological mandates. The United Nations is suddenly reactivated by its member states and the international community of multinational liberal interests to make sure that international politics represents a single international territory, the territory of the "universal social contract," not so much by enforcing such an imaginary, but by imagining and imaging it. Simply put, the UN becomes a framework of simulation and deterrence. The UN is a rediscovered "empty frame" that is asked to mobilize the appearance of collective security in a world that still looks disorderly. Techniques of simulation and visual reconditioning of appearances take over the UN to reshape the reality of international politics, with the hope that not only the UN, but also the "outside world," the actual undisciplined international landscape with its new threats, will fall for this play of reconstructed reality and, finally, will be deterred and (virtually) tamed.

THE RECOURSE OF SIMULATION

The critical perspective on the UN as a practice of international simulation and deterrence is influenced by Bartos's photographic vision of the international organization. It is also informed theoretically by Jean Baudrillard's writing on simulation. Simulation, as Baudrillard understands it, is opposed to representation. Both representation and simulation are modes of cognition, ways of dealing with reality. Both modes of cognition also turn to specific visual postures to capture reality. Before one considers the relationship between simulation and reality, one needs to clarify the role, technique, and strategic importance of representation as a mode of cognition that the advent of simulation supposedly brings to a crisis.

Reality and Representation

Reality may be understood as a field of experience, the so-called objective or empirical world that one encounters in one's daily and supposedly unaltered perceptions. It is the physical realm of sense-perceptions, an ideal state of material presence, where nothing interferes between the body and the stimuli present in the environment. Of course, such a degree of perceptual reality is, to some extent, a myth that no one, apart perhaps from die-hard naturalists, clings to anymore since it makes complete abstraction of other forces that may intervene in human perception and often distort it (the mind, psyche, media, etc.).

Representation is a way of capturing reality, of employing devices other than direct sense-perception to make sense of the surrounding world. These other devices can be anything from reason, religion, and desire to television, painting, or architecture (more obvious visual representations). Descartes's "methodological doubt," his distrust of the senses as a method of certain knowledge, is at the base of the recourse to representation in the modern era. Descartes performs a defining rupture between the world of reality and the senses (nature), and the world of reason (the cogito), in which reality is no longer immediately perceived but rather becomes re-presented by means of thinking/reasoning. As Descartes affirmed, "I knew from this [the moment of creative doubt that splits the ego as sensing being and the ego as rational thinking subject] that I was a substance the whole essence of which is only to think, and which, in order to be, does not have need of any place, and does not need to depend on any material thing."[18]

The Cartesian ontological moment introduces the human subject as a disembodied being and throws him/her into a world of representation. Starting with Descartes, representation is a process through which reality (the "objective" world) is given substance *in the mind,* in the domain ruled by the cogito. It replaces material reality and re-presents it (calls it back) in a form that has been reworked by interpretive formulas like reason, religion, television, and so on, from now on taken to give meaning to human existence.

The archetypal process of representation is perhaps to be found in modern liberal political theory, in the works of philosophers such as Locke or Rousseau. In the political thought of the Enlightenment, institutions like parliaments, governments, and their bureaucracies become the representatives of the sovereignty of the people.[19] In liberal political theory, these institutions hold sovereignty, but only by proxy. They represent or embody the common consent of the free subjects in the name of whom they are asked to act. These assumptions are well known to political scientists and practitioners who generally use the term "political representation" to identify these procedures.

Political representation is nothing more than one specific instance of a larger cognitive operation, an operation of "symbolic" representation that the Cartesian cogito announces.[20] Similar to the way one traditionally understands political representation, symbolic representation is a work of transference and selection. As Descartes intimated, it is a matter of transferring what is perceived to be outside the thinking subject, and supposedly unreliable and untrustworthy, into safe and recognizable categories inside which the perceived object (now becoming a conceived object; Descartes initiates a transfer from the perceptual to the conceptual) will gain a safe and final mooring.

Representation as a mode of (categorizing) reality is all-pervasive.[21] It has colonized modern thought processes (from rational idealism to positivism) and expanded to the multiple disciplines characteristic of the modern organization of knowledge, from semiotics to international relations as a field of study.

Semiotics, the study of signs or science of signification, is perhaps the most obvious example of representational logic. Modern semiotics assumes that signification (and linguistic signification in particular) is the product of an existing link between a sound or graphic form and a specific concept or object. Language, the privileged mode of signification, is what Ferdinand de Saussure calls a "system of signs expressing ideas,"[22] a "network of elements that signify only in relation to each other."[23] What Saussure, as a founding figure of modern semiotics, postulates is a principle of equivalence between what he calls a signifier (or sign) and a signified (or concept). On the basis of such an equivalent link (a chain of signification), every object or concept is granted an arbitrary but often exclusive sign that will from now on represent it, be its signifying agent, and become its forever engraved (in writing, in verbal language) mark. This mode of representational signification is, as Saussure indicates, conventional, not natural. Such an arbitrary structure of meaning may be necessary to create or solidify a community (a linguistic community first of all), as some have argued.[24] But it also has its shortcomings and problems. Indeed, it places knowledge within a clearly ordered and strictly delineated system that preexists human experience (from now on tied to the logic of representation) and disciplines cognitive processes (as Descartes did). As Roland Barthes has demonstrated, a signifying system, that is to say, a mode of representation at the level of language, always carries with it the burden of a certain ideology (expressed through the conventional relationship between signifier and signified),[25] and, of course, always starts with the postulate of supremacy of human reason (logocentrism).[26]

Simulation

Theories of representation postulate a principle of equivalence between the concept, the sign, and the real object. Simulation, by contrast, is radically opposed to representation, even if it remains a way of dealing with reality. As Baudrillard repeatedly mentions, with simulation, it is no longer possible to distinguish between a good and a bad representation, a correct or an erroneous interpretation, a truth or a falsehood. Simulation is defined as "the precession of the model . . . [which] allows for all the possible interpretations, even the most contradictory—all are true, in the sense that their truth is exchangeable, in the image of the models from which they proceed."[27] The conceptual categories that, in representation, allowed one to access reality are no longer available. In this sense, simulation is a play with reality without the recourse of the concept. It is an over-representation of the real (a hyperreal) without the interpretive devices provided by the Cartesian cogito. The simulacrum, the real of/in simulation, is no longer the product of interpretive mechanisms, but, rather, the outcome of operative media. The medium is the only device left to generate a reality effect that often looks "more real than the real itself."[28] Whereas representation was based on the premise (and the promise) that sense-perception had to be doubted, simulation aims at retrieving sense-perception (virtual reality requires heightened sensory capacities, for instance). But sense-perception in simulation is always already fooled by the fact that the "real" can never be trusted in the first place. In a way, simulation is an ironic reversal of representation. Whereas representation assumed that sense-perception was faulty, in simulation, the real, and the so-called cognitive principles derived from it, are always nothing more than traps, "trompe l'oeil" (literally, fooling of the eye) mechanisms, as Baudrillard suggests. This is what happens when simulation is read as a condition or context of reality/sense-perception.

But simulation can also be read as a strategy aimed at recuperating the real of representation in its absence. This is why, for Baudrillard, simulation also "masks the *absence* of a basic reality."[29] Representation was undoubtedly strategic to the extent that it sought to move cognition away from the realm of the senses and into the categories of the mind. Simulation can be strategic too. But its strategy is no longer about re-inscribing "empirical reality" in reason or thought, but of "reviving" reality through the hyperreal, simulated, visual, and virtual instruments offered by technological media. Recuperating reality through simulation becomes a technostrategic enterprise, a tactical move of late-twentieth century technotopia. By way of technologies of simulation (like virtual reality, for example), an idealized reality, an imaginary, may thus be (virtually) accessed. As William Bogard indicates, simulation is "the 'point' where the imaginary and the real coincide, specifically where the gap between virtual control and actual control disappears."[30] Simulation eradicates the gap between reality and the imaginary by providing an alternate mode of experience that can look like the imaginary (what could only be thought but is suddenly materialized) and yet can be just as convincing and true-to-life as empirical reality.

The Baudrillardian figure of the trompe l'oeil marks the link between simulation (as a strategy of recuperation of reality) and vision (a mode of cognition by way of the visual). Baudrillard writes that

[n]ature is not represented in the trompe l'oeil. There are no landscapes, no skies, no lines of flight or natural light; no faces either; neither psychology nor historicity. Everything here is artefact. A vertical backdrop creates, out of pure signs, objects isolated from their referential context. . . . Today the trompe l'oeil is no longer within the realm of painting. Like stucco, its contemporary, it can do anything, mimic anything, parody anything. In the sixteenth century, it became the prototype of the malevolent use of appearances, a game of fantastic proportions which eventually eliminated the boundaries between painting, sculpture and architecture. . . . In the murals or streets in the trompe l'oeil of Los Angeles, architecture is deceived and defeated by illusion.[31]

Simulation as a mode of visual cognition has no depth, no conceptual significance, no profound meaning. It is merely an image without an origin or an end. The trompe l'oeil is the visual labyrinth of reality. There is no way for the human eye to distinguish between a trompe l'oeil scene, a mediatically constructed visual/virtual reality, and a so-called real representation (presuming that metaphysically, if not cognitively, a difference may be maintained, which, as Baudrillard tells us, is no longer possible anyway). One day, one may crash into a trompe l'oeil without realizing it.

Simulation has entered the domain of "visual reality" through multiple contemporary modes of technological cognition. Virtual reality and computer simulation programs are some of the most common illustrations of such a perceptual mode. Such visual/virtual substitutes of reality are often put to efficient uses. For example, as James Der Derian has shown,[32] in the field of military defense and national security, visually simulated attacks or defensive postures created by computer programs and three-dimensional digital imaging have strategically replaced the need for a massive deployment of weapons, soldiers, and on-the-ground tactics in the good old real(ist) landscape of military preparation and war making. These strategic deployments can once again be placed in the larger context of "post-warring" regimes of international political deterrence. In the absence of large-scale physical or ideological warfare (no longer available after the collapse of communism), visual simulations keep the troops in a state of preparedness (they have to do something anyway), legitimate the enormous amounts of money spent on these programs (you never know if some day these simulated threats will become "real" or not), and, perhaps more importantly, maintain the pretense that war and power politics still matter in foreign affairs. What applies to the mode of preparedness of contemporary armies also works for sovereign states in general as simulation offers a substitute principle of reality, a way for states to modify their field of international perception.[33] Rather than face the multiple challenges of a highly disordered international landscape, today's nation-states, or at least those with the technological capacity to generate simulated realities, often choose to indulge in what looks like a fantasy-world of mediatically enhanced trompe l'oeils.[34]

As was suggested above, the United Nations, its peacekeeping, and the reality of its interventions in the 1990s rely on simulation too. Such a critical and perceptual take on the UN is not an isolated historical moment. It is rather the product of a long chain of institutionalist interpretations which, confronted with the "empty space" of the UN, have struggled to define the UN and its activities from the perspective of representation.

REPRESENTATIONS OF THE UN

The field and practice of international organization(s) in international affairs has been marked by the overarching predominance of representational modes of meaning. Over the past fifty years, institutionalist approaches have taken over the field to provide answers to the question "what does the UN represent?" The basic principle of representation associated with the UN is governance. The UN, as the only global international organization of the post–World War II era, was created on behalf of "the peoples" of the world to achieve governance in international affairs.[35] Unlike its domestic/national counterpart, international politics was interpreted as lacking government, that is to say, a structure of order and centralized authority. This fundamental absence of a centralizing principle of governance in the international system was directly to blame for the "scourge of war" characteristic of the early part of the twentieth century. The idea behind the UN was to replicate a mode of governance that could provide international politics with the same desirable effects of security and order achieved by national governments. Although realist scholars, intent on blaming internationalist utopianism for World War II, believed that the creation of worldwide governance by means of international institutions was a recipe for disaster and that, given this historically proven fact, states were better off devising their own means of individual preservation,[36] idealists and institutionalists posited that the only hope for world peace was to develop institutions of collective security. The ideal of institutionalism affirmed (and still does) that "only a collective effort can give states the framework and the strength to shape their own destiny."[37] In the wake of the creation of the UN and the rebirth of institutionalism in world affairs (institutionalism can trace its philosophical roots to Kant), international organizations became a tool of international order, and a rediscovered field of study, known simply as international organization (IO), emerged to "describe and explain 'how the modern society of nations' can govern itself."[38]

It is in such an early institutionalist context that the United Nations takes on its signification. For the institutionalists, the UN is a perfect formal edifice, an empty sign, that needs to be filled with visions of governance and collective security to take on global dimensions. The meaning of the UN is clearly exposed: it is to represent the "hope that the foundations for a new and more propitious international order [can] be constructed."[39] From the beginning, however, this representational mission reveals itself to be quite problematic. The vision or hope (of governance) that the UN is asked to signify is not a conceptual reality. The UN must represent international order in its absence. Furthermore, it must achieve this signifying mission in the context of an international system dominated by selfish realist (state) interests. The institutionalist vision of global governance is thus an imaginary. In the aftermath of World War II, there is yet no such thing as a referential presence of governance and collective security. Instead, there are self-interested states that are about to embark on an ideological struggle. Balance-of-power politics takes over the perceptual field of cold war international relations and leaves the UN and its approach to collective security as a utopian quest.

Faced with this situation, the story of the UN narrated through the discourse of international institutionalism is dominated by the dilemma of an impossible representation. Such an impossibility of representation—the inability to create meaning in international relations—gives birth to substitute strategies of meaning, alternate modes of signification. At first, alternate modes of (UN) signification remain within a purely idealist and internationalist mind-frame by suggesting that the UN can represent governance by means of peacekeeping. Such a narrative is very close ideologically to the type of internationalist and institutionalist optimism that reemerges today. Behind this early mode of institutionalist representation, what some have called formal institutionalism,[40] is the idea that "in place of the ideal of collective security, the UN [would] develop alternate means to mitigate certain conflicts under the term 'peacekeeping.'"[41] In this configuration, the UN still has meaning. It is not a dead sign. It cannot be an exact replica of global governance but it can approximate it. As a partial mode of collective security, UN peacekeeping affirms itself as a preliminary sign of international order. The work of UN peacekeepers—troops provided by member states to intervene as a buffer between warring parties (with the consent of the involved actors)—is viewed as a sign of hope in an otherwise anarchical world, a necessary first step on the way to a neo-Kantian universal moral community that (as Kant himself suggested) may take generations to achieve. Peacekeeping was not explicitly mentioned in the UN Charter. It had to be improvised, invented after the fact, as an afterthought, a proxy.[42] Thanks to peacekeeping, the UN was not left without meaning. Simply, it became a system of partial international representation. In certain situations, under certain conditions, the UN could be a meaningful, albeit limited, sign of governance and security. This was the hope that the early idealist institutionalists had to cling to.

If the idealist narrative of institutionalism places its (ahistorical) faith in a partial configuration of governance by means of UN peacekeeping, a second, more historically contextual trend chooses to displace the signification of the field/practice of international organization. Characteristic of the cold war era, a mode of functionalist and neofunctionalist institutionalism breaks with the idealist moment. Influenced by a realist context, functionalist institutionalism prefers to focus on the question of cooperation rather than governance. Functionalists operate a shift in the domain of referentiality of international organization by transforming the object/concept in need of representation. Governance can, at best, be approximated, not represented. But it can more felicitously be transmuted into another notion. Functionalists thus perform what Derrida has called a "sign-slide" by displacing the signification of the concept to another field of representation where meaning is made to appear more plausible.[43]

Functionalism's intervention in the mode of signification of international organizations and the UN is a semiological rescue mission. It is intended to save international organizations in general (and no longer specifically the UN) from their empty formalist and impossible representations by positing that it is no longer the form of institutions that matters. What counts, rather, is what kind of functions institutions are asked to perform. Instead of being empty signs ready to be filled with the latest idealist and utopian mood, institutions are functional clusters. They are the indicators of functionalist signification, the visible and effective proofs that "new powers can be acquired by functional accretion."[44]

With the functionalist redistribution of meaning (through a new semiology of international organization), what international organizations are called forth to represent is no longer governance (or the former dream thereof), but need. This need is a need of states that international institutions fulfill for states. In this perspective, the United Nations, among other international institutions, becomes the expression of the need (of states) to find, in certain occasions, a common solution to their problems by means of functional arrangements. Functionalists find an adequate and viable (surrogate) representation for the UN and its activities by erasing the previous spirit of idealist institutionalism. The UN does not have to approximate a (collective) reality that may never be. Simply, it is the sign of something else: the will of sovereign states to find a common resolve and cooperate only on certain issues.

A convenient way of explaining the development of economic unions and less formal common markets (such as the European Community), this new representational mode in international organization is perfected and updated by neofunctionalist institutionalist theories such as regime theory. Regime theory posits that international regimes, loose international arrangements whose function is to "condition patterns of social behavior" for states and create "standards of behavior defined in terms of rights and obligations,"[45] are the prototypical forms and functions of international institutions.[46] Regimes produce meaning by propagating norms of international behavior created by such clusters of global interdependence. Although its aim is to save the representational reality of international organizations by granting them a new, more realistic, and achievable mode of referentiality (to represent the need of states), the functionalist narrative reduces the role of formal institutions like the UN by showing that other informal and nonspecific international arrangements can be internationally significant and meaningful to states. Put simply, the new mode of representational reality is a matter of function, and the old formal arrangements and frameworks of governance do not matter anymore.

The subsequent modality of institutionalism (as a system of representational meaning in international organization) is what has come to be known in international relations circles as constructivism.[47] Constructivist institutionalism is a conceptual and semiological bridge between functionalist structures of meaning and the more utopian formalism of the early idealist period. Satisfied that international organizations, and the UN in particular, can no longer represent governance and collective security by way of peacekeeping, constructivist institutionalists nonetheless seek to refurbish formal international institutions. This constructivist move consists of affirming that function can have a transformative effect on form. International institutions do not simply condition state behaviors and, as such, provide norms and rules of international action. International organizations can also meaningfully "transform state identities and interests,"[48] the very nature of what states are and do in international affairs and, consequently, the nature of international anarchy too. By re-constructing state identities and the nature of their interests, international organizations (formal or informal) reconstruct the international system and lead it toward greater security, governance and order.

Whereas the task of the functionalists was a matter of semiological displacement (finding another referent), the mission of these constructivists is a semiological reconstruction. It seeks to rebuild the foundations of the previous mode of formalist institutionalism by filling the empty framework with a new dose of globalizing discourse that suggests that institutions of international life are "structures of collective meaning."[49] Unlike the early version of UN peacekeeping, these structures of collective meaning are not utopian or neo-Kantian figures of an internationalism that has yet to be materialized. They are, rather, the product of states' social actions, which, once established and fully functional, necessarily give new identities to the states that participate in these structures, and new meanings to state interests. In such a (re)constructivist scheme, states and international organizations are mutually (re)constituted. As states produce instances of conditioned and collective international identity, such structures, in turn, also produce states and re-present the meaning of security, governance, and order in international affairs.

Whereas functionalism sought to transform, constructivism wishes to reform. Constructivist institutionalism reinvents the UN as a reforming agent. UN practices reeducate states and show them how to act unselfishly. Such a representation of the UN brings international organization (as an international practice and a field of study) one step closer to a common acceptance of international order and global governance. International institutions like the UN reform the (selfish, realist) representations that states have of their international environment by providing them with a more interdependent and socially cohesive vision of international relations as a "society of intersubjective meaning."[50] It remains, however, that even if constructivism seeks to reframe the meaning of the UN as an "agent of change," it is still up to states, the reformed subjects, to act in accordance with the new modality of "international (re)education" that they are offered. There is still a dose of idealism in this reformist recipe.

The evolution of theories of international organization (including the UN) over the past fifty years is thus the story of a struggle. It is the story, discontinuous as it may be, of the impossibility of representing the UN or, more precisely, of ascribing a clear sense of referentiality to the UN as either a framework or a function. In the absence of a clear sense of institutionalist representation, substitute formulations have been offered and arbitrary semiological interventions have been performed. The end of the cold war marks a drastic shift in the semiology of both the UN and institutionalism. The formal emptiness of the UN is rediscovered. Yet, far from being an impediment to meaning, a crisis of representation, the emptiness of the UN, its revelation as a system of objects only, becomes an incredible opportunity. It opens up the possibility of deploying strategies of meaning behind plays of appearances to produce international reality by means of trompe l'oeil devices and techniques. At the UN, (impossible) representations give way to simulations.

SIMULATIONS OF THE UN

Post–cold war neo-institutionalism is the latest trend in United Nations and international organization theories. It is a trend that keeps up with the spirit of the (postmodern) times by turning to simulation to give "a second chance" to the UN.[51] All of a sudden, institutionalist discourses are given the visual and technological capability to make complete abstraction of the representational crisis of the past forty to fifty years. Collective security can be "realized" despite the numerous international threats that proliferate in the post–cold war international landscape.

Simulation penetrates the United Nations by way of its hyperreal diplomacy: peacekeeping. Peacekeeping is no longer interpreted as a partial representation of collective security. Rather, it becomes a simulation of (collective) force and power. Without any referential support apart from textual and rhetorical markers (neoidealist theories and neoliberal ideologies), peacekeeping is a self-generated force: "an effective *projection* of military power under international control [whose?] to enforce international decisions against aggressors."[52] It is a mode of international force and global power only because it looks like one. Peacekeeping is a (visual) projection! More real than realist diplomatic strategies, more universal than superpowers' hegemonic schemes, more powerful than power politics itself, UN peacekeeping is a (Baudrillardian) trompe l'oeil. The post–cold war imaginary of UN peacekeeping "precedes the realist realities of realpolitikers with a code of aestheticized images, imaginary artifices, or recurrent dreams that 'envelops the whole edifice of representation as simulation' (Baudrillard)," as Timothy Luke suggests.[53] UN peacekeeping simulates a real landscape of ordered international politics, a New World Order, by trying to multiply the scenes of peaceful intervention and humanitarian assistance throughout the mediatically envisioned domain of international politics. Working mostly at the level of the global mediascape, that world of visual cognitive sense-perception created by high technology through which events, no doubt, are "more real than the real itself" (hypermediatization), UN peacekeeping saturates the scopic regime of postmodern Western states with snapshots and videobytes of heroic, blue-helmeted soldiers/workers/volunteers that impose the vision (artificial as it may be) that there is nothing else to the real but this blatant (dis)play of appearances. UN peacekeeping as a trompe l'oeil strategy is simple and obvious. In the early 1990s, everyone could relate (necessarily had to relate) to it, even beyond the West, because it was affirmed as the most readily available visual expression of post–cold war international politics: UN signs and colors across the globe, UN blue-helmets restoring order and patrolling the streets of Port-au-Prince and Sarajevo, Pakistani troops working for the UN running after rebel clan leaders in Mogadishu, UN relief personnel in a camp of Rwandan refugees in eastern Zaire. The simulation was everywhere. The simulation was the UN.

IDEOLOGY AND DISCIPLINE

Simulation is the mode of cognition that best applies to the postmodern "visual ontology" of the UN. There is, however, a conceptual/perceptual blind spot in the notion of simulation. There is a dimension of simulation that Baudrillard mentions all too briefly, in passing, and that postmodern commentators have rarely remarked on. This ignored dimension of simulation is ideology. At the beginning of *Simulations,* Baudrillard notes that the fact that "present-day simulators try to make the real, all the real, coincide with their simulation models" is a matter of imperialism.[54] Beyond this statement, Baudrillard never returns to the question of the place of ideology (as imperialism over ideas and forms) in simulation. Some of Baudrillard's readers have tried to compensate for the oversight by offering a parallel between Lenin's notion of imperialism (as the highest stage of modern capitalism) and the imperialism of simulation in contemporary practices/discourses of the state (as "the highest stage/endgame" of postmodern capitalism).[55] Such readings have not systematically looked at the relationship between simulation and ideology. They have suggested that simulation may be taking the place of imperialism in late-twentieth-century transnational capitalist games. But they have not questioned the place, effect, and modality of simulation in ideological processes in general (surely, even today, there is more to ideology than capitalism). In short, for Baudrillard (writing on simulation) and some of his commentators (writing on Baudrillard on simulation), the question of ideology is not taken to be a crucial moment of simulation. Post–cold war practices of UN peacekeeping push us to seriously reconsider the link between ideology and simulation and, by the same token, allow us to sharpen critical/postmodern analyses on simulation.

Strategies of simulation are never innocent. They may never be completely self-referential either. Just as representation was a capable mode of production of political/ideological meaning, so is simulation. The United Nations is not simply an empty spot where self-referential plays of images take place. It is the place where, in a post–cold war era, transnational and global ideologies are mobilized by means of simulation. Specifically, United Nations peacekeeping is not simply a (virtual) mode of reactivation of governance and collective security in contemporary visions of international politics. Rather, such a re-creation of international reality, of the reality of international security, is always already an ideological enterprise.

As previously mentioned, the original discourse on international organizations (and on the UN too) was institutionalist idealism or globalism. In the 1990s, such a discourse returns and is conveniently fused with other globalizing tendencies and practices (market liberalism above all) to give birth to a specific ideological formation: disciplinary liberalism. Disciplinary liberalism is the dominant (global) ideology of post–cold war international affairs, one that permeates most of the contemporary world order/global governance discourses and practices. As Stephen Gill suggests,

> [t]he present world order involves a more "liberalized" and commodified set of historical structures, driven by the restructuring of capital and a political shift to the right. This process involves the spatial expansion and social deepening of economic liberal definitions of social purpose and possessively individualist patterns of action and politics . . . [s]ome fundamental aspects of neoliberal market civilisation . . . constitute a temporary politics of supremacy in the emerging world order . . . Although the governance of this market civilisation is framed by the discourse of globalising neoliberalism and expressed through the interaction of free enterprise and the state, its coordination is achieved through a combination of market discipline and the direct application of political power. . . . [N]eoliberal globalisation is the latest phase in a process that originated before the dawning of the Enlightenment in Europe, and accelerated in the nineteenth century with the onset of industrial capitalism and the consolidation of the integral nation-state . . . [This] politics of supremacy implies a fusion of economic, political, cultural elements of society . . . into a political alliance or coalition that combines coercion and consent.[56]

Gill's critical analysis of today's world order places the core of contemporary international ideology in the ever-growing capitalist market, in what he calls disciplinary neoliberalism. It is an ideology which, following the dictates of corporate capital, is constantly looking for expansion and control.

Gill's notion of disciplinary neoliberalism is on target, but his analysis of ideology is economistic. It all too conveniently attaches ideology to the global requirements of the capitalist world market. What Gill fails to emphasize, despite the fact that he mobilizes the term, is that it is the "disciplinary" part of disciplinary neoliberalism that matters (the disciplinarity of the capitalist market rather than its essence). It is discipline that anchors modern and postmodern ideologies. It is the regime of disciplinarity in general (in which capitalist practices are no doubt embedded) that fashions ideology. Following Foucault's analysis, we may define discipline as the more or less explicit exercise of a regime of knowledge and power, based on specific techniques (from brutal force and physical marking, to spatial delineation and epistemological ordering), which, far from simply coercing, negating, and restraining, seeks to produce desirable social effects of governance, subjection, and normalization.[57] Foucault's work has shown that disciplinary techniques have often shaped modern state ideologies (the ideology that supports the liberal democratic state in particular). The disciplinary regime of power/knowledge and its determination of ideology can be traced to the days when the Enlightenment ideal of a harmonious relationship between free subjects and an ordering state was formulated. In eighteenth-century philosophical and political treatises that link the welfare and freedom of the individual to the necessary disciplinary order/organization of the state and its agents, one may detect early versions of this contemporary ideological formation that I call disciplinary liberalism. In Rousseau's *Social Contract,* for example, disciplinary liberalism is the product of the sovereign's general will. Rousseau's central tenet is that "each of us puts his person and all his power in common under the supreme direction of the general will, and in our corporate capacity, we receive each member as an indivisible part of the whole."[58] But because this will, representative of the community of freely consenting subjects, must remain boundless and can never be altered (otherwise the social compact would simply vanish), the consequence is that "whoever refuses to obey the general will shall be compelled to do so by the whole body. This means nothing else than that he will be forced to be free."[59] This last statement by Rousseau is a clear formulation of the fundamental link between disciplinarity and ideology, between the exercise of social coercion and the creation of human governance. Disciplinary liberalism is an ideology that promises individual freedom and welfare in society through the implementation of disciplinary modalities of power. It emerges as a human need when social harmony is no longer traditionally/naturally based. Since the early days of modernity, and with different degrees of refinement, discipline has been the favorite mode of construction of liberal-communitarian orders. Disciplinary liberalism has become the normal way of things social and political in Western societies not simply because of the coercive power of economic markets (as Gill would have it), but because of the productive ingenuity of disciplinary regimes in general.

The ideology of disciplinary liberalism, no doubt also embedded in the globalizing tendencies of market liberalism identified by Gill (it is truly difficult to disentangle the two tendencies nowadays), no longer has to compete with communism as an alternate vision of social order. Left on its own, disciplinary liberalism can take over the field of post–cold war international politics/economics and impose its ideologico-disciplinary modalities in a global manner. It is in such an ideological context, relied upon by states, transnational business interests, and individuals worldwide, that United Nations peacekeeping has to operate too. I argue that it is also for the purpose of facilitating the deployment of this ideology all over the global landscape (or mediascape perhaps) of the 1990s, the use of simulation by the UN is an ideological and disciplinary strategy. The mode of visual simulation of the UN is not simply a matter of recuperating the referential significations of governance, order, and collective security in the absence of clear representations. Simulation at the UN is also a mode of propagation of disciplinary liberalism as the dominant ideological formation of post–cold war international affairs. To use Louis Althusser's terminology,[60] the simulated regime of UN peacekeeping is an "interpellating" technique that hails sovereign states and other international organizations (the subjects of international politics) and individuals and business corporations (the subjects of global policies) into adhering to the mandates of disciplinary liberalism.

In a sense, ideology is the contemporary supplement of simulation, of the regime of international cognition that emerges from the ruins of representation. Ideology and discipline are, then, constants of both representational and simulated systems of signification. Through ideology and disciplinarity, one may no longer see simulation as a radical opposition to representation (as Baudrillard saw it), but as a refined succession, as yet another tactical move mobilized to retrieve the real of representation which, however, has no other choice but to rely on machines and media, on a visual system of objects, to find meaning.

Methodologically, where ideology and discipline supplement simulation, the sociopolitical analyses performed by Foucault and Althusser complement Baudrillard's understanding of technology and the visual. To put it another way, both Foucault's and Althusser's more referential works (grounded in discipline and ideology) give Baudrillard's simulation a reality principle, so to speak, one that is not necessarily anchored in a system of subjective representation,

but rather in an "objective" world, that of states, disciplines, apparatuses, and institutions as machines. Those "celibate machines," to
use a Deleuzian terminology,[61] often beyond the rational or cognizant mastery of the individuals who run them, are generally at the
origin of the visions and simulations that condition the contemporary global landscape. It is also through them, through ideology and
discipline as much as through simulation, that the reality of today's
social, economic, political, and cultural scene can be read.

LEVELS OF READING

How, then, does one read this book? There is, of course, no right or
wrong way of reading the following chapters, no predetermined direction either, apart perhaps from the theoretical suggestions offered
in this introductory section. The reader, however, may wish to identify three complementary levels of reading. These three levels of
reading can be differentiated from one another. They may or may
not remain at the end of this study. Simply, they provide three specific points of entry into the text, three somewhat coherent narratives that can be pursued throughout the entire volume.

The first level of reading is, to use a Barthesian terminology, the
most denotative.[62] It is also the most readily available for a more orthodox audience of international relations scholars, international organization theorists, foreign policy observers, and media pundits. Indeed, this reading still operates within the code of representation (or
referential signification). It is a level of analysis that looks at this text
as, simply, a critical interpretation of the post–cold war peacekeeping interventions of the United Nations Organization. Starting from
this premise, this category of readers will find in this text a critical
analysis of post–cold war United Nations diplomacy anchored in
traditional realist/neorealist approaches to international relations in
general (chapter 1), a study of the United Nations' strategies of
global and panoptic surveillance as they apply to North Korea and
Iraq (chapter 2), an interpretation of the failure of the joint UN-U.S.
peacekeeping mission in Somalia (chapter 3), a subsequent reading of
the relationship between the United Nations and NATO in the context of the largely unsuccessful UN humanitarian operation in Bosnia
(chapter 4), and an empirical as well as a theoretical description of
the Rwandan humanitarian crisis of 1994, a crisis during the course
of which the humanitarian and peacekeeping efforts traditionally

displayed by the UN since the end of the cold war were, by and large, absent and replaced by the work of medical NGOs (nongovernmental organizations) (chapter 5). Throughout these various interventions, the theory of UN peacekeeping is put to the functional test (Does it work? Does it achieve governance?). These five chapters, read as different case studies of UN interventionism, offer explanations about the function of UN peacekeeping, its modes of implementation, its strategies, its victories (when there are any), its failures (which are often more visible). This level of reading allows the reader to gain a conceptual and practical understanding of how the United Nations system, in the context of post–cold war peacekeeping operations, works, and how it interacts with other agents present in the post–cold war international scene, such as sovereign states, other international organizations, nongovernmental organizations, and civilian populations.

A second level of reading is much more connotative,[63] tracing the presence of ideology through the primary level of interpretation of UN peacekeeping (from a classic normative and institutionalist perspective). This level of interpretation is assuredly critical of specific representational strategies, discourses, or visions. But it never really steps out of representation altogether. It denounces and criticizes, but rarely problematizes or even transcends representation. Critically approached, the ideology of disciplinary liberalism, as it expands all over the world, is diagnosed. The way such an ideology deploys force, coercion, subjection, and hegemonic discourses, in an overt or covert fashion, is clearly documented in each of the above mentioned cases. A Foucauldian reading of global governance and world order outlooks through the UN's interventionist actions is performed. It reinscribes UN peacekeeping into a larger ideological mode of disciplinarity, normativity, carceralization, and normalization. Such an approach is often compatible with an Althusserian context of critical Marxist-structuralist theory which details, through processes like interpellation and subjection, how ideology functions in practice.

A third level of reading is cognizant of the postmodern modes of textuality and reality. Inviting itself to simply be a supplement of the first two readings (and perhaps never more than that), the postmodern text highlights the visual strategies and the simulations (the real/visual is read as simulation, no longer as representation) that are deployed in the exercise of UN peacekeeping. Based on textuality (as in chapter 1, where the analyzed text is Hobbes's philosophy and realist international relations discourses) and on visuality (in the other chapters where the "texts" are specific instances of UN visual simulation), the postmodern reading deconstructs the strategies and policies of UN post–cold war diplomacy, and the ideological formations mobilized by it, by merely rereading these processes from their points of rupture, their discontinuities and aporias, the points where the hegemonic structures created by UN peacekeeping slowly but surely start to undo themselves. This is also the moment where plurality is restored, where the regime of meaning and certainty imposed by the hegemonic system (of diplomacy, ideology, textuality, visuality) becomes unstable and undecidable. If nothing else, the postmodern approach/supplement to the two previous readings works inside the text as a provocative and destabilizing agent (to the extent that it draws the attention of the reader to the places where the dominant system/order is fundamentally unstable).

The three levels of reading can be maintained in their autonomy, perhaps even their dualities (normative and descriptive approach to the UN versus critical theories of ideology versus postmodern approaches to the textual and the visual). But they may also be read as a whole, as one single reading, one that remains aware of the specific strategies present in each level of interpretation, but which, nonetheless, takes the text as an entity, a unique object perhaps. As such, this volume and text may finally give the reader the impression of a blend of various strategies, ideologies, epistemologies, theories that build upon one another without exhausting the meaning of any of the singular components. At times, in some instances of the text, the process of writing may have privileged a level of analysis to the detriment of others. But the reader, in a mode of active rereading of this volume (a writerly text, as Barthes would suggest), may freely choose to privilege another level in the same instances. To put it bluntly, as much as it is strategically feasible, the text is left open, constantly playing between those different levels which do not have to be one.

1

Destabilizing Leviathan: Revisiting the Order/Anarchy Debate through a Postmodern(ized) Hobbes

To an international observer, it may appear that the events of the past decade have left humankind in a condition reminiscent of that situation, prior to the creation of the modern state, that Thomas Hobbes described in *Leviathan*.[1] Some of the most blatantly alarmist depictions of world politics that have emerged over the past years—from John Mearsheimer's prognosis of a future multipolar chaos in Europe to Robert Kaplan's prophecy about a "coming anarchy"[2]—are clear indications that one of Hobbes's most celebrated constructs, the "state of nature," has found a contemporary application. Today, human nature, left by itself in those places that once were organized by the logic of cold war politics, has once again turned for the worst. From the former Yugoslavia to Rwanda, from Somalia to Haiti, life in large areas of the world appears "solitary, poore, nasty, brutish, and short."[3] Of course, not everyone in the world experiences such a resurgence of "natural life." Despite increased urban decay, social violence and pockets of extreme poverty, most Western democracies still enjoy the benefits of the "rule of reason" under the guidance of securing welfare states (even if some of the most pessimistic "prophets" of international politics announce that, eventually, Western states will be affected too).

Disciplinary liberalism—arguably, the dominant ideology/discourse of contemporary international relations—builds upon such a commonly accepted vision of what may be called an "anarchic south" (which, more and more so today, includes the former communist bloc countries of Europe and Central Asia) versus a supposedly well-ordered and stable north (which mostly refers to the old "Western bloc") to justify its will to "enlighten" global politics. In such an ideological perspective, the figure of Hobbes, mobilized in international relations theory to underscore the importance of a dialectic of order versus anarchy, is complicit in disciplinary liberal strategies. Although I offered the philosophical example of Rousseau as a foundation for disciplinary liberalism in the introduction, I suggest that the specific "order versus anarchy" debate that continues to delineate the space of (disciplinary liberal) international affairs in a post–cold war era can best be explored by turning to another liberal tradition, that of Thomas Hobbes and *Leviathan*.

HIDING, ORDERING, REPRESENTING

Images have an advanced religion; they bury history.
— ALFREDO JAAR, CATALOGUE, "REAL PICTURES:
AN INSTALLATION BY ALFREDO JAAR"

The multiple interpretations of contemporary international affairs that rely on a clear dichotomy between order and anarchy are at times attractive and eye-catching. They are often validated by the most gruesome mediatic reports and televisual images that have overflooded public opinions in the West. Pictures of naked slain children in Rwanda, of disfigured refugees in Bosnia, of tortured prisoners in Somalia may not only reveal "pure evil" and a capacity of destruction present in human nature, but, more importantly, may indicate that nobody is in control "out there." The meaning of such graphic reports is supposedly easy to determine: there is no order, only fear and death.

It is in such a (global) context that Chilean photographer Alfredo Jaar has decided to provocatively alter the vision that most Western observers have of these episodes of post–cold war international "anarchy." Jaar spent months in Rwanda in 1994, taking thousands of pictures about the ethnic massacres between the two local rival factions, the Tutsis and the Hutus. Jaar, apparently, photographed everything he could see: mostly people, bodies (dead or alive), scenes of "everyday life under anarchy." His photos probably do not show more than what we have already seen in newspapers or on television in the summer of 1994. Back from Rwanda, Jaar then decided to exhibit his pictures. His exhibition entitled "Real Pictures" opened on January 28, 1995, at the Museum of Contemporary Photography of Columbia College, in Chicago. Instead of displaying his images from Rwanda, shot after shot, on a wall, for instance, Jaar put all his pictures in sealed black boxes so that nobody could actually see them. The entire installation simply consisted of a geometric display of small black boxes, grouped together or separated from one another, with only the description of the pictures supposedly contained in the boxes on top. The exhibit was also sparingly lit, with only a ray of artificial light falling on the black boxes, thus giving the visitor the impression that she or he was walking into a war memorial or a tomb.

Jaar's display is seductive, yet pathetic. Why bother going to Rwanda, taking pictures, and later concealing them from the visitor's eye? Alfredo Jaar's intention, his message perhaps, is for the Western observer to look differently. His exhibit is at once a cynical representation of how the West looks at the disorder(s) of the "other" world and a sadistic plea to abandon the Western vision. It is a cynical representation of how Western viewers, and by extension international political observers and theorists, look at what is beyond order, what is beyond the domestic community and beyond the feeling of security granted by the sovereign nation-state. Put bluntly (but is it any blunter than Jaar's exhibit?), when the Western observer looks at the "international realities" of the post–cold war scene, what she or he gathers is a flood of images, often transmitted via televisual technology, that are fetishized and taken for granted as yet another visual commodity of the late-capitalist age. The Western observer, Jaar intimates, never sees the pictures of Rwanda, the gazes of the victims (and the supposedly specific reality of the situation over there). What the Western viewer sees rather, through his/her daily overdose of images, is the reproduction of a same logic, a logic of dialectical identity and mediatic representation which posits that international disorder is necessarily opposed to domestic or national order. This vision, Jaar insists, is a blind vision, the blind spot of the West's global outlook. Putting everything that is visually seen and characterized as being "outside" the West under a single category, the category of the Same, of anarchy and chaos, is like seeing nothing at all. To put it another way, we see only black boxes. We,

Western observers, apply over and over our same visual frames, our small black boxes, on the "outside."[4]

As a critical visual analysis of the post–cold war international visions and visual consumptions of the West, and, for this present analysis, as a tempting allegory of the way international relations theorists envision their post–cold war (dis)order, Jaar's project is undoubtedly powerful and compelling. Yet, as a sadistic demand to look at Rwanda differently, Jaar's exhibit also carries a suspiciously responsibilizing message that deserves mentioning. One may suggest, in fact, that Jaar is not only interested in critically interpreting the Western gaze. He also holds tremendous power out of his visual presentation. Indeed, he possesses the gaze about Rwanda, has control over the "truth" about the real out there, what his images seen only by him reveal. Jaar hopes that the visitor to his exhibit will desire to move beyond his everyday consumption of images, will seek to see what actually is in the box, and yet will never be able to do so. Empowered by his visual stratagem, Jaar perversely controls the gaze and aesthetically announces the revenge of the "other" world.

It may not be the place here to expand the critical analysis of Jaar's project. Suffice it to say that, understood in these terms, Jaar falls back within the same simplistic structural logic of the Same (the West/the non-West; those who hold the gaze/those who consume images; those who see and live their daily anarchical lives/those who are blind) that is supposedly privileged by the Western observer whom he hopes to challenge.

For the purpose of this book, a more important issue is whether Jaar's politico-photographic display can work as a possible allegory for international relations after the cold war. In many ways, as R. B. J. Walker has already noted,[5] international relations theory reproduces the structural logic of Sameness/Otherness visually denounced by Jaar. This is certainly not a new phenomenon. Rather, as Walker eloquently shows, this "inside/outside" delineation overdetermines much of the past and present discourse of the "international relations" episteme. For realist international relations theorists in particular, the domestic-national domain of political and social activity has traditionally been the privileged model. For realists—but it is also the case with many idealist thinkers[6]—the inner vision of order and hierarchy present within the Western democratic nation-state is the privileged image.[7] By extension, every vision that does not belong or correspond to an image of order or stability in politics falls under the undifferentiated category of the "outside," the "other," the international, the disorderly, and the anarchical.

Post–cold war visions of international relations practices and theories may not vary much from past tendencies. Yet, Jaar directs our attention in a (post)modern era of world politics toward the importance of the visual, toward the role of images, and toward the question of how post–cold war images participate in the reshaping of preconceived beliefs and dichotomies. In other words, the visual frames (often mediatically enhanced) relied upon inside the Western state to truthfully represent the real of global politics, and the dogmatic "blindness" inherent to those frames (as Jaar would claim), are structurally juxtaposed by international theorists and foreign policy analysts to visions of the "outside." The visual post–cold war strategy of the West that Jaar challenges here, a strategy of "looking outside" after the collapse of communism perhaps, is a strategy of continuity and permanence that hopes to visually make sense of the New World (Dis)order. It is a visual strategy that, for Jaar, is still based on a reappropriation of good old (modern) atemporal oppositions between order/chaos, community/anarchy, security/fear, domestic/international, life/death.

Seen through Jaar's allegorical project, the dilemma over post–cold war visions and images, and over the production/consumption of the visual today, echoes the dilemma faced by Hobbes in the midst of the seventeenth century. Both projects are indeed interested in the power of symbolic representation. In particular, both Hobbes and Jaar, in quite different ways, investigate the relation between representation and the possibility of order. Of course, Hobbes and Jaar deal with the question of representation from seemingly antagonistic poles. Whereas Hobbes is trying to build a perfect model of order/security (the modern state) to move away from the "state of nature," Jaar is hoping to show how images, that is, visual representations, are capable of either representing or distorting the real, and of either highlighting or erasing any contingent and singular form of human life that can be found in a state of naturelike condition (which Rwanda exemplifies for Jaar). Yet, both Hobbes and Jaar deal with the visual at a level of (closed) interpretation. As will be shown later, Hobbes's modern project is to impose the sovereign state as a powerful figure capable of holding supreme representation, as a single source of interpretation of the Law. For Jaar, the problem with images is not in their production but rather in their interpretation or their consumption. Thus, interestingly enough, both Hobbes and Jaar embody two different, yet similar in their finality, projects of modernity. Both Hobbes and Jaar end up closing representation(s)—within a sovereign state for Hobbes, and within small black boxes for Jaar. It is not too far-fetched to suggest that both Hobbes's and Jaar's projects are driven by a (modern) fear of dissemination of meaning and by the desire to regulate, in their distinct ways, such an anxiety.

Starting from these allegorical concerns but linking the debate more precisely to international relations theory, this chapter provides the reader with a theoretical and discursive foundation for the subsequent critical and postmodern investigation of the visual ways according to which international relations practices—specifically, peacekeeping interventions—represent post–cold war international politics. This investigation is initiated in this chapter through a theoretical prologue that analyzes, criticizes, and pluralizes the notions of order and anarchy. The problematic of order versus anarchy has traditionally been at the center of most political, theoretical, and disciplinary debates in the field of international studies and continues to be so today. Although the critical/postmodern work of this chapter is performed against the background of Hobbes's political theory and against the background of traditional uses of Hobbesian politics by international relations scholars, it does not hold that most of our post–cold war international visions depict a dilemma easily resolved by Hobbes. Instead of reaffirming, or even criticizing, the validity of a "Hobbesian" approach to contemporary international affairs, the reading performed in the following pages seeks to problematize the need, prevalent among certain international relations theorists, to return to Hobbes in order to close off (within international relations' own "black boxes" perhaps) the representations of international realities that have emerged of late. Instead of foreclosing the interpretation of the visual-scape of international politics and relations by mobilizing Hobbes as a master-signifier of order and anarchy, this chapter opens international relations representations to potential revisions by performing a deconstruction of the Hobbesian text. Far from considering Hobbes as the holder of a sacred truth and mechanism about order and stability in political life (both domestic and international), a classical claim that allows international relations scholars to reproduce the same atemporal models/conceptualizations of international life, I have elected, rather, to showcase the deconstructive work performed on *Leviathan* by Frederick Dolan and, specifically, to draw on Dolan's reading of Hobbes as a philosopher of "ambiguities" and "inconstancies."[8]

As a text in which ambiguities and discontinuities proliferate, Hobbes's *Leviathan* may no longer be a monolithic bloc of truthful doctrine about political order in an overall condition of anarchy that international relations theorists are so eager to apply to their research.[9] It may rather be a pleasingly unexpected text, where meaning is never easily fixed, and from which international theorists, if they choose to revisit Hobbes's text instead of always coming up with the same predetermined and predictable interpretations, may learn important lessons about their representations of international politics.

THE MODERN HOBBES

Hobbes initiates one of the grand projects of modernity: writing human existence from the point of view of the rational subject. Hobbes's project starts with a reinterpretation of God's "state of nature," no longer seen as a paradisiac kingdom from which sinful beings have been expelled and that they desperately long to recover, but rather as a satanic and beastly human condition, what Dolan calls an "ironical inversion of the Story of Genesis."[10]

Cleared of Christian beliefs in "metaphysical" (the term used by Hobbes) forms of authority, Hobbes sets out to correct the disorders, anarchies, and low lives encountered in the "state of nature" by proposing the creation of a mortal and artificial deity, born out of man's reason: Leviathan, or the civil state. Hobbes's "modern God" is much more material and human than the earlier metaphysical constructions of divine authority that he rejects. Leviathan is man's divinity, not created out of nothing; nor is it postulated prior to the existence of human beings. Rather, the civil state becomes a supreme authority (a "common power") grounded in the everyday experience of human individuals. It is a God-like civilian figure that exists only to the extent that individuals have freely consented to leave their "poor, nasty, brutish and short" natural life behind and have commonsensically accepted to form a mutually beneficial union (or Covenant), marked by the presence of Laws,[11] and safeguarded by the protective presence of the state. Read as such, Hobbes's philosophy does find its place within a liberal tradition that emphasizes human rationality and free choice. Dolan summarizes Hobbes's "materialism"[12] and this (liberal) ontological moment as an "attempt to invent a new anchor and a new ground [that] relies upon a privileging of capacities that are adrift owing to qualities inherent in the ground-creating, world-interpreting being, Hobbes's 'natural' individual."[13]

Hobbes's mechanistic materialism assumes that individual beings possess the qualities needed to rationally conduct their own existence. Yet, in the absence of security, protection, and well-being, individual existences will remain in a permanent state of fear, disarray, and destruction. Influenced by the Civil War that he was witnessing at the time of his writing, Hobbes characterizes such a living condition as "the war of all against all." This observation is summarized in this famous passage:

> Hereby it is manifest that during the time men live without a common Power to keep them all in awe, they are in that condition which is called Warre; and such a warre, as is of every man, against every man. For Warre, consisteth not in Battell onely, or the act of fighting; but in a tract of time, wherein the Will to contend by Battell is sufficiently known.[14]

In the absence of a state or sovereign, war and disorder prevail, and greed, survival instincts, and fear of violent death overcome men's capacities of reason.

If human reason (interpreted as everyday common sense by Hobbes rather than as an abstract cogito) pushes individuals to seek protection by creating common Laws and by submitting their Rights to a sovereign power, fear is really what for Hobbes is directly conducive to the creation of Leviathan. It is fear that gives rise to the state as a structure of order and certainty. It is out of fear (of being physically hurt and, finally, killed) that "natural" individuals, reflecting upon their everyday conditions, just as Hobbes was reflecting upon the Civil War perhaps, decide to accept the civil state as an omnipotent source of authority and order. In other words, it is fear, derived from the real conditions of existence of human beings in the "state of nature," that initially triggers the contractual creation of the Sovereign. Finally, it is also fear that moves individuals away from a privileging of their individual capacities, disorderly and chaotic as they may be, to a common acceptance of a unique text of Laws (a Covenant) that will unequivocally interpret and discipline the everyday activities of individual beings. Thus, the making of Leviathan is a panic reaction by nonetheless free and rational human beings.

Moving away from chaos and instability into a realm of order, centralized power (the civil state), and certainty is the project that Hobbes attributes to humankind. Accepting to do so (out of fear rather than out of a recognition of individual free will), individuals allow themselves to become the subjects of a sovereign state, arbitrary as it may be, that will be vested with the supreme task of interpreting and implementing the Laws.[15]

Hobbes's project does not consist in rejecting early metaphysics (Christian theology and Plato's theory of the Forms in particular) in order to unearth the contingent realities of individual existence, even though Hobbes recognizes that experience and knowledge are conditional and circumstantial,[16] and that contingent realities are what make Leviathan possible (if one were not in particular temporal and spatial conditions of danger and insecurity, one would not need a power to "keep us all in awe"). His modern project is rather to recover the living conditions of humankind to better reorder and rechannel them, to recode life in fact, under the sign of a superior authority and master text: the modern state and its ability of interpretation. Dolan explains that

> for Hobbes, "truth consisteth in the right ordering of names" (105) and not in the direct mirroring of an uninterpreted reality. The very idea of uninterpreted reality is, for Hobbes, a legacy of the "Vain Philosophy, and Fabulous Traditions" that he attacks in Chapter 46 of *Leviathan*.[17]

For Hobbes, accepting to live within the Law of the sovereign presupposes the "free submission" of the members of the Commonwealth (the citizens of the state) to a strict discipline. Discipline may be understood here in the Foucauldian sense mentioned in the introduction. To reiterate this previous point, a discipline is a normative and coercive construct, characteristic of the modern project, that seeks to homogenize human existence by producing structures of knowledge that will normalize the human body, the mind, and the psyche. The discipline imposed by Hobbes, as Dolan reveals, is a linguistic and nominalistic discipline. Hoping to get rid of previous religious beliefs in "fantasy figures," abstract creations, and metaphysical determinism, Hobbes plans to reach a necessary condition of peaceful and ordered existence by means of what he calls a "right ordering of names" (as we shall see momentarily). Hobbes proposes nothing more than the implementation of a discursive police. In a closed semiological and linguistic system, in which each sign can have only one specific and strict definition, known by all, the sovereign or state produces "social" life by making it linguistically and normatively homogeneous and unambiguous. The political mission of the sovereign, from which the sovereign gains its unmatched power, is deduced for Hobbes from its interpretive/linguistic role: purging social/domestic life of any possible ambiguity; making human contingencies clear, constant, and secure. Dolan concurs with this analysis:

> Making good the Hobbesian critique of separated essences depends upon constituting a subject of knowledge who can "remember what every name he uses stands for," and who can "place it accordingly" (105); it depends, that is, upon fixed definitions and unambiguous distinctions purged of figural language.[18]

The implementation of such a discursive method (only that which can be defined/worded is meaningful and is worth experiencing), what Hobbes at times calls the creation of a "political science," allows the state to normalize and control its subjects through its sovereign and uncontested power of interpretation.

This discursive method announces also, and perhaps more importantly, the birth of a supreme capacity of symbolic representation for the state. Functioning on the basis of a clearly delineated semiological system—where meaning is ascribed by the sovereign to specific and describable objects and subjects, where signs are unambiguously interpreted and can hold only one signification—the state emerges as both master-signifier and master-signified, as the only mode of wording and the only source of meaning in the newly created political community. Yet, the capacity of symbolic representation of the state, its ability to produce/derive meaning in society, is not a "natural" and unchallengeable process. It is rather, as Hobbes's "ordering of language" shows, a very artificial, arbitrary, and fragile construction (the artificial construction of the "Artificiall Man" perhaps) that depends upon the coercive exercise of a discursive police, and, above all, upon the fact that the inherent ambiguities of language, like those of human existence (found in the state of nature), will not be revealed. If the ambiguities of discourse/language were to be acknowledged, in other words, if polysemia were to be allowed inside Hobbes's construct, meaning produced by the modern state would no longer be the only possible way of envisaging sociopolitical life. Plural and antagonistic views and preferences in the modern community would possibly be given voice, and the sovereign figure of the civil state (its sovereign capacity of representation) would probably have to resort to overtly physical means in order to maintain its supremacy. This, a return to brute power *without the alibi of the text/Law* to cover it, could easily foreground a return to the "natural" individual relations of force described and feared by Hobbes.

If the strength and reliability of Hobbes's mechanism of political order, represented by the modern state, depends upon the implementation of a linguistic/discursive discipline, the weakness of Hobbes's state/Leviathan is also evidenced by language itself (and particularly by Hobbes's own language), and by the failure of Hobbes's discursive police, as a postmodern reading of Hobbes will now show.

THE POSTMODERN(IZED) HOBBES

A postmodern understanding of Hobbes relies upon a critical analysis of the modern Hobbes. But a postmodern reading of Hobbes's *Leviathan* is not interested in formulating a radical rejection of the Hobbesian project. Its aim is certainly not to uncover a hidden meaning about Hobbes's text either, one that would consist in revising all the previous interpretations of Hobbes's philosophy to arrive at a better one. Rather, the interest or curiosity of a postmodern approach is to offer a close reading of Hobbes's text and, by pointing to some inconsistencies, ruptures, excesses, and ambiguities within his discourse, to let the (old or novel) interpretations about Hobbes proliferate.

A postmodern reading starts with the suggestion that Hobbes is in fact very lucid about the contingent difficulties and inherent aporias of his trying to construct an almighty and unambiguous sovereign out of material/mechanical practice, language, and human existence. In other words, a close reading of Hobbes's text shows that, while he still hopes to build a model of order and security able to reconcile individual preferences and differences, the chaotic and material basis (the state of nature) from which his entire modern project stems is hard to supersede, even with the help of a discursive police.

Dolan's deconstruction of Hobbes's text drives the analysis toward similar destinations. By paying close attention to Hobbes's tropes, and to their polysemic deployment within the text, Dolan suggests that Hobbes is aware of the constant supplementation of language, of the fact that once a term is introduced it is open to plural interpretations and uses. This lucid recognition on the part of Hobbes—the realization that he "became increasingly troubled by the depth of the divergence between the prescriptions and premises of his theory on the one hand, and the realities of human nature and politics on the other"[19]—is reason enough for him to fear that the ordering/disciplining project centered around the modern state will not succeed without the implementation of a method capable of thwarting the proliferations of language, without what Dolan calls "an unambiguous political vocabulary."[20]

Dolan's deconstruction operates an ironic reversal of Hobbes's linguistico-political project. Where Hobbes seeks to advance order, certainty, and sovereignty, Dolan mobilizes the inconstancies/inconsistencies present in Hobbes's political discourse. Where Hobbes dreams of establishing a discursive police, Dolan points to the "ambiguities" of Hobbes's own vocabulary. Dolan concludes his deconstructive analysis in the following terms:

> *Leviathan* attempts to establish an unambiguous political vocabulary on the basis of figures whose multiple meanings necessarily thwart any such project. At each stage, the hoped-for "constancy"— political, psychological, metaphysical—appears compromised by the resources of the figures in which Hobbes chooses to state it, and must be guaranteed by supplementary measures.[21]

This textually inherent instability of Hobbes's project, the instability of Artificiall Man perhaps, deserves more attention and may be the object of a supplementary deconstructive analysis (a textual analysis that, opened up by Dolan's own deconstruction, supplements both Hobbes's and Dolan's texts).

The notion of "textual instability" is an important one. Not only does this notion pluralize Hobbes's discourse, but furthermore, it puts into question the entire (modern) project, prevalent among international relations theorists as will be shown momentarily, which consists in interpreting Hobbes as the founder of an infallible mechanism of political order and stability. In other words, by putting to the fore some "instabilities" present in Hobbes's text, the will-to-order reproduced by contemporary theorists of domestic and international politics from a so-called Hobbesian model appears just as compromised and dogmatic as Hobbes's will-to-constancy through language.

The "instability" of Hobbes's politico-linguistic enterprise stems from his understanding of language. Realizing that, despite his intentions, language is never completely closed but on the contrary always already open to interpretations and reinterpretations, Hobbes is at a loss when it comes to proving that language is a necessarily fixed and stable basis of knowledge. His "discourse on language" and his "right ordering of names" seek to impose a strict and rigid mechanism of knowledge. Yet, supplements and excesses end up creeping into Hobbes's text and, like a loose thread, undo the entire discursive edifice.

Knowledge, Hobbes insists, exists only to the extent that understanding can be transcribed into words whose definitions are unambiguously posed to start with. With such an arbitrary linguistic structure (Hobbes discovers language as an arbitrary code), connections can be made between different terms, unambiguous resolutions can be taken, and a knowledge of the right ordering of things can be arrived at.[22] Hobbes's discourse on language is best summarized in the following paragraph:

> Seeing then that *truth* consisteth in the right ordering of names in our affirmations, a man that seeketh precise *truth,* had need to remember what every name he uses stands for; and to place it accordingly; or else he will find himselfe entangled in words, as a bird in lime-twiggs; the more he struggles, the more belimed.[23]

In an ironic reversal of his own discourse and construct, however, Hobbes turns out to be like one of those "birds" and "finds himself entangled in words" that slide beyond his tightly organized project. A few pages later, Hobbes is pushed to realize that language is often deployed in a much more chaotic and pluralistic manner. Indeed, if "public opinions are volatile,"[24] their modes of communication and expression are too. Hobbes, then, has to address the possibility that language is an unstable ground upon which to establish a lasting and solid political system. Hobbes gives this unstable language the name of "absurdities" or "inconstant signification." By naming this plural usage of language "absurdity" or "inconstancy," Hobbes hopes to reinsert these linguistic supplements to his "right ordering of names" into his nominalistic system. However, by recognizing that language evolves and varies according to practices and uses, Hobbes shows the artificiality and fragility of his discursive construct. In a sense, Hobbes deconstructs his own enterprise. Aware of the contingent deployment of language by "public opinions," and of the fact that imposing a "constant language" on every human activity would be nothing more than a return to religious or metaphysical languages (Hobbes's perpetual enemies), Hobbes falls back into "ambiguity" (Dolan) and his text ends up being a delightful irony. The following passage may be read as the emblematic mark of irony in Hobbes's work:

> The name of such things as affect us, that is, which please, and displease us, because all men be not alike affected with the same thing, nor the same man at all times, are in the common discourses of men, of *inconstant* signification. For seeing all names are imposed to signifie our conceptions; and all our affections are but conceptions; when we conceive the same things differently, we can hardly avoyd different naming of them. For though nature of that we conceive, be the same; yet, the diversity of our reception of it, in respect of different constitutions of body, and prejudices of opinion, gives everything a tincture of our different passions. And therefore in reasoning, a man must take heed of words; which besides the signification of what we imagine of their nature, have a signification also of the nature, disposition, and interest of the speaker; such as are the names Vertues, and Vices; For one man calleth *Wisdome,* what another calleth *feare*; and one *cruelty,* what another *justice*; one *prodigality,* what another *magnanimity*; and one *gravity,* what another *stupidity,* &c. And therefore such names can never be true grounds of any ratiocination. No more can Metaphors, and Tropes of speech: but these are less dangerous, because they profess their inconstancy; which the other do not [Hobbes's emphases].[25]

Read in direct contrast to Hobbes's earlier passages on language, the notion of "inconstant signification" destabilizes the rigidity of Hobbes's discursive project. This paragraph exemplifies the tension in Hobbes between his recognition of individual differences (which naturally proliferate) and his attempt at discursively creating a sovereign power (the mark of antidifference). This inner tension in Hobbes's work (recognizing difference versus imposing a mastertext) slides to the level of language, where for Hobbes everything has to be decided. Anticipating some postmodern moves, Hobbes realizes that knowledge (including knowledge of life in society) can never be placed outside language (textuality, discursivity). But Hobbes tries to rechannel language toward specific ends which, as a deconstructive reading shows, is nevertheless a vain enterprise. By sliding to the level of the text, this major tension between (natural) differences and (artificial) sovereignty produces textual instability. This tension indeed leads to discursive *aporiae* and textual "ambiguities" that destabilize Hobbes's project. Against his desire to impose a discursive mechanism conducive to truth, "inconstant significations" are the direct expressions of how individuals conceive of the world around them. And because individuals are placed in different situations and have different ways of expressing their perception of the real, the words they pronounce, inconstant as they are, cannot be trusted to form a common ground of knowledge (as the above passage emphasizes). Yet, Hobbes never reconciles the fact that individuals' "inconstant significations" are the same language, the necessary linguistic basis that makes possible the "right ordering of names" and the creation of "Artificiall Man." Built on a shaky nominalistic foundation, both the "right ordering of names" and Hobbes's sovereign are doomed to remain unstable and inconsistent. Hobbes's only way out is to quickly move to the assumption that the sovereign is created (by a mutual pact that magically supersedes the inconstant significations of individuals in society).[26] Once the sovereign is created, signification and interpretation of the law are arbitrarily placed on his side. But this magical intervention (words are no longer pronounced by individuals but by an Artificiall Man who speaks for individual beings) produces a language, a "constant signification," that may have nothing to do with the language of the people, the different "inconstant significations" "naturally" produced by individuals. Given such a *décalage* (discrepancy) in language, how can a discursive political community be meaningful and last? Given this possible nonidentification or misrecognition of the sovereign's language, of his Law, only discipline, an executive and discursive police, and the blind overt power of the sovereign can coercively solidify the modern political community.

Thus, a deconstructive reading of Hobbes's "discourse on language" suggests that, in the inner fight that haunts Hobbes's work (proliferation of natural differences versus order and security guaranteed by the state), it is the proliferation of difference(s), expressed through an "inconstant" and "unstable" language, that ends up being privileged. Creeping through Hobbes's own textual inconstancies, differences and instabilities end up dominating the Hobbesian politico-linguistic system.

Seen at this angle, it is more than ironic that contemporary political theorists have relied on Hobbes to provide a durable model of political order. Theorists of the modern state and sovereignty, for example, have traditionally acknowledged a Hobbesian heritage.[27] These theorists are not interested in problematizing Hobbes's work. Assuming that Hobbes's texts have nothing surprising or unexpected to offer anymore, they do not see the necessity of rereading his theories. A postmodern revisiting of Hobbes, as was shown above, does not desperately look for novelty and surprise in his texts either. Nevertheless, returning to Hobbes's writing several times as if, every time, it were a brand new text, a reader with a postmodern approach is willing to accept the unexpected if it arises. In contrast to the postmodern reader, what most modern political interpreters of Hobbes do is impose a dogmatic frame over the Hobbesian text and theory. For modern theorists who wish to uncover a theory of the modern state in Hobbes, surprise gives way to predetermined interpretation. Treated as an unproblematic text and doctrine of state power or sovereignty, Hobbes's political theory may appear to be unambiguous. By highlighting only what in Hobbes's text validates their own particular projects, modern political theorists turn Hobbes into a defender of atemporal mechanisms of power and into a structural thinker of order and security (the way realist international relations theorists like to read Hobbes). Through such a facile caricature, Hobbes becomes a thinker who relies on binary oppositions to implement his political model (state of nature versus common power, anarchy versus order, differences versus ordering of names, Rights versus Laws). This binary thinking is no doubt part of Hobbes's thought. Yet, as was suggested above, there is more to Hobbes than a political theory intent on opposing order to anarchy. Indeed, through the Hobbesian text itself, this opposition of order to anarchy is revealed to be artificial, fragile, and inconsistent.

Beyond a structural framing that emphasizes Hobbes's binary thinking, other interpretations may thus be envisaged. But this play of differences and interpretations offered by Hobbes's text is often buried under the desire of political theorists to use Hobbes as the founder of basic truths about sovereignty, power, and order. Such a narrow reading of Hobbes is exactly the type of reading (or lack of open-ended reading) that has been privileged by many theorists of international politics. International relations theorists have traditionally simplified Hobbes's analysis and directed it toward their own preoccupations.[28] Above all, they have insisted on treating Hobbes as the purveyor of a fundamental point of departure for any valid theorization about international politics: the notion of anarchy. It is toward a critical reading of this notion, supposedly borrowed from Hobbes by international relations theory, that this chapter now turns.

HOBBES AS A THEORIST OF INTERNATIONAL ANARCHY

In international relations theory, realist scholars are, by and large, responsible for the appropriation and banalization of Hobbes's thinking. To give but a recent illustration of such an epistemological takeover, John J. Mearsheimer's somewhat paranoid vision of post–cold war international security challenges is clearly affirming a so-called Hobbesian heritage. Mearsheimer writes that we may soon end up "lamenting the loss of order that the Cold War gave to the anarchy of international relations. For untamed anarchy—Hobbes's war of all against all—is a prime cause of armed conflict."[29] Mearsheimer's comments are a typical form of "Hobbesian realism" in international relations. Realist scholars generally find in Hobbes the basis for their understanding of the importance of order and anarchy (or order as opposed to anarchy) in international politics. Applying what they call a "domestic analogy," realists like Mearsheimer argue that the international environment of states is in a condition similar to that of Hobbes's "state of nature." Realists reappropriate for their own enterprise the canonical Hobbesian vision of "natural life," a vision according to which, prior to the Covenant, human existence is governed by competition, fear, diffidence, and greed.[30] In such a natural state, conflicts arise and the need for self-preservation (what realists transcribe into national interest) is exacerbated. By analogy with Hobbes, realist authors thus decide that world politics should be viewed as a "war of all against all." This is perhaps best summarized by Hans Morgenthau, arguably the most ardent defender of post–World War II realism, who declares that "the essence of international politics is identical with its domestic counterpart. Both domestic and international politics are a struggle for power."[31]

In a Hobbesian spirit, it would appear that the only possible solution to the permanent state of war would be to appoint a sovereign. Such a supreme being, capable of holding unmatched power and centralizing fear, would allow the individuals living under the new Covenant to develop into a peaceful and ordered community. Unfortunately, the international system, realists tell us, is composed of individually sovereign, equal, and powerful states. As such, international politics cannot hope to see the fulfillment of Hobbes's version of the rule of Law. This is no doubt the drama of international life. And this is what explains, in a perpetual international "state of nature," the permanence of anarchy. In the absence of Laws, anarchy is the conventional truth about international politics as realist scholars understand it. Put in other terms, under an international system composed of multiple Leviathans, the creation of a super-Leviathan does not belong to the realist reality of international politics. Lack of order is a fateful consequence. Content with the fact that states are and will remain the sovereign actors in international politics, international relations scholars suggest that the only possible outcome out of a general state of war is for states to continuously rely on their power capacities as a guarantee for their survival. By constantly acting as independent subjects with an autonomous capacity of power, states may end up balancing one another's threats and may avoid direct conflicts. Thus, just as individuals in a "state of nature" are the basis for what follows for Hobbes, in a condition of international anarchy, the presence of the state as a power-seeking and power-enacting agent is the cornerstone of the realist vision of international politics. This classical interpretation of Hobbes through a "domestic analogy" is relatively coherent. It certainly is not aimed at problematizing or pluralizing Hobbes's text. Rather, it uses Hobbes as a "father figure," a master-signifier, which serves to reinforce classical realist conceptualizations of world politics. Beyond this analogical reading of Hobbes, in the margins of the realist use of Hobbes, some questions need to be posed. It is the task of critical and postmodern readers to work from the margins of international relations theory and pose potentially disturbing and provocative questions. In the present context, the critical/postmodern reader wishes to ask what is at stake for international relations theory in using Hobbes as the political thinker of international anarchy, and what kind of stable theoretical and political ground Hobbes's theorization of order against anarchy provides for realism.

Recent works by David Campbell[32] and R. B. J. Walker[33] have begun to address these questions. These studies suggest that international relations theorists are not interested in remarking the complexity and possible "inconstancy" of the concept of Hobbesian "anarchy." Rather, they are concerned with what the mobilization of the notion of "anarchy" offers for international relations and the practice of foreign policy making. In these critical views (which refuse to be satisfied with a realist reappropriation of Hobbes and, instead, choose to return to the Hobbesian text to problematize current concepts and practices), Hobbes's "anarchy" is revealed as a powerful alibi for realist international relations. Presented as an irrefutable truth, "anarchy" is a notion that guarantees the perpetuation of structural visions about international politics. Hobbes's "anarchy" is a "strategy of otherness"[34] that allows the domestic model, that of order and community safeguarded by a sovereign, to be privileged. For Campbell, foreign policy is a (realist) practice of international politics that reaffirms "anarchy" as a mode of structural othering, as an arbitrary legitimation for the constructed separation between domestic and international, between "the 'state' and 'the international system'."[35] Foreign policy, and its anarchy/otherness–producing effects, is truly the realists' transposition of Hobbes's attempt at making Artificiall Man. It is an all too convenient reproduction of the Hobbesian *fiat* which now becomes a "let us make international relations" type of creation. Walker adds to this critical insight by indicating that the use of Hobbes as a master-text on anarchy facilitates the deployment of an "inside/outside" divide, whereby "the distinction between an authentic political community within and an absence of community between states" is reinscribed.[36] Constructed as such, the so-called Hobbesian anarchy is indeed never problematized by classical international relations theory. Whatever "anarchy" means, what "anarchy" represents, what different positions are encompassed under such a categorical "outside," what plural political possibilities are offered by the deployment of "anarchy" are perspectives or questions that remain "foreign" to international relations and foreign policy practices as realists understand them. Similarly, the inner tension present in Hobbes's work between differences and the possibility of order is never addressed. Rather, Hobbes's "anarchy" is resolved as a fixed position for the development of realist politics. Far from being a point of rupture, where inconstancies, instabilities, and differences emerge, "anarchy" becomes a stable ground.

A convenient displacement from "anarchy" to the notion of "domestic analogy" is what allows realists to stabilize "anarchy." The "domestic analogy" of international politics is a notion that may not be directly attributed to Hobbes,[37] but is at least often derived by international relations scholars from Hobbes's account of politics, as was shown above. "Domestic analogy" is a structural method that allows international scholars to resolve the ambiguities/instabilities of Hobbes's "anarchy." "Domestic analogy" is an interpretive framework, conceptually and normatively limited, that seeks to deproblematize "anarchy." It is yet another disciplinary construct (with its own discursive police, i.e., the realist rhetoric)[38] that hopes to remodel "anarchy" so as to make it fit within the parameters of the modern state and foreign policy discourses. Hence, through the imposition of a model of "domestic analogy," "anarchy" is simplified, universalized, and tamed. "Anarchy" is no longer the insuperable name for human differences, public opinion's inconstancies encountered by Hobbes. It now becomes the "other side" of order, its antagonistic other, which has to be rejected, not explained (visually commodified, and not actually looked at, as Jaar would put it). "Anarchy" via the "domestic analogy" of the realists becomes that against which domestic order, the state as opposed to the international system, is meant to prevail. As usual, this entire operation is attributed to Hobbes himself, whose text is not allowed to proliferate but, on the contrary, is restrained within the bounds of dogmatic realist interpretations.

HOBBES AGAINST THE WILL-TO-ANARCHY

Hedley Bull's summary of Morgenthau's approach is appropriate to the present investigation. Bull writes that "[o]ne way of looking at Morgenthau's work is to see it as an attempt to restate the view of international politics contained in the works of Thomas Hobbes—to make it fully explicit, to systematize it, to expound it in the idiom and to relate it to the preoccupations of another generation."[39] In the light of what was said above, what Bull describes is the need to extract "anarchy" out of Hobbes's text and context, and rhetorically apply it (or "expound it in [a new] idiom") to more current (realist) observations. In other words, realists seek to refer to Hobbes in order to continue to impose a will-to-anarchy onto the discipline and practice of international relations. The will-to-anarchy is a guarantee of order and status quo in the realist version of international politics. Realists "will" anarchy, as Bull notes, because it allows the same concepts (state power, the domestic community as the model for order, national interest as a guide to foreign policy) to be reproduced and to remain unchallenged.

The will-to-anarchy of realist international relations works as a metaconcept. It is a sovereign notion and construct from which all meanings are derived. Here sovereignty may be understood in a sense that is very close to Hobbes's notion. The will-to-anarchy is the sovereign mechanism of international politics as realists see it because it is a mechanism that discursively mobilizes and centralizes fear. Similar to Hobbes's sovereign "civil state" (able to monopolize fear), the will-to-anarchy of the realists pushes states and their foreign policy makers to perpetually replicate similar types of attitudes if they want to survive in a supposedly inimical surrounding. "Anarchy" (the "outside") is what is to be feared for states. Order (the "inside") is what has to be preserved at all costs. The will-to-anarchy is thus fundamental to the success of the will-to-order that guarantees the continuous domination/preservation of the state and its hegemonic structures.

It may be seen that Hobbes is the thinker who a posteriori introduced the will-to-anarchy into realism (hence, Hobbes with anarchy). However, one may also read Hobbes as one who is less concerned with international politics and its conflicts than he is with what he considers to be the terrifying possibilities of domestic civil disorders (hence, Hobbes against anarchy). Far from "restating the view of international politics contained in Hobbes's work" (Bull), realists are once again providing a bad caricature of Hobbes's text. This may be shown by suggesting that Hobbes, when he actually talks about international relations (only a few passages are denotatively devoted to international politics), is not trying to impose the notion of "anarchy" at all. Put in other terms, Hobbes does not characterize the "outside" as a realm of fear and danger. Hobbes writes:

> But though there had never been any time, wherein particular men were in a condition of warre one against another; yet in all times, Kings, and Persons of Soveraigne authority, because of their Independency, are in continuall jealousies, and in the state and posture of Gladiators; having their weapons pointing, and their eyes fixed on one another; that is their Forts, Garrisons, and Guns upon the Frontiers of their Kingdomes; and continuall Spyes upon their neighbours; which is a posture of War. But because they uphold thereby, the Industry of their Subjects; there does not follow from it, that misery, which accompanies the Liberty of particular men.[40]

For Hobbes, international relations and conflicts are no "miseries." Rather, they are phenomena that cannot be ignored, or simply cast "outside." International relations are activities that states should necessarily indulge in, for they help to reinforce the domestic community. We find here with Hobbes a notion that is also present in Machiavelli. The Prince or sovereign should look to gain or maintain power not so much for the sake of possessing power or authority, but rather because power is necessary to protect the domestic community from internal divisions and foreign invasions.[41] Once again, the international side of politics is used as a way of reinforcing or comforting its domestic counterpart, and, ultimately, of solidifying the civil community. But Hobbes does not need to establish "anarchy" as a universal "other," as a permanent evil in international politics, to arrive at the conclusion that the "Industry of the state's Subjects" is the supreme good that must be preserved. Hobbes does not need to rely on a will-to-anarchy to produce a will-to-order. This view suggests that Hobbes actually places more trust, or optimism perhaps, in international politics than realist scholars are willing to do. Of course, prudence and diffidence will continue to dominate the international affairs of states, but international politics is not the "state of nature." It is not the supreme mark of a "solitary, poore, nasty, brutish and short" life feared by Hobbes. It can rather be seen as an arena of politics (a specific practice/art of politics) that is full of opportunities for the state. This is precisely what Walker notes too:

It is possible to go even further with this line of reasoning. Given that states are not as vulnerable as individuals, prudence and fear suggest not the necessity of a global Leviathan but the need for some rules of co-existence; principles of sovereignty and non-intervention, for example, or mechanisms like the balance of power. In teasing out these themes, Hobbes begins to slide out of the realist camp and becomes a prime example, like Bull himself, of a theorist of interstate society, rather than interstate anarchy.[42]

Walker's point is congruent with a reading that suggests that Hobbes's so-called model of international politics is much more "ambiguous" than stable. It has perhaps less to do with "anarchy" than it has to do with a desire to find a system of cohabitation among states.[43] This reading, pushed further, indicates Hobbes's willingness to study international affairs not as a monolithic and undifferentiated "outside" sphere, but rather as a domain of political life where the presence of different realities pushes the state to prudence. Once again, a dilemma may be seen to emerge in Hobbes's work at this point. On the one hand, states continually behave the same way in international politics. Protecting the domestic commonwealth is their primary motive. Yet, on the other hand, international politics is potentially less frightening and harmful than domestic "anarchic" politics (civil war) and, as Walker notes, possibilities can arise for different situations to be envisaged. This dilemma is unresolved by Hobbes and unresolvable in his text. It is, however, easily resolved by theorists of international relations who interpret Hobbes as a thinker of international "anarchy." Acting as stereotypical "political scientists" (in Hobbes's sense), realist international relations scholars have simply decided to "purge" Hobbes's work "of its ambiguities."

Given the apparent absence of a formulation of "anarchy" in Hobbes's vision of international politics (or, at least, the absence of a formulation of the realist notion of "anarchy"), one has to conclude that it is once again the "domestic analogy," and not "anarchy," that governs the realist model. It is an arbitrary juxtaposition of Hobbes's description of the "state of nature" with international politics as realist authors wish to understand it that, in fact, authorizes their views. This is no doubt the way international relations theorists have decided to "stabilize" Hobbes's political edifice. Resorting to arbitrary structural devices (like the "domestic analogy") and mobilizing so-called Hobbesian signs even when they are not visible, the realist enterprise of international relations theory is an erroneous representation of Hobbes's political philosophy. Realism misrepresents Hobbes as a stable ground or origin for a theory of order and anarchy in international politics because, in fact, in the Hobbesian text, there are more instabilities and ambiguities than fixed positions. The next section extends the exploration of the "Hobbesian theme" in international relations by examining the situation of the realist representation of "anarchy" (or what is left of it) now that, in a post–cold war era, structural binaries, the view of an "inside versus an outside," are faced with growing claims to globalism or globalization. Specifically, a particular focus is placed on the suddenly rediscovered practice of United Nations peacekeeping and on how such a strategy of international action, in a renewed but transformed "Hobbesian spirit" perhaps, seeks to redefine the boundary between order and anarchy, inside and outside, in an era when global politics supposedly faces global problems.

FROM STRUCTURALISM TO GLOBALISM, OR WHEN LEVIATHAN GOES TO THE UN

Peacekeepers have to learn how to deal with a multiplicity of authorities; the leaders of such groups are often inaccessible and their identity even unknown; chains of command are shadowy; armed persons are disowned; discipline is non-existent and brutal; and everywhere there is an evil proliferation of arms.

—UN SECRETARY-GENERAL BOUTROS-GHALI,
"EMPOWERING THE UNITED NATIONS"

All this confirms that we are still in a time of transition. The end of the Cold War was a major movement of tectonic plates and the after-shocks continue to be felt. But even if the ground beneath our feet has not yet settled, we still live in a new age that holds great promise for both peace and development.

—UN SECRETARY-GENERAL BOUTROS-GHALI,
SUPPLEMENT TO *AN AGENDA FOR PEACE*

The overall condition of post–cold war international relations is best summarized by these two quotations from former United Nations Secretary-General Boutros Boutros-Ghali. After the collapse of communism, the fixed ground of realist international relations becomes, in Boutros-Ghali's words, an "unsettled ground" that can hold only the promise (not the reality) of order and security. Until such a promise is realized, post–cold war international relations is doomed to encounter the type of chaotic and unsettling phenomena described in Boutros-Ghali's first quotation. The artificiality and "inconstancy" of realist structural constructs are all the more noticeable as images of disorder, chaos, and multiple identities broadcast throughout the global mediascape exacerbate the feeling of widespread insecurity. Yet, far from moving away from Hobbes, international relations scholars continue to pose basically Hobbesian (in form if not in spirit) questions: how can order and stability be reintroduced in the international practice of states? Where can international relations find a "stable ground" now that the realist binaries have been superseded by the end of the cold war and submerged by a flow of recognized events that, at first glance, do not appear to make (structural) sense?

Although "anarchy" was believed to be a settled matter,[44] its specter now resurfaces through the image of a proliferation of evils, through a notion that some have alarmingly started to call a "coming anarchy."[45] Order and anarchy are no longer structural guarantees.[46] The old discourse of (structural) realism, reliant on a certain understanding of Hobbes, is no longer able to offer the "right ordering of names" required for the new period. For international relations theory, the post–cold war era does not only continue to pose "Hobbesian" questions about order. Rather, the current theoretical debate is at the very core of Hobbes's unresolved dilemma between the proliferation of (natural) differences and the need to impose a sovereign mechanism of antidifference. The problem, however, is that contemporary international relations theorists feel that they no longer have the "right ordering of names" inherited from the cold war, or, at least, that such a realist "ordering" no longer seems to master the current realities.

It may be the case that the New World Order requires a new word order.[47] A new "right ordering of names" is required to rediscover order out of the post–cold war's global instabilities. Such a discursive project is exactly what Boutros-Ghali is hoping to inaugurate with the two above-quoted statements. Interestingly, just as Hobbes was arguably establishing the "state of nature" as a "dire prospect" that everyone would want to stay away from and "from which his radical presumptions [could] be judged a worthy pursuit,"[48] Boutros-Ghali needs to brandish the banner of insecurity, chaos, and absolute danger in order to, later, by way of contrast, justify the necessity for a new formulation of international order (which he believes he has discovered). The second of the two quotations already marks the passage from the "new anarchy" to potential order under the form of a promise to come. This new promise of order, this new way of taming "anarchy," is the subject of Boutros-Ghali's seminal work, his *Agenda for Peace*. In *An Agenda for Peace,* Boutros-Ghali reveals the secrets of the new recipe for international order: globalization, the UN, and peacekeeping.

In *An Agenda for Peace,* Boutros-Ghali's visionary thinking is clearly deployed. Boutros-Ghali's overt optimism contrasted to the "dire prospect" of anarchy constitutes the theoretical foundations of this essay. In response to the "changing context" of international politics, Boutros-Ghali introduces a new vocabulary and new definitions, a "new ordering of names" in the practice of world affairs, which shall cover more thoroughly and accurately the extent of global changes. Faced with plural transformations and contingent situations that the discipline of international relations cannot fully integrate (at least, in a classical realist fashion), the United Nations and its support of what becomes known as the New World Order are given by Boutros-Ghali a novel discursive posture. For Boutros-Ghali, it is diplomacy that has to be redefined, discursively restructured, in a (verbal) way that is able to accommodate the necessary presence of the UN and the central function of its peacekeeping policies.

With this scheme in mind, Boutros-Ghali maps four supposedly different discursive fields of post–cold war UN activities: preventive diplomacy, peacemaking, peacekeeping, and postconflict peacebuilding.[49] These four activities of United Nations interventionism are basically similar in practice. They simply refer to the UN and its armed operations (conducted by blue-helmets) before (preventive diplomacy), during (peacemaking and peacekeeping), and after (postconflict peacebuilding) an international crisis. These four domains represent what is traditionally known today as peacekeeping. Although peacekeeping is supposed to be distinct from the other three activities (but it is never clearly explained how and why it is distinct), peacekeeping is the more generic wording for this new mapping of UN post–cold war diplomacy. It is indeed a matter of using terminology to delineate, of linking the practice of wording to the practice of mapping. The four diplomatic domains are inscribed as a new geography of international relations. They reintegrate state relations inside supposedly specific domains of UN interventionism[50] by rhetorically slicing up the field of international relations into four supposedly important, complementary, and exhaustive components of diplomatic activity. Global order will become the logical outcome of such a diplomatic discursive reorganizing, not so much because Boutros-Ghali gives this recentering (around the UN) of diplomatic efforts actual means of effectivity (this mapping is mostly an ideal-scape of global affairs, not a practical strategy), but rather because this reordering of diplomacy, effected by a reorganizing of concepts, casts the very possibility of war, disorder, and "anarchy" away. Boutros-Ghali's new diplomatic wording conjures away the possibility of war and redrafts post–cold war international relations as a coherent and secure diplomatic domain. Boutros-Ghali writes: "these four areas for action, *taken together,* and carried out with the backing of all Members, offer a *coherent* contribution towards securing peace in the spirit of the Charter" [my emphasis].[51]

Boutros-Ghali's text is a discursive performance that seeks to shape a new all-encompassing vision of international diplomacy to which all states should adhere. If the coherence of this system is not achieved by the practical effectivity of the methods offered (once again, no specific suggestion on how to operate these four domains is given), the so-called coherence of Boutros-Ghali's system is merely ideological. It is ideologically coherent because it clears the very possibility of war, chaos, and "anarchy" off the new diplomatic picture. It offers the impression that inside this new mode of international diplomacy, which supposedly encompasses the new reality of international affairs, peace is eternally realized (or, at least, realizable). By rewording and reworking the field of meaningful peaceful action (and the meaning of peace and order as well) around the UN and the four "areas for action," Boutros-Ghali initiates the recolonizing process of all the contingent events and elements of post–cold war international politics. Simultaneously, he discursively authorizes the deployment of a New World Order ideology (call it disciplinary neo–liberalism if you will), shared by member states and extended to the confines of UN diplomatic peacekeeping/making/building/enforcing mandates. Through Boutros-Ghali's *Agenda for Peace,* the world of the UN, unclearly defined and yet depicted as if it covered the entire surface of world affairs, must become the new hegemonic international system, the next ideological structure of world order. The values traditionally associated with the UN (and recognized in its founding Charter)[52] will provide the rationale (or alibi) for the creation of such a new order.

The "new ordering of names" attempted by Boutros-Ghali is also supported by emerging concepts and patterns of international relations theory. The debate around the question of order and discourse is reproduced today, in the theory of international relations, by what has recently been called neoidealism or neoliberalism which, to some degree, comes to the rescue in the absence of a "realist vision." This supposedly new perspective on international affairs, championed by Charles Kegley in particular,[53] is prima facie a return to idealist universalizing tendencies in international affairs (global democracy, human rights, peacekeeping, etc.). By resurrecting universal visions of world affairs (global solutions for a global planet), neoidealists seek to reorder the post–cold war age and its proliferation of "evils" in the absence of evident structural binaries.[54] Neoidealists reiterate the visionary discourse of idealism, that of Woodrow Wilson for instance,[55] in order to determine the contours of a new global order (as a not yet realized and, thus, imaginary global landscape) in which conflicts, disorders, instabilities, ambiguities, proliferations, and differences are resolved. As such, this neoidealist discourse also hopes to solidify the theoretical basis of Boutros-Ghali's "new diplomatic model" centered around the UN's four modes of post–cold war interventionism. In the early to mid-1990s context of international relations theory, it is this specific discourse, with clear universalist penchants, that suggests that the United Nations can look like a successor to Leviathan in an endless search for global order. It is not a question of materially re-creating the UN as a Leviathan, as a world government capable of using force, coercion, and discipline to impose order. Rather, it is a matter of forming a rhetoric, a new discursive platform, that will make possible the belief (or the promise) that the UN can indeed fulfill the mandate of a Leviathan in international politics, even if it does not possess the physical capacities that were necessary to the original Leviathan to centralize fear. As Boutros-Ghali's previous diplomatic reordering demonstrates, and as the neoidealist visionary spirit intimates, the United Nations is highlighted as the central location where independent Leviathans of the old age may now, in the 1990s, find a safe haven, a place where they can safely relax and let another structure achieve order and security on their behalf. From independent and sovereign Leviathans to the UN as an instrument of global order, from the realists' Hobbes to Boutros-Ghali and neoidealism's discourse on globalization by means of the UN, a "new word order" seeks to affirm itself through the disruptions of the discipline of international relations in a post–cold war era. This new word/world ordering is perhaps no longer a matter of casting away "anarchy" outside the bounds of a domestically stable sphere of state sovereignty. It is, rather, a matter of colonizing anarchy, of conquering this categorical "outside" by expanding the limits of the liberal state under the ideological formula of disciplinary liberalism on a global scale. Simply, it becomes a matter of "glocalization," as some have ironically put it.[56] This takes the form, announced in the introduction, of a global will to UN-iformity, a universal will-to-purity,[57] which hopes to deter the proliferation, hyperrealization, and hybridization of signs, images, bodies, and nations in contemporary international life by globally recolonizing them. As was previously mentioned, this work, performed under the sign of the UN and globalization, is necessarily an ideological and disciplinary task. It is a global enterprise that returns contemporary international relations theory to concerns with ideology and hegemony, and with the new technologies and media through which ideology is now mobilized (the work of simulation, for instance).

With the overt choice made by the new hegemonic discourse (Boutros-Ghali's or Kegley's) toward a recolonization and a globalization of the "outside," another technique of ordering is revealed. In an important supplementary manner—particularly so in a post–cold war era where visual technologies proliferate, visual recognitions of knowledge take precedence over more classical linguistic or verbal forms (the impact of the Internet, for instance), and ideological intimations take on visual and virtual shapes (television hailings condition sociopolitical behaviors as much if not more than rules and modes of interaction imposed by more traditional apparatuses)—the New World Order is *no longer not only*, if one may use such a neology, guaranteed by a "new word order." The New World Order supported by the new United Nations diplomacy is no longer based on a "right ordering of names" only.

Rather, as Jaar allegorizes, the New World/Word Order is supplemented by what may be called a "right ordering of images."

As Hobbes tried to dogmatically and nominalistically demonstrate, order may be achieved through naming. The story or fiction narrated by Hobbes's sovereign and written in the normative language of disciplinary power is no doubt an efficient means of control and stability. Yet, in a contemporary perspective (Hobbes in the 1990s), his blatant metaphoric depiction and imagery of the sovereign as a body composed of individual subjects[58] would perhaps be just as compelling. Interestingly for contemporary representations of knowledge and power, Hobbes had already supplemented his discursive construct of political order with a pictorial rendition, with what can be called a recourse to visual allegorization. In the 1990s, Hobbes would be able to use CD-ROM technologies and, no doubt, have his own web-site (Leviathanet?) to enhance his theory of power and politics.

The allegory of the small black boxes is not simply anecdotic or illustrative of a so-called "Hobbesian condition." It also reveals one of the changes that has recently occurred in the rhetoric of international order. Jaar's display moves the critical analysis of the will-to-order, omnipresent in contemporary international relations debates, away from a reading of international relations as a "right ordering of names" and toward a revisiting (or re-envisioning) of this field as a discursive and linguistic enterprise supplemented by visuality. Beyond a structural realist discourse in which observations and images (Waltz) were confined within the bounds of the realist text, images have now found a way of escaping the "real world" of the realist text. Today, the hegemonic discourse of disciplinary neoliberal globalization conveyed by the UN has to find a way of reinscribing them, while taking into account the advent of visual technologies and recognizing the somewhat fateful hybridization of textuality and visuality, of words and images. To some extent, this is the dilemma at the core of the several attempts by disciplinary liberalism, through the UN's peacekeeping interventions (described and analyzed in the following chapters), at recolonizing/re-ordering the post–cold war international landscape.

The post–cold war order is perhaps "beyond Leviathan."[59] It is perhaps beyond Hobbes's modern "ordering of names." But it is still haunted by an order versus anarchy problematic. Today, this debate may best be reworded or re-envisioned as a global discourse/vision (that of global disciplinary neoliberalism supported by UN peace-keeping strategies) versus a proliferation of images (of visually mobilized singularities) debate. The focus of the following chapters is directly placed on the relationships and confrontations between the textual and visual strategies deployed by disciplinary liberalism in the practice of post–cold war international relations and the so-called "anarchy" (inconsistencies, ambiguities, differences, plural modalities) of international life, including human life worldwide, which today often takes the shape of a proliferation of images and signs. As the centralizing agent of disciplinary liberalism, the UN finds itself at the heart of the battle. Envisioned by Boutros-Ghali, among others, in the position of the Hobbesian sovereign, the UN is in charge of imposing a "right ordering of names" (inscribing and mapping a new global diplomacy), but it also needs to consider how its peacekeeping operations can satisfy the requirements of a "right ordering of images." In the next chapter, I suggest that, in the early 1990s, as the new spirit of global order and peacekeeping is emerging, panopticism is one of the first techniques used by the UN (in North Korea and Iraq above all) to perform its "right ordering of the visual."

2

Space Quest: The UN and the Politics of Panoptic Surveillance

An omnivoyant eye, a power from above, capable of encompassing by its constant gaze all life on earth and of simultaneously controlling and regulating with a most detailed perfection the existence of individuals, animals, plants, machines, institutions placed under its inspection: the myth of an omnivoyant and omnipotent center of surveillance has persisted, from Christian mystics of the late Middle Ages to nineteenth-century liberal utilitarians, from technocratic fictions (Orwell's *1984*) to some of the most recent global governance and planetary sustainability utopias (late-twentieth-century environmentalism). Jeremy Bentham first formulated[1] the myth and, later, Michel Foucault theorized it as a panoptic society.[2] The panoptic society or Panopticon is a model of human and/or technological organization governed by three principles: clarity, surveillance, and discipline. The central eye/power of such a control mechanism sees all and everything at once. Privacy, selfishness, individual pulsions are eliminated by the mere fact that the omnipresence of the controlling eye is a sure reminder that punishment is always possible. God (or an equivalent principle of authority and governance) knows all and sees all. And the wrath of God can strike at any moment. In such a universe of perpetual control and immanent/imminent punishment, bodies can be disciplined with minimum power and, at the limit, without physical force. Bodies need not be tortured. Simply, they are docile. The panoptic mode of governance is a marvelously efficient

61

"system of certainty," as Foucault puts it, that allows a dominant ideology/order to be productive and reproductive without having to constantly fight to maintain its hegemonic status. This Panopticon is not only Bentham's utilitarian dream of a well-managed and self-perpetuating socio-economic infrastructure. It is also a dream of governance for societies that have placed their organizing principle, the raison d'être of their governed individuals, under the sign of an all-surveilling and all-ordering eye of power like God, the modern state, or more recently, institutions of international governance.

This chapter offers two illustrations of the visual surveillance model. One, Cardinal Nicholas de Cusa's "Vision of God" (*De Visione Dei*),[3] is a classic of fifteenth-century Christian theology. The other, the image of the United Nations' panoptic eye in recent cases of global monitoring of dangerous weapons and nuclear deterrence, is exemplary of recent practices of global surveillance and governance in international relations. Despite their apparent temporal discontinuity (de Cusa's text can be chronologically classified as premodern whereas the UN's panoptic interventions are characteristic of late-modern New World Order policies), both visions display striking analogies. Both models reveal an obsession with high visibility and power. In both cases, a disembodied organism is the bearer of life for the subjects governed by these visions. God or the UN presides over the destinies of lowly existences on earth. The difference, however, is that the surveilled subjects are Christian faithful in the case of de Cusa's text and sovereign states in the case of UN panopticism. But despite the fact that the interpellating mechanisms may be different (for one, the interpellating principle is faith, for the other it is sovereignty), the panoptic construct forms, in both models, a community built on surveillance and punishment.

The presentation of these two visual models serves as a starting point for a critical and postmodern reading of the United Nations's global surveillance and governance policies. Going back to the Cusian theological model, and turning to a complementary analysis of Bentham's utilitarian system in order to anchor the study in a larger context of modern liberal ideologies, this chapter examines how the current mode of panoptic surveillance deployed by international organizations like the UN has emerged as a contemporary visual practice in international relations. Tracking down the formation of contemporary international panopticism (in its specific shifts, additions, and redistributions) to determine what it owes or does not owe to previous panoptic modes allows, moreover, expansion of the critical focus of this study to an exploration of the relation between theories of global governance and techniques of visual simulation. This chapter thus performs a theoretical task, too, by expanding the postmodern and critical debate over surveillance technologies to include currently popular international relations theories (New World Order literatures, humane governance models), while critically detailing these recently predominant concepts.

THE SINGLE EYE

The Single Eye, the title of the first English version of Nicholas de Cusa's *The Vision of God,*[4] is indicative of the author's intent. In this work, "an easy path to mystical theology" as de Cusa suggests,[5] the basic principles of modern panopticism are already displayed. At a time when God's presence as an ordering principle of life was increasingly being challenged and was in need of reinforcement,[6] Cardinal de Cusa proposed to revive faith in God among believers. Augustine's vision of the "City of God" was no longer in order.[7] Rather, throughout Western Christianity, ways were developed to find individual paths to God. In the history of Christianity and of medieval thought, this movement was known as mysticism, that is to say, the development of psychic states and meditative experiences that allowed subjects to form a direct and personal relationship with God. It is in this context that de Cusa came up with "a fiction of God," a painting that would represent God in such an aesthetically enhancing manner that belief in God and in his grace could always be reaffirmed. The "Icon of God" would function as a propping mechanism that could facilitate the deployment of mystical encounters with God.

The technique of such a painted device is simple. It consists of "an image which is omnivoyant—its face, by the painter's cunning art, being made to appear as though looking on all around it."[8] The material reinforcement of God's power depends on a painting technique. By the painter's "cunning art" of drawing the eyes of the represented face in such a way that, from wherever you look at the picture, you are still assured that it looks back at you, the "Icon of God" places the faithful (transformed into idolaters) under the all-viewing (albeit fictional) power of God. De Cusa intimates that the picture's gaze has the ability to follow all of the onlookers' motions:

> this picture, brethren [de Cusa's writings are primarily addressed to other monks and Christian mystics who, according to him, are the most likely to benefit fully from his theological revelations], ye shall set up in some place, let us say on a north wall, and shall stand around it, a little way off and look upon it. And each of you shall find that from whatsoever quarter he regardeth it, it looketh upon him as if it looked on none other. And it shall seem to a brother standing to eastward as if that face looketh toward the east, while one to southward shall think it looketh toward the south, and one to westward, toward the west. First, then, ye will marvel how it can be that the face should look on all and each at the same time. For the imagination of him standing to eastward cannot conceive the gaze of the icon to be turned unto any other quarter, such as west or south. Then let the brother who stood eastward place himself to westward and he will find its gaze fastened on him in the west just as it was before in the east. And, as he knoweth the icon to be fixed and unmoved, he will marvel at the motion of its immovable gaze. If now, while fixing his eye on the icon, he walk from west to east, he will find that its gaze continuously goeth along with him, and if he return from east to west, in like manner it will not leave him.[9]

The panoptic model is rooted in de Cusa's description of the Icon of God. The panoptic gaze, that of the iconized God for de Cusa, is omnipresent but immovable. It controls everyone's motions, fills them with a creative grace, and never abandons its central and fundamental position. By means of a painter's "cunning art," the gaze of God becomes an unmoved mover, a creative truth. For de Cusa, this iconic representation of God must be so pregnant that it shall accompany the idolaters (the brethren) even if they leave the sanctuary where the picture stands. Having been reaffirmed in their faith and replenished with God's grace thanks to their visual contact with the Icon, the mystics are constantly governed by the gaze of God which, as an after-image, always "lives" with them no matter where they are. Should the brethren start to lose the feeling that they are governed by such an aesthetically mobilized grace, they can always return to the sanctuary where the picture stands and get another (visual) injection of God's presence. The Icon of God constitutes for the Christian mystic a material bridge (what de Cusa calls a perceptible image) into the divine realm. It is the visible guarantee that the sovereign power of the invisible does exist. It provides the metaphoric certainty that God supervises and protects his devotees.

With such a model, a fiction of "Absolute Sight" is rendered. God's panoptic powers are given universal dimensions: his sight "springeth, surpasseth in keenness, in speed, and in strength the sight of all who actually see and who can become capable of sight."[10] Human sight has a limited visual as well as conceptual field. It cannot even come close to experiencing what it means to have "Absolute Sight," which God only (as his Icon reveals) possesses. For de Cusa, and all proponents of panoptic structures in general, this is the natural fate of humankind. Human subjects cannot be omnivoyant. They cannot know all and, as such, will never be able to reach the perfection and universality of eternal life. From their birth, human subjects are ill-construed beings whose only hope is to fall under the protection of the Divine and his "Absolute Sight." Deprived of universal vision and leading imperfect (hence insecure) lives, individual subjects must be surveilled and guided by a most perfect, yet invisible, life, a life who knows all and (fore)sees all. God is indeed the perfect Panopticon. It is a fitting model for all the future panoptic systems that will come afterward.

The Icon of God as a "bridge into the divine realm" is a metaphorical construct in charge of interpellating individual subjects into a more certain and supreme power of sight, into the power of the Single Eye. It also holds tremendous suggestive power of identification and self-recognition. Indeed, as Božovič suggests, it is the necessary "first step on the path that culminates in the insight that I exist because God is looking at me and that the moment God turns his gaze away from me, I will cease to exist."[11] This notion of the subject existing only to the extent that the Single Eye looks back at him/her is a key element of panopticism. Panoptic systems do not only achieve control and surveillance by means of metaphorical intimation. They are also identity-producing devices that subject the individuals submitted to them to a recognized and accepted mode of allegiance.

De Cusa's *Vision of God* opens up a field of experimentation for panoptic mechanisms and for the fictional constructions that they rely on, and that seek to turn abstract principles or invisible creators into effective structuring powers of everyday life. From early to late modernity, the figure of de Cusa's omnivoyant and yet extremely detailing gaze of God (or of his icon) often reemerges, even if it is put to different uses and gives rise to divergent practices. But the basic principles of vision, surveillance, and subjection remain. I now turn to the second illustration of panopticism. This second example is, in a sense, at the other end of the panoptic spectrum. Whereas de Cusa represents the emerging moment of panopticism (with visual constructs that can only be achieved by means of individual and mystical imagination), the late-modern mediatico-technological surveillance devices deployed by the UN in its weaponry monitoring and nuclear compliance and control missions in North Korea and Iraq are some of the most up-to-date versions of panoptic surveillance. In these recent cases, an individualized capacity of imagination or a mystical will-to-believe are no longer necessary to fall under the gaze of panoptic devices. Technology from space or high in the sky is now presented as a "reality" that leaves nothing to the (mystical) imagination.

SPACE QUEST, CAMERA MONITORING, AND ON-SITE INSPECTIONS IN NORTH KOREA AND IRAQ

In the early 1990s, North Korea and Iraq had a lot in common. Both countries fell under the category of what, in 1993, the Clinton administration started to call the "rogue states." The "rogue doctrine," as Michael Klare explains, started as a uniquely American notion.[12] It was a way for the United States, after its success in the Gulf, and with the arrival of new president Bill Clinton, to redefine its defense strategy. According to Les Aspin, Clinton's first secretary of defense, American defense policy in the 1990s would be geared toward containing states with "rogue leaders set on regional domination through military aggression while simultaneously pursuing nuclear, biological, and chemical weapons capabilities."[13] The two nations of North Korea and Iraq fit the description perfectly and, as such, would have to be prime targets of U.S. containment.

As a mostly U.S. strategy, the "rogue doctrine" was never officially adopted by the UN as one of its post–cold war mandates. Although Boutros-Ghali's *Agenda for Peace* recognized that international conflict was pervasive and that some states were more likely to cause trouble than others, it contained no mention of the "rogue doctrine" and certainly did not provide a list of potential regional aggressors or weapons violators. Yet, even if the notion was not inscribed in its founding post–cold war era text, in practice, the UN was going to become a staunch defender of the United States–originated "rogue" doctrine. In fact, in its actions and surveillance operations in Iraq and North Korea, the UN would reveal itself to be more than simply an ally to the United States in the context of such a new version of global/regional (or globally regional) containment. In both countries, the UN's presence was to become a key element in the propagation of the United States–based "rogue" doctrine. Thus, de facto if not de jure, the UN was to subscribe to the view that both North Korea and Iraq were "bad subjects" of the international "family of nations" which, because of their potential for regional violence and for building prohibited weapons, needed to be constantly surveilled. As comembers of the "rogue state" clan, North Korea and Iraq would also have to share a common experience: they both would be placed under the close technological scrutiny of the United Nations, its specialized agencies, and its member states.

North Korea

Between March 1993 and June 1994, North Korea's threat to block on-site inspections by the International Atomic Energy Agency (IAEA)[14] of its suspected nuclear-weapons sites revealed North Korea as a number one "rogue state." Despite signing the Nuclear Non-Proliferation Treaty in 1987 and agreeing to what is traditionally known as a safeguards agreement imposed by this treaty,[15] North Korea suddenly decided to discontinue the international legal process that entitled IAEA and UN experts to control and verify North Korean sites at any time and under any circumstance. The IAEA generally ensures that a state party to the Non-Proliferation Treaty does not conduct illegal operations (i.e., does not attempt to build nuclear weapons) by placing remotely monitored cameras in each of the declared or potential nuclear sites. These cameras, placed in the nuclear sites of the countries that have signed the treaty, provide images in "real time" (via satellite) or videotapes that are periodically examined by international officials. In addition to these permanent visual reports, the IAEA conducts on-site inspections on a regular basis. It can also mandate "challenge inspections" (short-notice inspections on demand) if it believes that illegal activities are taking place.

On March 12, 1993, the DPRK (Democratic People's Republic of Korea) announced that, contrary to its previous engagements, it would withdraw from the Non-Proliferation Treaty.[16] North Korea's sudden decision was not an irrational act, as it was then suggested in the West. As Han S. Park explains, this decision found its justification in the North Korean national ideology of *Juche,* an ideology of national self-sufficiency, autonomy, and autarky that views foreign impositions (including international treaties) as imperialistic invasions.[17] If such a decision may have been justified on the basis of *Juche* (and on the grounds of self-protection), the earlier signing of the NPT back in 1987 was, then, an illogical act, for it was a violation of the *Juche* doctrine. The ideological explanation used by North Korea was not irrational, but it was not consistent either. In fact, the international context had a lot to do with the DPRK's choice of blocking the inspections. Back in 1987, when it signed the NPT, North Korea believed that it could rely on the Soviet Union for support.[18] In the early 1990s, the international context had changed. After the fall of the USSR, Kim Il Sung, the North Korean leader, took notice of the isolation of his regime (despite China's nearby presence) and chose to make the nuclear armament program the cornerstone of his country's survival. In the summer of 1993, the North Koreans went one step further in their open defiance to what they considered to be Western imperialism by letting the cameras placed in strategic nuclear sites run out of film.[19] IAEA officials ordered North Korea to let international inspectors visit the testing sites and reload the cameras.[20] No longer having visual access to the North Korean sites, and suspecting that this lack of visibility could be masking an illegal activity, the IAEA, after consultation with the UN, decided to mandate on-site "short-notice inspections." Additionally, with the support of the UN's Security Council, the IAEA turned to U.S. spy satellite photos to try to see what, as was suspected, the North Koreans were attempting to hide.[21] Those spy photos, indirectly provided to the IAEA by the CIA, showed that, at an undeclared but suspected test site, North Korean workers were apparently covering with artificial and natural camouflage what appeared to be nuclear reprocessing equipment.[22] Thus, while the negotiations with the North Korean leaders continued in the hope that the DPRK would not reject the NPT and allow inspectors to return, what could no longer be accessed by means of on-site inspections or cameras was nonetheless still made partially visible by means of surveillance techniques.

The talks between the IAEA, the United States and North Korea seemed to make progress, and the Pyongyang regime was on the verge of allowing the return of inspections when, in May 1994, the crisis exploded again. All of a sudden, reversing the more conciliatory trend of the past months, North Korea decided to "shut down its 25-megawatt reactor" and "with IAEA personnel barred from the site, removed all of its fuel rods, thereby precluding any future efforts to determine how much plutonium was extracted after the 1989 shutdown."[23] This second showdown with the West was more serious. The United States, on the one hand, behind its "rogue" doctrine, was willing to ask the UN to impose economic sanctions on North Korea. Kim Il Sung, on the other hand, was ready to engage in a military intervention against South Korea. Meanwhile, spy surveillance was still actively deployed to search for traces of illegality, even if such a mode of imagery was certainly not able to provide as much evidence as on-site inspections could have produced.

Beyond the issue over the shutdown of the nuclear reactor and North Korea's compliance with its international obligations, the May 1994 crisis had another dimension. For the West (the United States, the UN, and the IAEA), the crisis was about imposing transparency into an anachronistically hermetic society (the last survivors of the Stalinist era) that still refused to abide by the principles and rules of the international community. As Hans Blix, the General Director of IAEA, had made clear, the IAEA inspections regime was as much about imposing principles of "openness and transparency," as it was about nuclear non-proliferation. This was the mission that, in the perspective of disciplinary liberalism, had been assigned to the UN and its agencies in North Korea and other "rogue" countries. Blix declared that "it is important . . . to retain the notion that openness and transparency about nuclear activities is the essential requirement to maintain confidence. . . . Full cooperation in implementing required safeguards is a way of achieving such openness and transparency."[24] For North Korea, the standoff was an ideological battle too. It was a matter of preserving North Korea's own ideology of self-sufficiency and self-defense in an era when calls to globalism and globalization were more and more pressing. The nuclear program, including the ability to create weapons of mass destruction, was once again seen by Pyongyang as a question of anti-imperialist resistance and national survival. This, as Park notes, was based on the view that North Korea's "self-defense [was] morally right and ideologically correct" and that "the IAEA and the United States [were] morally misplaced."[25] But North Korea also sought to expand its ideology beyond its borders and, by its example, reach "the traditional nonaligned bloc of the Third World."[26] In a naïve fashion, Pyongyang believed that its *Juche* could serve as a model of resisting ideology for all the other nations of the world that, like North Korea, resented the oppression of disciplinary liberalism and global capitalism. In short, North Korea hoped to trigger the revenge of the rogues.

In order to bring transparency to North Korea the nuclear threat had to be mobilized. The worst thing that these "rogues" could do was destroy humankind by means of their secretive, but nonetheless powerful, nuclear capabilities. More than the conviction that North Korea could build such weapons, potential sites needed to be seen, explored, surveilled, penetrated, and, if need be, destroyed. Gaining access to North Korea through those nuclear sites was the only guarantee for transparency. Satellite surveillance pictures had previously revealed the presence of something (the international community did not quite know what it was since it had been camouflaged) that authorized penetration and intrusion by foreign experts inside North Korea. Once inside, the international community would find it easier to try to bring the North Korean regime to transparency and visibility.

In the months that immediately followed the May 1994 standoff, the threat of economic sanctions was presented as the primary form of response by the West if Pyongyang were to maintain its hard line. But, as Park notes, economic sanctions would have been meaningless since North Korea had very little economic contact with the international community. Most economic relations were with China, which, even if it were not to veto a UN Security Council vote against North Korea, would have a hard time stopping the food and commodity items trade across its border with the DPRK.[27] Economic sanctions were by and large an idle threat which, if applied, could have been taken as yet another imperialist aggression by Pyongyang (and could have pushed the North Korean regime to close its doors even more than before). Openness and transparency had to be achieved by other means. Instead of deeper isolation, Pyongyang had to be connected to an inescapable web of global transactions (economic, cultural, mediatic, strategic) so that it would become increasingly difficult for such an isolated nation to retain its beloved ideology of self-sufficiency and self-defense. North Korea had to be hooked to the rest of the world and made ready for the penetration by diverse economic and ideological transnational currents and currencies.[28] More than really trying to avert a military crisis or an economic impasse, the strategies used by the West to force Pyongyang to accept the regime of IAEA inspections and restart its reactor in the spring-summer of 1994 were deployed in such an ideological spirit.

In this ideological context, the "international family of nations" sent some of its most charismatic (ideological) preachers to Pyongyang. Reverend Billy Graham had already been sent in January 1994 supposedly to give Kim Il Sung a message from Bill Clinton, making clear that the United States was serious about the question of on-site inspections.[29] Jimmy Carter was sent in June 1994, after the crisis had exploded, to try to convince Kim Il Sung to "freeze North Korea's nuclear efforts in return for a promise of fresh talks with the United States."[30] Carter's trip helped ease the crisis and "opened a new door for North Korea."[31] A few weeks after his departure, Kim Il Sung, with whom Carter had started to develop a close friendship, died. Shortly before Carter's visit, the first major contract allowing international TV crews to film scenes of North Korean life had been signed. U.S. emissary Bill Taylor brought CNN and NHK (the Japanese TV network) along with him during his official trip to Pyongyang aimed at encouraging the North Korean regime not to reject the NPT treaty altogether.[32] While North Korea was still denying access to its sites to Western inspection teams, the idea was that global TV links could offer a surrogate visual access. Things changed with the death of Kim Il Sung. After a short period of mourning, his son and successor Kim Jong Il agreed to negotiations. In August 1994, North Korea appeared to suddenly reject its previously defensive posture and the dictates of *Juche* to finally accept the full application of the safeguards agreement that allowed IAEA inspection teams to return and proceed with all the necessary verification and monitoring exercises.[33] On October 17, 1994, the final piece in the West's regime of transparency in North Korea was put in place "with the signing of an even more sweeping agreement, under which North Korea [would] terminate its nuclear weapons program entirely in return for massive infusions of U.S. economic and technical assistance."[34] In the fall of 1994, with a new leader, Pyongyang had apparently abandoned its doctrine of self-reliance and self-defense and accepted a more dependent posture within the network of the "family of nations." By accepting U.S. economic and technical assistance, in exchange for its nuclear program, North Korea was turned into a tamed "rogue" within the new global surveillance/governance order.

Iraq

What has taken place in Iraq since the end of the Gulf War is relatively similar to the North Korean case even if the techniques used to assure visibility and transparency have been deployed in a different strategic context. Whereas North Korea was a closed and secretive nation in need of openness and enlightenment, Iraq's record as a "rogue" speaks for itself. Iraq is a recognized aggressor, a felon state, whose "open" foreign policy under Saddam Hussein has been geared toward invading foreign lands (as happened in Kuwait) and whose domestic politics is in blatant violation of basic human rights principles (retaliations against the Kurds and the Shiites). Unlike the situation in North Korea, the panoptic means of surveillance and transparency deployed in Iraq are not linked only to the nuclear non-proliferation program. Rather, surveillance techniques employed there are more directly and overtly placed under UN control and are extended to different domains of post–Gulf War monitoring. Iraq is the most obvious illustration of the fact that UN global governance policies rely on very detailing and extremely encompassing watching methods.

Resolution 687 of the UN Security Council[35] is the key document on visual surveillance and punishment by the international community in Iraq. It is a document that, officially, provides "for the inspection and removal, destruction or rendering harmless of all weapons of mass destruction in Iraq and of all materials and facilities which can be used for weapons of mass destruction including the means of delivery most apt for their use."[36] The scope of intrusive activities authorized by this document is larger than anything that took place in North Korea. Here, it is a matter not only of disciplining a potential outlaw but, moreover, of punishing it for its previous actions. The "roguery" has already been committed and the culprit must be punished. There is no need, in Iraq, to try to negotiate. Preemptive action, on the contrary, is what is necessary. As Clinton once put it, "we will not allow Saddam Hussein to defy the will of the United

States and the international community."[37] The regime of Iraqi punishment is clear. Iraq has no choice but "to accept inspections in
order to verify the declarations and set a time limit for the destruction . . . of the relevant materials."[38]

In order to monitor such a regime and make sure that Iraq does
not rebuild a dangerous chemical, biological, and nuclear warfare
capacity, the IAEA was once again asked to intervene. This time,
however, it was necessary to expand the scope of the inspections beyond nuclear disarmament. To fulfil this task, a Special Commission
of the UN (UNSCOM) was created. Whereas the IAEA would provide experts (nuclear energy specialists), UNSCOM would provide
inspectors (officials with weapons monitoring training directly
working for the UN) to the Iraqi surveillance operation. UNSCOM's
role would be to "oversee" (the term may be taken literally) the removal and destruction of all weapons of mass destruction.[39] According to this mandate, UNSCOM and IAEA inspectors would be deployed all over the Iraqi territory to form a vast net that could collect
illegal weapons, concealed material, secret documents, and valuable
information to the benefit of the UN and the members of the coalition of states that took part in the Gulf War. Specifically, six commands were given to the inspectors of this mission: measure, evaluate, assess, identify, search, and supervise.[40] Furthermore, for the
duration of this mission, sovereignty principles otherwise in place in
traditionally sovereign nations would be lifted. IAEA and UNSCOM
inspectors could come and go to and from Iraq without any visa.
They could carry out inspections "at any locations and facilities at
any time" and, in this process, have "full and free access to all locations, persons and information." They could take samples, equipment, place any devices deemed relevant to the monitoring process,
make copies, take pictures, and prevent local transport of material
by the Iraqis.[41] The conditions of inspection imposed on Iraq were,
no doubt, those imposed on a defeated nation. Having lost the war,
Iraq would have to pay the dear price of having an almighty foreign
power intrude and do whatever it wished on its territory, beyond any
dilemma of sovereignty. UN Resolution 687 and its inspections
regime had nothing to do with international justice and lawful diplomacy, as some more idealistic observers were willing to believe.[42]
What was imposed, rather, was a regime of reparative conditions and
heavy sanctions. Under such a regime, Iraq was not to be given the

benefit of the doubt. Despite the fact that its military arsenal had been severely damaged during the Gulf War, if "monitoring operations [were] to detect *any sign* of secret efforts by Iraq to rebuild their WMD [weapons of mass destruction] capabilities,"[43] preemptive strikes and a tightening of the economic embargo would certainly ensue. The January 1993 launching of Tomahawk missiles by departing U.S. President Bush on an Iraqi nuclear weapons plant (almost two years exactly after the Gulf War) clearly sought to demonstrate this position.

Beyond the immediate objectives of the inspections (finding and destroying weapons of mass destruction), UNSCOM and IAEA's international police regime in Iraq was officially designed to implement a system of trust and certainty. Since the Gulf War, Saddam Hussein had been treated by Western diplomats and the media as someone who could never be trusted, a cheater, a back-stabber who certainly would not hesitate to return to his previous imperialistic and genocidal policies. In the West, the general assumption was that, as long as Saddam was in charge, lying and deceiving would continue to be the official political doctrine of the Iraqi nation. The defeat in the Gulf had reduced Hussein's arrogance, but he had been able to transfer his blatantly offensive strategy into what some started to call a "cheat and retreat" tactic.[44] Seen as a pathological liar, the only type of policy likely to succeed against Saddam was forceful deterrence. As Thomas Friedman put it, "Saddam Hussein is the reason God created cruise missiles."[45] Short of compliance, the inspection regime and the conditions imposed by Resolution 687 would remain a masquerade. It is doubtful, however, that the international community really wanted Saddam to be out. Despite the stated intentions, maintaining a defeated and humiliated Hussein in power in Iraq was seen as a guarantee that Iraq would not break into multiple Muslim states, which, from a Western (U.S.) perspective of containing "rogue states," would be even more difficult to control. Furthermore, as some have noted, Saddam Hussein was also able to provide a buffer against a resurgence of Iran in the region.[46] In short, in an age of post–cold war panopticism, a disciplined but united Iraq could serve the objectives of the West better than a multiplicity of Iraqi kingdoms, or than a *retour en force* (return in force) of an economically stronger Iran in the Middle East. Yet, with Hussein in power, a trust system based on transparency could not be realized either. Trust, then, would have to be enforced. And the way the international community proposed to enforce trust in Iraq, per UN Resolution 687, was by imposing, among other things (economic sanctions went hand in hand with that as well), a vast regime of weapons inspections. If Iraq was not yet able to come home to the New World Order of democratically enlightened states, at least the international community would be able to come to Iraq by means of its most legitimate but also intrusive agent, the United Nations. To build trust in Iraq, the UN would have to make sure that the international "family of nations" knew everything about Saddam's regime despite its propensity to play "hide and seek" with the international community.

In this ideological spirit, and in accordance with UN Resolutions, on-site inspections started to be deployed in 1991, immediately after Iraq's defeat. At first, however, and to the dismay of the international community, UNSCOM and IAEA inspectors did not catch anything in their nets. The UN's monitoring efforts were frustrated as the Iraqis spun "a web of deception"[47] along the inspectors' way, something that they would continue to practice with consistency over the next six years. Gary Milhollin recounts the typical frustration of a UN weapons inspector in Iraq:

> the inspector is discouraged, and so are many others. For almost a year, they have found practically nothing new. The Iraqis are outfoxing them at every turn, harassing them, and making it more and more likely that Saddam Hussein will wriggle out from under the current embargo with large parts of his A-bomb effort intact.[48]

The unwelcome UN inspectors were thus put under constant pressure by their Iraqi hosts. Ironically, the inspectors were constantly spied upon during their stay in Iraq, an interesting reversal effect of what was supposed to take place.[49] In some cases, nuclear inspections provided indirect intelligence leads but "the inspectors [often] had to violate IAEA policies to get [evidence]."[50] Thus, with the only recourse to on-site inspections, the IAEA, the UN and their inspectors were vulnerable. No visible proof of Iraq's noncompliance could be clearly identified. Yet, the overall feeling that Saddam was hiding something remained. At times, using strategies reminiscent of childish taunting maneuvers, Iraq itself acknowledged that it was creating and testing dangerous weapons (chemical and biological above all).[51] Although such admissions could provoke severe sanctions, they also sought to show that Saddam was actually still capable of sadistically toying with the West (for the inspectors could not find clear evidence whether the admissions were true or not). In addition, repeated accounts by defectors (in particular Saddam's son-in-law) reinforced the view that the Iraqi regime was still actively building chemical and biological weapons.[52] Finally, despite the "web of deception," UN inspectors were able to find a few things too.[53] Yet, the inspection regime was, by and large, limited and the leads were often incomplete, thus leaving the UN in a mode of suspicion and uncertainty. Over the years, Iraq's strategy of obstruction of on-site inspections would lead to repeated crises with the UN and the United States.[54]

Faced with the apparent limitations of on-site inspections in Iraq, the UN had to devise a different strategy of control. To circumvent the local obstacles placed in the way of the inspections, the UN soon discovered that "overhead imagery" could be a more efficient technique.[55] By 1992, to counter the "web of deception" on the ground, a web of visual control from above was deployed (it was to be perfected in the following years). Intended to be a supplement to the on-site inspection regime, the overhead imagery would often reveal itself to be the only mode of penetration and intrusion, particularly for those sites declared "off-limits" by Saddam Hussein. Johan Molander summarizes the situation by indicating that, faced with the problem of on-site inspections, UNSCOM had "requested and received additional information from a number of governments, including satellite photography and line drawings of declared and non-declared suspect sites in Iraq from the U.S. government." Yet, Molander continues, "gradually, the need for independent aerial inspections became more evident."[56]

The UN and the IAEA did not (yet) possess the technological means to deploy such a system of overhead imagery on their own. In order to ensure its mode of "sky-surveillance," UNSCOM had to turn to American technology. In the context of its new "rogue doctrine" of defense, the United States had placed the emphasis on the development of "airborne intelligence units." Klare explains that the Bottom-Up Review of U.S. defense strategy initiated by Secretary of Defense Aspin in 1993 had "favored accelerated procurement of the Joint Surveillance and Attack Radar System (JSTARS) aircraft, the MILSTAR satellite communications system, and an upgraded version of the E-3 Airborne Warning and Control System (AWACS)."[57]

In Iraq, the UN directly sought to benefit from the U.S. military's new high-tech surveillance gimmicks by first relying on U.S. satellite technology. Once satellite photography had isolated potentially suspicious sites, UNSCOM would look more closely by using U-2 spy planes (lent to the UN by the U.S. government) and helicopters.

Overhead imagery proved more successful to UNSCOM and the IAEA than on-site inspections, even if complete clarity was not achieved. As "the Iraqis [were] watched by satellites, by U-2 spy planes, and by UN helicopters flying out of Baghdad,"[58] space-scanning (from high in space or lower in the sky) allowed the UN to get images, no matter what the Iraqis would do to try to prevent direct access on the ground. By 1993, Milhollin recalls, these images revealed that "the Iraqis went to hiding places in the desert, dug up giant machines for processing uranium, loaded them on trucks, and drove them to a site called Abu Gharib, to which the inspectors had been denied entry."[59] The importance of overhead imagery borrowed by the UN from the American military was not so much to show what Iraq actually had or not, or what Saddam was truly trying to hide (for the actual content of what Iraq was hiding would have to be physically verified, which, once the inspectors gained access to the discovered site, was often too late to ascertain). It was enough for overhead surveillance to demonstrate that, as had been suspected, Saddam Hussein was trying to cheat by not complying with the inspection regime. Overhead imagery confirmed the truly important point that Saddam could not be trusted, that Iraq was still to be treated as a "rogue" nation, and that, finally, the Iraqi regime was in need of more durable surveillance and constant punishment (maintaining the economic sanctions).

In Iraq, the aim of visual surveillance was to demonstrate that transparency could not be achieved and that, short of a safe opening of Saddam's regime, isolation would have to be maintained. By contrast, in the North Korean case, UN panopticism was used as a way of ensuring transparency in a hidden and secretive country. In New York, Washington, or Seoul, it had been decided that it was necessary to render North Korea transparent and penetrable so that transnational flows (of information, Christian and liberal evangelism, capital) and neoliberal ideology (championed by the UN) could reach this hidden country. Since, in the early 1990s, it became anachronistic for a society not to be open to worldwide mediatic and technological culture, inspecting, monitoring, and surveilling North Korea were the methods chosen to pull Pyongyang out of its frozen cold-war status. The program of Iraqi surveillance was different from the North Korean panoptic structure. In Iraq, the idea was rather to negate the possibility of transparency by means of overhead imagery. Visual surveillance in Iraq gave further evidence that Saddam was still up to his old games of treachery and deception, and that, given this reality, every effort would have to be made and maintained to discipline and punish him. Although transparency by means of overhead surveillance played contradictory roles in North Korea and Iraq, the two countries remain exemplary cases of post–cold war United Nations panopticism. As panoptic subjects, both countries can attest that technological panopticism from space (high or low in the sky) is a powerful instrument of global governance.

God or the UN

The rules of formation of panopticism identified in de Cusa's system (surveillance, clarity, subjection) are reproduced and technologically enhanced by the UN in its post–cold war surveillance missions. The fiction of an all-seeing eye (God for de Cusa) that regulates the movements of individual subjects, no matter where they are, is efficiently replicated by the UN, its agencies, and its member states. In a New World Order where liberal principles (of law, political organization, social life) have become a necessity, a requirement in fact, every nation must know that it cannot indulge in activities that have not been ideologically validated by the international community. Despite such a warning, if a nation nonetheless chooses to follow its own path (as North Korea did for so long), it will become a "rogue" and will have to be surveilled and possibly punished. The visual-scape of the post–cold war international community championed by the UN imposes itself as a no-escape mechanism.

An omnivoyant center of international life requires allegiance, compliance, and sacrifice. Elements of international life, like Iraq or North Korea, which prefer to play their own anachronistic and idiosyncratic ideological or strategic games, must be controlled and tamed. The refusal to abide by the will-to-believe in a better future of global governance imposed by the UN is not acceptable and, as in the most perfectly technocratically ordered societies, "resistance is futile." Perhaps more than ever before, the post–cold war age of

panoptic governance is one of primal purification and normalization. A global inquisition by means of surveillance is orchestrated by
the UN and its enlightened policies while, in the shadow of the UN's
sacrificial justice, Western states are patiently waiting. The UN has
not only retained the lessons of panopticism offered by de Cusa's
metaphorical model; it has added to it an ideological dimension by
turning global.

Yet, in the story of the evolution of panopticism (from de Cusa to
the UN) presented up to this point, there is a missing link. There is a
link between de Cusa and the UN that allows mostly individualized
panoptic constructs to become global ideological "war machines."
Bentham's liberal-utilitarian reconstruction of panopticism (of the capacity of omnivoyance) is the missing link. Bentham is the utilitarian
ghost that haunts contemporary global governance literatures and
ideologies. Before proceeding any further with the analysis of panopticism in current regimes of global governance and peacekeeping, a
detour through Bentham's vision of the Panopticon is in order.

DREAMS AND FEARS OF PANOPTICISM

Practices of visual surveillance have often been traced to Bentham's
Panopticon. If de Cusa can be credited for providing the creative moment of panopticism, Bentham's theory of how panoptic modes can
be put to good and efficient uses has a more concrete and contemporary resonance. De Cusa's version of panopticism offers an ideological space, the space of surveillance as a mode of behavioral compliance (effectively used by the UN in both Iraq and North Korea).
Bentham's model, by contrast, provides a meticulous know-how,
with tools and instruments that can make panopticism work in all
cases. With Bentham, the capacity of seeing (all and everything) becomes a "user-friendly" strategy employed in larger ideological
schemes. In Bentham's (liberal reformist) age, the proponents of the
dominant ideology of the liberal modern state directly benefit from
(and hope to use) panoptic devices. In today's practice of international relations, the proponents of the dominant ideology of disciplinary liberalism on a global scale seek to apply Bentham's practical
lessons to more ideological panoptic purposes too.

Bentham's Panopticon is well known to scholars who have written
on various aspects of postmodern culture, politics, and philosophy.
Foucault's work on the "birth of the prison" since the late Middle

Ages has largely contributed to the renewed interest in Bentham's Panopticon. Bentham's Panopticon is a reformed prison-house whose novelty lies in its architecture. Architectural designs were the late-eighteenth and early-nineteenth centuries' favorite means of efficiently redressing pathologies and producing normality.[60] Bentham, an archetypal British utilitarian, did not miss the opportunity provided by these new architectures. Foucault has eloquently described the architectural principles of the Panopticon:

> we know the principle on which it was based: at the periphery, an annular building; at the centre, a tower; this tower is pierced with wide windows that open onto the inner side of the ring; the peripheric building is divided into cells, each of which extends the whole width of the building; they have two windows, one on the inside, corresponding to the windows of the tower; the other, on the outside, allows the light to cross the cell from one end to the other. All that is needed, then, is to place a supervisor in a central tower and to shut up in each cell a madman, a patient, a condemned man, a worker or a schoolboy. By the effect of backlighting, one can observe from the tower, standing out precisely against the light, the small captive shadows in the cells of the periphery. They are like so many cages, so many small theatres, in which each actor is alone, perfectly individualized and constantly visible. The panoptic mechanism arranges spatial unities that make it possible to see constantly and to recognize immediately. In short, it reverses the principle of the dungeon; or rather of its three functions—to enclose, to deprive of light and to hide—it preserves only the first and eliminates the other two. Full lighting and the eye of the supervisor capture better than darkness, which ultimately protected. Visibility is a trap.[61]

The architectural structure of the Panopticon gives the "essence," as Bentham puts it, of this vast machine of vision: "the centrality of the inspector's situation, combined with the well-known and most effectual contrivances for *seeing without being seen.*"[62]

Although Bentham, like de Cusa, seeks to achieve surveillance, subjection, and self-disciplinization by turning to the power of the visual, Bentham's Panopticon is a reversal of de Cusa's Icon of God. Whereas de Cusa hopes that the "cunning art" of the painter will render God's presence visibly evident to the believers, Bentham's panoptic model of efficient control is based on invisibility ("seeing without being seen"). The center of power (the warden watching in the tower) must not be seen by the prisoners. For de Cusa, power had to be made visible, present on earth by means of a fiction. By contrast, for Bentham, power must remain abstract, almost unreal. Bentham declares that power is based on "the *apparent omnipresence* of the inspector (if divines will allow me the expression) combined with the extreme facility of his *real presence*."[63] The "real presence" of the inspector is not meant to be seen. Nor is it meant to stay. Rather, it must be felt by the prisoner. The prisoner will see the shadow of the warden once or twice. But, from now on, knowing that the shadow of the inspector may always be there is sufficient to guarantee compliance. Simply, this panoptic model allows its user to "exploit uncertainty"[64] as there is no way for the prisoner to ascertain whether he is really being watched. In the Panopticon, the "apparent omnipresence," the fiction of presence, takes over. Appearances prevail over reality.

Whereas de Cusa sought to bring God down to earth by painting his portrait, Bentham ironically tries to elevate power by never allowing the incarcerated subjects to see who or what watches them. In fact, Bentham's exercise of "invisible visibility" allows for the possibility that nothing watches at all. It does not matter whether a person or any other watching device is actually placed in the tower. The central place of the omnivoyant power may well be empty (the inspector may even be replaced by a puppet). In fact, for Bentham, it may work optimally this way since the apparent omnipresence of the central power is what perpetuates the system. What matters for Bentham is, to use a turn of phrase developed by William Bogard, the "simulation of surveillance"[65] that maintains the guarded subjects in a perpetual condition of docility. Whereas de Cusa's Icon *represents* God (by metaphorically reviving his image), Bentham's panopticon *simulates* power and its central presence. It relies on a potential absence, a vacuous space technologically made to look like a watchful eye, to condition subjects into believing that all their actions are examined, measured, interpreted, controlled, and possibly used against them. Bentham's Panopticon is a "dead center of simulated power."[66]

Bentham is not interested in the proliferation of ideology by means of visual surveillance and compliance. What he is interested in, rather, is the production of deterrence. Foucault is right to point out that the (panoptic) discipline imposed by Bentham is one that relies on positivity (producing subjects, docile bodies), not negativity (coercing by violence, possibly death). Corporeal punishment does not serve Bentham's liberal-utilitarian enterprise. Bentham compared his system to the old incarceration techniques by stating that "[t]here you saw blood and uncertainty [whereas] here you see certainty without blood."[67] Simulating presence (of power, surveillance, inspection) is a cost-effective way of nevertheless assuring compliance. The work gets done at a minimal cost or, as Bentham put it, "certainty, promptitude, and uniformity are qualities that may here be displayed in the extreme."[68] The deterrent surveillance mechanism that Bentham creates moves away from reality (by simulating it) to better recolonize it. His Panopticon works for society (the outside world) as a surrogate principle of reality. As Miran Božovič ironically suggests, Bentham's ultimate dream would have been to construct a fully simulated penitentiary-house, with nobody living inside. Screams could be heard once in a while. However, they would not be the screams of the prisoners, but of people hired specifically for the task.[69] A complete simulation of disciplinarity would thus produce deterrent effects (as Bentham, the reformer, wanted) into society as a whole. Bentham's dream was that of a society where technology could be used as a substitute for real life, as a means to construct fictional situations and characters to prevent catastrophes from really happening. Bentham's fear (like Hobbes's before him) was caused by a recognition of the weakness of the human body (as a potential victim of violent actions). To remain free from (physical) suffering, Bentham tried to devise fictional ways of producing disciplinarity.[70] His universe of social fictions (like his Panopticon) revealed an attempt at managing everyday existence by placing it under optically generated mechanisms of order and certainty. His belief that "appearance outweighs reality"[71] is perhaps the reason why, in the absence of television, cinema, or virtual reality, Bentham was left with theater as his preferred model. As he once put it, "in a well-composed committee of penal law, I know not a more essential personage than the manager of a theatre."[72]

Bentham thus takes panopticism one step closer to what contemporary techniques of visual surveillance achieve by designing a model, based on simulation, that guarantees that the disciplined subjects are always docile, even when they stray away from the "Single Eye." Bentham creates a more durable system of panopticism than de Cusa, who ultimately had to rely on a will-to-believe (the belief that the brethren would always desire to return to the Icon). At the end of his quest for efficient compliance, Bentham found the perfect panoptic model in a system reliant upon simulations and motivated appearances. The principle of panopticism as a simulation of surveillance is today coupled with a more elementary model of omnivoyance (reliant upon a necessary will-to-believe) to produce contemporary visions and fictions of global surveillance.

FICTIONS AND VISIONS OF GLOBAL SURVEILLANCE

The end of the cold war has witnessed an unprecedented surge of global surveillance scenarios. Classical spying intrigues may have dissipated. But the new era of international affairs is replete with political issues that, in a disciplinary liberal tradition, require sovereign states to join forces to limit the effect of international disorder. Such a new "family of nations," the latest version of a "universal community" in the making, is today faced with threats like environmental catastrophes, ozone layer depletion, population growth, and, of course, "rogue" nations' aggressive and terroristic tactics, which, because of their emphasized global reach (even if it all starts locally), must be dealt with collectively. The international community, in its infinite post–cold war wisdom, has given itself a set of international instruments designed to study these issues, remedy the damage caused by some of these threats, and prevent these globally represented new forces of post–cold war "anarchy" from spreading their destructive influence all over the international landscape. In the language of international affairs, these instruments of global subsistence and governance are called international organizations.

Beyond Territoriality: International Organizations

International organizations were born long before the fall of Communism and the end of the cold war.[73] The United Nations system, heir apparent to the previous League of Nations, was created after World War II. Yet most international organizations, particularly those built in the interest of global governance or collective security, never had the opportunity to assert their global mission as long as the international politics of hegemonic blocs was dominating international life. Today, with the apparent absence of ideological opposition (Western liberalism is no longer threatened by Communism or the classical

Fascisms), international organizations of global subsistence, governance, and surveillance are given the green light by sovereign states to achieve global stability and, in this perspective, to design the security and protective measures necessary to reach this goal.

It is in this late-modern context of international life that panopticism enters the realm of post–cold war international politics and, specifically, the dominant vision of global governance promoted by international organizations like the UN. Panopticism in contemporary international affairs is the dream, formulated by sovereign states, of having international organizations peacefully control and dominate the entire spectrum of international activities, at any time and in any place, by multiplying global surveillance mechanisms. These international organizations of surveillance have no actual life of their own. Rather, they are the panoptic agents, the all-seeing and detailing lenses, of liberal states that find in these mechanisms the ultimate dream of a completely disembodied (deterritorialized) yet omnipotent sovereignty, a postmodern transference of their power from territorial unity and integrity to technocratic visibility and fiction.

For the state in a post–cold war age, territoriality means death.[74] The state can no longer survive in its enclosed sphere of jurisdiction because all that used to be contained within this spatial delimitation has now escaped and become transnational and transdimensional (capital, population, information, crime, etc.). The state must abandon its modern, all too modern outfit in order for its Leviathanic authority to continue to yield a power-effect over those governed. To compete with sociocultural forces that have gone deterritorial (from being ascribed to one place to circulating in space), the postmodern virtual life of states is technologically fused in the globally controlling and surveilling capacities of international organizations. There, as a collective body of scattered bodies, a cyborganic Super-Leviathan,[75] states can hope to compete with information networks, transnational capital, computerized technologies that already have taken the minds and bodies of the individual subjects formerly governed by states. By going "territorially virtual" through the surveillance technologies of international organizations, states are attempting to join the global cyborganic family in order to recolonize their prodigal subjects.

International organizations of global surveillance and the laws (of certainty, normality, disciplinarity) that they produce are the culmination of social governance models (Rousseau's social contract made universal, Kant's "Perpetual Peace" realized), the happy conjunction of Nicholas de Cusa's technical artifice and Jeremy Bentham's utilitarian simulation. Nowhere is this more obvious than with the United Nations, whose specific intrusive inspection policies have been described above.

Simulating United Nations Surveillance

"Surveillance is also a fantasy of power," writes Bogard.[76] If surveillance aims at organizing, controlling, or even producing (docile) subjects, it is also, as Bentham revealed, the dream of a not yet realized or realizable configuration of order and power. The simulation of surveillance facilitates the deployment of what Bogard calls a "social science fiction," the implementation of a structure whose effects are not real (on the body) but rather virtual (on-screen).[77] Thus, as much as institutions of surveillance (like the UN) aim at achieving real effects of power, coercion, order, or transparency (as happened in both North Korea and Iraq), they also seek to produce "reality effects" which, more than effectively coercing, provide the appearance of coercion at a minimal physical cost. This is nothing more than the outcome, made possible by means of more sophisticated technologies of simulation, of Bentham's panoptic dream. Surveillance is at once real and hyperreal, panoptic and "hyperpanoptic" (Bogard).[78] In the perspective of global governance/surveillance by means of international organizations, the UN deploys its panopticism as both an effective mode of power and coercion (the force of the Single Eye) and a virtual mode of governing/ordering international politics. The UN, heir apparent to de Cusa's Icon of God and Bentham's Panopticon, is both a Single Eye and a simulation of surveillance. As a simulation of surveillance (or an "imaginary machine of surveillance," as Bogard puts it), the UN is an "apparently omnipresent" watchful eye that hides the fact that, behind its optical intrusiveness, there may be no such thing as a realized principle of global governance. Nowhere is this interpretation of the UN as an "imaginary machine" of surveillance-as-simulation more firmly asserted than in technologico-strategic literatures on global security and governance whose authors, in the early 1990s, sought to come up with different versions of UN panopticism. Bruce Poulin's "An Early Warning Apparatus for the United Nations" is possibly the most intriguing of these new technoscopic literatures.[79]

Poulin's utopia of the UN as an "imaginary machine" of surveillance, able to see everything without being seen by inspected states, is comparable to Bentham's Panopticon. Poulin, a captain in the Canadian Armed Forces and a graduate of the School of Advanced International Studies at Johns Hopkins University, considers himself to be a reformer who—just as Bentham was trying to convince the British government of the need to implement his model penitentiary—wants to encourage the Canadian government to support his policy prescriptions and champion his vision at the UN.[80] Having prepared it for the United Nations' fiftieth anniversary, Poulin saw his project as his own birthday gift to the international organization and as a benefit to humankind. His gift is a technologically enhanced panoptic system, what he calls a "UN-sponsored early-warning apparatus."

Poulin's vision of the UN is simple. In the aftermath of the cold war, the UN has to become a watchtower. To make sure that the UN is an effective warden, four deputy secretaries-general need to be created to improve the current inspection regime. "One of these deputies would be in charge of political, security and peace affairs" and "would oversee a global watch on developments in peace and security, peacekeeping and good offices, disarmament, arms control and regional security, the servicing of the Security Council and General Assembly on political and peace and security matters as well as the Military Staff Committee Secretariat," says Poulin.[81] Like Bentham's warden in his central tower, this new UN deputy would have "an operations room or an information management centre manned 24 hours a day, seven days a week."[82] The implied idea is that, with such a mechanism, the inspected states as well as UN officials themselves would always know that they are watched at any time (or potentially watched), and that information can always be collected from them (the entire system assumes mistrust and deception). To facilitate this deputy's mission, a technological arsenal of super-vision would be at his/her disposal. An electronic eye known in UN jargon as ORCI (Office for Research and the Collection of Information) would have to be remodeled and placed at the deputy's service in order to provide visibility and detailed precision in the darkest and most remote regions of the "world of the UN." In such a "global watch" scheme, ORCI's role "would be to observe and report on events around the world and it could use much of the knowledge and experience already accumulated by the UN's Regional Remote Sensing Program (RRSP) [functioning as some type of probes periodically sent by the UN in certain regions to bring back information on the way a country complies with UN resolutions] and perhaps modelled on the Pentagon's 24-hrs command centre."[83]

Poulin's reformed system of UN surveillance comes, in fact, as a direct response to the recognized failure of the UN's on-site inspections in Iraq and North Korea. In these two cases, human intelligence (what Poulin calls HUMINT) by means of on-site inspections and aerial reconnaissance by U-2 planes and helicopters were not sufficient to demonstrate that both countries were not abiding by UN policies. Space surveillance, often offered by the United States, had been needed to provide visual evidence against and visual access to these two nations. To remedy these imperfect situations, full panoptic vision from space (by means of satellite photography) is what Poulin wants to enforce, with the help of the Canadian government, at the UN. "The growing number and complexity of recent peacekeeping operations coupled with the associated costs suggest that advanced technology—namely, PHOTINT [photo intelligence]—should be included as an effective adjunct to these operations, thus forming an effective triad for confidence spirit."[84] With Poulin's project, Bentham's simulation of surveillance goes global. A most rational, effective and useful system of surveillance (PHOTINT), based on technological supremacy, shall bring happiness and remove pains for the sum total of individuals on the planet. Placed under the protective umbrella of a new "triad for confidence building" (the new holy trinity of late-twentieth-century international life),[85] individuals of all cultures become united, not by a communitarian drive, but by their submission to a globalizing optic technology that virtually frees them from pain and suffering by imposing transparency and docility. The dream of a technocratic world where sophisticated machines have clarified and purified all that could locally bring destruction, fear, and diffidence is, no doubt, corollary to Poulin's global surveillance simulation.

Similar to Bentham, Poulin wants to avoid having to use physical coercion. Deterrence can be achieved because elements of international life, starting with "rogue" states, know that they are under the constant monitoring of PHOTINT. "PHOTINT would raise the expense required to achieve deception and increase the risk of detection thus deterring states from any potentially aggressive behaviour," adds Poulin.[86] A system of certainty would be based on the fact that states can never tell whether they are watched or not. There would be no need to send UN inspectors to monitor on the ground. No need for planes either. These can be easily detected. No real presence would in fact be required. The UN would not be seen but felt, and, thus, not antagonized in the real landscape (as in Iraq) but revered in the sky. PHOTINT, ORCI and the UN deputy in his watchtower would simulate the UN's power and, through it, the divine and inescapable dictates of disciplinary liberalism. For high in the sky, the UN would not have to demonstrate its power. With the technological arsenal that it would receive, the UN simply would deter and order. Knowing that "a discredited UN would only aggravate international disorder,"[87] inimical states and their subjects would never dare to test the powers of this newly imposed Single Eye of international life (of course, some of the most influential states in the Security Council, those that have decided to rely on international organizations in the first place, would still retain access to this simulated deity and directly benefit from the advantages it brings).

Poulin's vision of the UN as a technological panopticon is certainly not the only technotopia of global surveillance that has been formulated of late.[88] Yet, Poulin's optimistic approach to the simulation of surveillance is original because it seeks to reinvent the UN as a virtual center of power (by means of omnivoyance). In Bogard's words, Poulin creates a (social) science fiction of the UN and invites us to look at the UN as both a real and an imaginary surveillance machine.

This latest vision of the UN, coupled with the earlier operations in North Korea and Iraq, introduces the UN and its post–cold war peacekeeping interventions into an era of superpanopticism. Superpanopticism is a global formation that, in the absence of a world government (or super-Leviathan), nonetheless offers the (simulated) ability to organize, steer, and govern international affairs through the discipline of real/imaginary surveillance. This simulation of governance by means of surveillance also generates what may be called (drawing upon Foucault's analysis) a carceralization of international life.

THE CARCERALIZATION OF INTERNATIONAL LIFE

Even though, as Der Derian once remarked, "in an anarchical society [supposedly characteristic of international relations] there is
no central watchtower to normalize relations, no panopticon to define and anticipate delinquency,"[89] fictions of global surveillance still
hope to simulate the UN as a superpanoptic center. In the aftermath
of the cold war, the UN has proven to function better as a super-
Panopticon (a simulation of order and discipline) rather than as a
super-Leviathan (a world government). The UN as super-Panopticon
may well be the alternative to the lack of a super-Leviathan in
post–cold war international life, just as the reliance on global surveillance is possibly a technological substitute for the actual incapac-
ity of the UN to provide states and their subjects with actual conditions of global governance. As international anarchy ("rogue" states
like Iraq or North Korea continue to implement their selfish strategies) cannot be resolved by the simple goodwill of the UN and its enlightened officials, an alternative scenario consists of constructing
the UN as a panoptic organization whose methods of surveillance
and visual deterrence will make up for the lack of effective governance. UN panopticism provides an alternate mode of reality (hyperpanoptic reality) that replaces the less attractive reality of international affairs where the confrontations with "rogue" states or other
recognized international threats do not always produce the desired
results. As Poulin's imaginary UN machine suggests, panopticism applied to strategies of global governance and international order aims
at simulating (if not achieving) normality. It hopes to condition
humankind, above all the surveilled subjects, to a normal state of
things by means of coercion perhaps, but more likely by means of
(science) fiction.

   Thus, the "normalizing gaze of the Superpanopticon"[90] is the
strategy used to artificially make up for the recognized and deeply
felt presence of international disorder (or absence of international
order). Conversely, the recognition of so-called international disorders and threats is what legitimizes the deployment of superpanoptic
regimes. Presented as such, the dilemma of international order and
governance is not about transcending what was once called "anarchy." It is rather about finding the most adequate, efficient, and
"true-to-life" means of disciplining "anarchy."

The disciplinization of international "anarchy," of the recognized (if not clearly identified) post–cold war threats, by means of (super) panoptic strategies is, in Foucault's jargon, a practice of carceralization. What Foucault calls the "carceral archipelago"[91] is a general principle of panoptic surveillance. The carceral archipelago is panopticism and surveillance applied to the entire social domain, realized, and finalized (Foucault does not really question whether such a finalization of panopticism is actual or virtual). The carceral thus becomes the outcome of panopticism, the normal everyday discipline/ simulation of visual surveillance, compliance, and control that can no longer be questioned but must simply be accepted by the subjects themselves.[92] Far from ever realizing the presence of this mode of disciplinarity over their everyday lives, the observed subjects become their own self-regulators by reproducing the very panoptic structures that normalize them. They become the replicators of the system of surveillance, their own (invisible) wardens. Carceralization is the ultimate goal/dream of surveillance techniques. Once normal behavior is achieved in this manner, the harmonization of the subjects (transformed into type-beings responding to specific stimuli and codes) is facilitated and larger ideological enterprises can be realized without having to face the obstacle of idiosyncratic preferences and differences, and, of course, without having to use violence.

The carceralization of international life is the task assigned to the UN by means of panopticism. Of course, in mainstream literatures, such a notion is more conveniently hidden behind constructs such as globalization, globalism, or global governance. Carceralization is nonetheless the ideological end-result of UN superpanopticism. Whether it is physically enforced (UN peacekeeping missions as direct compliance as shall be seen in the following chapters) or visually intimated (UN panopticism as a simulation of surveillance), globalization-as-carceralization is a trap.[93] Critically revisited, globalization is a set of ideological processes which, beyond their professed liberal, economic, moral and political justifications,[94] seeks to deploy various technologies aimed at normalizing and ordering the lives of sovereign states and, beyond, of individuals, institutions, and civilizations that necessarily find themselves subjected to these processes. Stephen Gill has described globalization, by and large, as a transnational economic strategy. Globalization, characterized by "the cumulative aspects of market integration and the increasingly expansive structures of accumulation, legitimation, consumption and work," is "largely configured by the power of transnational capital."[95] Globalization undeniably marks the link between global capitalism (pancapitalism and its deterritorialized regime of transactions) and universal liberalism as an ideology of sociopolitical governance. Yet, as was noted in the introduction to the volume, there is more to globalization (and liberalism) than these economic dimensions. The ideological process (or set of processes) of globalization is also, and perhaps more importantly, a discursive formation. As a discursive formation—a field of interpretation where meaning is inscribed by certain ideological/political/cultural representations—globalization is the point where the discourse(s) of global governance (economic, geostrategic, environmental, moral, etc.) and the disciplinary practices of global carceralization by means of surveillance converge. Discursively and pragmatically, globalization is more than a phenomenon that, along its way, creates international structures and institutions of neoliberal subsistence.[96] Globalization-as-carceralization is also a structure of meaning whose ideological representations (or simulations, as the case may be) demand that the subjects "governed" by such practices adhere to stated principles/policies/ideologies that will transcend localized, individualized, and particularized experience. Globalization ends up being a prescribed life strategy imposed from outside, a desired, accepted, forced, or simulated transfer of meaning from private experience to collective existence. These postulated discursive and ideological effects of globalization are clearly displayed in recent global governance literatures where the carceralization of (international) life is a taken-for-granted formation.

Lawrence Finkelstein, for example, suggests that global governance is "governing, without sovereign authority, relationships that transcend national frontiers."[97] Such a definition introduces global governance as a search for transnational order without, however, the imposition of a sovereign ("without sovereign authority"). Global governance, in other words, is international government without a super-Leviathan. This vision of governance is quasi-magical. Global governance imposes order and rule (of law, reason), and normalizes international relations without having to rely on a centralized mechanism of power. This mostly metaphysical vision of global governance is contradicted by Finkelstein himself who, in the next sentence, argues that "global governance is doing internationally what governments do at home."[98] In this second statement, global governance simply becomes a transposition into international affairs of the type of hierarchical structures already present within a (liberal democratic) state. This second version reveals Finkelstein's own indecision and imprecision about the so-called reality of global governance. After all, as he puts it, "global governance appears to be virtually anything."[99] Finkelstein remains uncertain about this transnational ideology, constantly wavering between a notoriously idealist position (global governance is self-evident and does not require authority structures) and a Waltzian neorealist stance (global order can only be achieved by reproducing domestic structures of power). But this apparent contradiction between Finkelstein's two statements is resolved if we take him to signify something else. When he posits that "global governance is doing internationally what governments do at home," Finkelstein may in fact have something different in mind. Global governance is a different discursive formation and modality of governance and government. Global governance is what "governments do at home" because what they do at home is impose modes of disciplinarity. Governments may govern by imposing a rule of law (Hobbes), but they also discipline, as Foucault has shown, by means of diverse institutional and ideological structures that condition subjects to adopt a normalized status. These structures produce the subjects themselves and the relationship between the subjects and the recognized authorities. Thus, as Foucault suggests, acts of governments are first and foremost formations of/in "governmentality." Governmentality refers to the ability to "apply techniques of instrumental rationality to the arts of everyday management."[100] Such a capacity is not proper to governments. It is the expression of the discursive formation (the field of ideologico-political meaning/ representation) of governance in general, a formation that national governments have mobilized to establish their power, among other techniques.

Although its historical origins coincide with the development of modern governments, the principle of governmentality cannot be restricted to state formations and disciplines. Its forms vary, evolve, and follow different historical patterns. In the context of contemporary global governance, as Finkelstein suggests, it is adapted to the deployment of global processes for which governmentality is no longer a question of "targeting" a single population (the population of a given nation-state that is regulated by such practices), but rather a question of reordering or redistributing multiple elements of international life. This is how Finkelstein understands global governance. For him, global governance is what states "do at home," and what they do is apply principles and techniques of governmentality that seek to carceralize individual subjects. Global governance as governmentality is similarly a discourse/practice whose purpose is to carceralize elements of international politics by normalizing them into "good" states (as opposed to "rogue" states) and disciplined subjects (of such tamed states).

Seen at this critical/postmodern angle of analysis, governance does not require the permanent presence of a sovereign or super-Leviathan. Simply, panopticism and surveillance performed by appropriate institutions can achieve governance as a practice of governmentality, and lead humankind to its desirable liberal apogee (to govern: to steer, to drive) in the absence of a central power (but with the realized and/or simulated presence of a central warden). This view on global governance is consistent with the phenomenon of UN panopticism in the 1990s. It is also congruent with other post–cold war practices/formations of governance-as-governmentality such as global environmental regimes.[101] Panopticism allows global governance to be any kind of order achieved by surveillance that may facilitate worldwide compliance to recognized liberal principles. After all, as Finkelstein notes, global governance

> applies whether the subject is general (e.g., global security and order) or specific (e.g., the WHO Code on the Marketing of Breast Milk Substitutes). It is flexible enough as to reach; it applies whether the participation is bilateral (e.g., an agreement to regulate usage of a river flowing in two countries), function-specific (e.g., a commodity agreement), regional (e.g., the Treaty of Tlatelolco), or global (e.g., the NPT). The definition [of global governance] accommodates both governmental and 'sovereignty free' actors.[102]

Another key example of the triangular relationship between carceralization, governance, and panopticism is James Rosenau's recent essay on global governance.[103] In this short visionary work (Rosenau's idea is "to anticipate the prospects for global governance in the decades ahead"[104]), global governance is presented as a finality, a universal goal. Globalization is not simply the product of the expansion of capital, technology, and information worldwide (a common signification that the term has come to take of late). Rosenau's piece has the merit of trying to disentangle the nature of the process of globalization from the many commonplace usages that have been ascribed to the notion. Simply, globalization is a process or set of processes that facilitates the advent of global governance. Global governance, Rosenau claims, can be realized thanks to the implementation of "control or steering mechanisms."[105] Globalization is such a mechanism in charge of "modifying attitudes," transforming realities, rendering the international system uniform. In a system redefined by techniques of globalization,

> some actors [later, Rosenau enumerates the various types of institutions and international organizations involved], the controllers, seek to modify the behavior and/or orientation of other actors, the controllees, and the resulting patterns of interaction between the former and the latter can properly be viewed as a system of rule sustained by one or another form of control. It does not matter whether the controllees resist or comply with the efforts of the controllers; in either event, attempts at control have been undertaken. . . . Rule systems and control mechanisms, in other words, are founded on a modicum of regularity, a form of recurrent behavior that systematically links the efforts of controllers to the compliance of controllees through either formal or informal channels.[106]

Globalization is a process in charge of "realizing" global governance as a carceral(ized) order. It is once again a matter of governmentality. In such a vision of a globally facilitated life, the work of the "controllers" and of their regulating "rule systems and control mechanisms" (over the "controllees") establishes, just as Foucault maintains, "a slow, continuous, imperceptible gradation that makes it possible to pass naturally from disorder to offense and back from a transgression of the law to a slight departure from a rule, an average, a demand, a norm."[107] Rosenau's institutions of globalization (from NGOs and multinational corporations to state-sponsored machineries like the UN, the European Union, or NAFTA) are to give ideological, bureaucratic, and logistical substance to the myth of global governance by constructing (or simulating) an order of power and knowledge, a carceral archipelago, "with its many diffuse or compact forms, its institutions of supervision and constraint, of discreet surveillance and insistent coercion."[108] For Rosenau, global governance is clearly the result of superpanopticism, and perhaps nothing else, as the regime of globalization "knows no boundaries— geographic, social, cultural, economic, or political."[109] Global governance is international life reduced and simplified to a norm (universal liberal order, loosely defined and rather imprecise, and hence arbitrary as well), and objectified under the constant perforating discipline of superpanoptic machines like the UN. All of this is done (or dreamed of) under the pretense that all of humankind will, at different levels, be enhanced by this vast regime of carceralized life.

The simulation of (global) surveillance is the paradigmatic model of global governance. Superpanopticism, as both fictive and real, is the exemplary regime of international governmentality in a post–cold war era. As both Finkelstein's and Rosenau's texts reveal, superpanopticism permeates (if not defines) global governance literatures, which, in turn, become all too convenient scholarly covers for an intensified carceralization of international life. Carceralization, surveillance, and disciplinization are, of course, never overtly advocated by any of these discourses and practices. But governmentality is, and Foucault has shown that carceralization is often the outcome of governmentality formations. Through the notion of governmentality extended to global international practices/literatures, the illusion of liberal values is preserved while controlling and disciplining mechanisms are implemented or imagined. The visions of governance championed by these texts open up a new era of international affairs, a new discursive field where, in both theory and practice, the promise that "anarchy" can be ordered and contained by means of surveillance is made. UN panopticism as a mode of (actual or simulated) governance is thus an indispensable component and a key moment of disciplinary liberalism.

3

From a Hopeless Situation to Operation Restore Hope, and Beyond: Suture, Ideology, and Simulation in Somalia

REALITY-FILM-IDEOLOGY

Somalia was a John Ford—not an Oliver Stone—movie.
— SIDNEY BLUMENTHAL, "WHY ARE WE IN SOMALIA?"

With cameras switched on in nose cones, a high-tech machinery of war had been launched into the emptiness of the sky, heading toward a land without people, in search of a cartoon version of evil.
— TOM ENGLEHARDT, THE END OF VICTORY CULTURE

The United Nations intervention in Somalia from January 1992 to April 1995 offers itself to us as a movie. Reading Somalia as a cinematographic fiction is not only made possible by the explosion of visual media that this post–cold war intervention triggered.[1] It is also influenced by the actors themselves, the level of reality at which their actions take place, and the staged scenarios that they try to follow. In fact, Somalia is one of the first locations where the United Nations has actually been given the opportunity to demonstrate its acting talents. Reinvested by George Bush's post–Gulf War vision of a New World Order, the United Nations has been given in Somalia a chance to perform as an undisputable "international actor," as a symbolic and legitimate power to be reckoned with as the century draws to an end. In Somalia, the UN's task is not simply to mobilize strategies of visual surveillance and panopticism (as was the case in North Korea and Iraq). It is rather to show the international community that it can actively construct and organize the neoliberal world order through its peacekeeping interventions. Somalia, in fact, inaugurates a series of peacekeeping missions that will require the UN to transcend panopticism in order to achieve global governance in practice in certain regions of the globe where, as will be argued, a more forceful intervention is required. Unlike panopticism, the strategies of visual simulation relied upon by the UN to achieve its ideological objectives are now intended to be highly visible. To put it bluntly, the UN will have to act, and it will have to be seen.

This chapter highlights the apparently rediscovered capacity of the UN to act, a position that Boutros-Ghali had already tried to sketch out (albeit in a visionary fashion in his *Agenda for Peace*). This "acting capacity" of the UN, however, is not simply a matter of international agency or diplomatic activity. It is also, and more importantly, a form of acting that is directly modeled out of cinematographic performance. The UN's acting capacity in Somalia recalls the performance of an "actor" on stage or, more precisely, of a "film star" placed under the spotlight of a camera. As Sidney Blumenthal's introductory metaphor suggests, the cinematographic context of the Somalia crisis conditions this post–cold war UN-U.S. joint operation. If, as Blumenthal would have it, Somalia needs to be interpreted as a movie, the UN in one of its supposedly defining post–cold war missions has to be regarded as an actor featured in what looks to be a prescribed film. Indeed, when the UN "acts" in Somalia, it is as if its movements, expressions, and declarations were following a previously agreed upon scenario, a scenario no doubt highly influenced by ideological connotations of global governance, nation building, and peace enforcement.

From a visual and filmic point of view, the UN operation in Somalia recalls the staged U.S. intervention in the Gulf War against Iraq. A few months earlier (January–February 1991), the United States, behind then-President Bush, had intended to rediscover a "narrative of triumph"[2] by means of a high-tech visual war against a "cartoon version of evil" (as Englehardt suggests).[3] In Somalia, the UN will try to deploy the same type of strategy in the ideological emptiness of the post–cold war order. The United States partially succeeded in rebuilding a culture of triumphalism in its war against Saddam Hussein. Now, in the aftermath of such a symbolic success, the UN is in charge of making visible the triumph of neoliberalism on a global scale by intervening in war-torn Somalia. If the UN's intent is slightly different from what the United States hoped to achieve in Iraq in 1991, the technique is nonetheless very similar (perhaps because the United States, in the post–Gulf War euphoria, has a vested interest in such a mission too). The idea is to try to impose a "reconstructive image of images" that can prove a perfect "antidote to [international] discontrol."[4] In short, the UN will have to act out order, control, and governance for the resurrected (triumphalist) good of the international community in the sands of Somalia.

Denotatively, this chapter renarrates the story of the UN in Somalia by following the steps of the main actors (the UN, the United States, and the Somalis) as the plot thickens. The plot, once again, is about imposing and affirming peacekeeping as an ideologically motivated mode of global governance (reorganizing societies toward the global, the international, the ideologically hegemonic neoliberal) that could be reproduced in the future should similar situations develop. Somalia must set an example for what the UN can do now and in the future. Somalia must demonstrate what roles the (reactivated) UN can play in a post–cold war era.

What is expected of the UN in Somalia is a closing of reality.[5] The UN is supposed to foreclose the ideological representation(s) of the New World Order by means of visual simulation, by imposing a "reconstructive image of images." In psychoanalytic terms, this closing of reality by means of visual devices is what is known as a process of suture. Here, suture is mobilized, by means of cinematic, televisual, and symbolic devices, in order to give meaning to the actions of both the United Nations and its member states (the United States above all) on stage or, if one prefers, in the everyday practice of military and humanitarian interventionism in Somalia. Suture is designed to give the peacekeepers a clear and reassuring identity, a nonambiguous sense of what they are supposed to achieve. However, a process of (cinematic, psychological, symbolic) suture is not only about regaining a safe and certain identity (for the actors themselves) and meaning (to their actions). It is also linked to more encompassing ideological projects and constructs.[6] In the case of Somalia, suture is also the means through which neoliberal world politics is visually constructed as an irrefutable and totalizing condition of humankind. In such an ideological context, Louis Althusser's notion of ideological "interpellation" will be called forth to explain how the Somali suture of post–cold war international politics seeks to (visually) condition humankind to a mode of political and ideological globalization (and to show how UN peacekeeping is necessarily an ideological complement to global surveillance strategies as well).

It is well known by now that the peacekeeping precedent that the UN was supposed to set in Somalia did not take place. Instead of following the scenario, some of the actors (mostly the Somalis) prefer to improvise and follow their own scripts. Intended to become a triumphalist film, the UN mission in Somalia turns out to be yet another "quagmire" film.[7] This Somalia "quagmire" (the end of the story) can still be read from the perspective of suture. The discontinuities of the visual projections coming out of Somalia (and showing among other things tortured U.S. Marines dragged down the streets of Mogadishu) produce ruptures in the suturing process. The revelation of the UN's operational lacunae in Somalia is a foretaste of things to come (as will be seen in Bosnia). It is the point when the Somalis refuse to abide by the UN's visual strategies, when the suturing visual code breaks, and when the ideological edifice of global peacekeeping reliant on the UN may be interpreted as an unsuccessful simulation. There is, then, a fatal return of suture as well, of the notion of suture and its relation to practical experience, to what, perhaps, it always already was. Ironically, beyond ideological recodings, suture always was already nothing more than the trace of an incompletion or an imperfection. A suture as a visual/psychological/ideological device never goes beyond what it physically looks like as a surgical procedure implanted on an injured, imperfect body: it is a seam, an awkward dotted line that, far from (en)closing, points to the ruptures/discontinuities that it surgically tries to patch. Thus, what I suggest toward the end of this chapter is that suture operates a fateful reversal. Instead of being a "reconstructive image of images," suture is a deconstructive process of images. It is a visual construct that contains its own excesses and impossibilities (or its own possibilities of deconstruction, not reconstruction) which, sooner or later, are bound to be blatantly exposed.

But before these critical questions are considered, we must turn to the (visual/filmic) narrative. As we now join the action in Somalia, we find ourselves inside a movie theater. We are in Mogadishu, in the summer of 1993. Most of the people in the audience are American soldiers and international blue-helmets. A few Somalis are sitting in the back. The movie that is shown today: *Delta Force.*

CINEMA MOGADISHU

"At the Cinema Equatore in Mogadishu, Somalis put aside their guns and let Clint Eastwood do the shooting."[8] This is how Donatella Lorsch, special envoy in Mogadishu for the *New York Times,* described the last stronghold of Western values in the middle of wartorn Mogadishu: Cinema Equatore. Cinema Equatore reopened in the early days of 1993, a few months after the landing of U.S. Marines. Its charismatic owner, Ali Hassan Mohammed, a graduate of Brandeis University, found a new life after the announcement of the deployment of Operation Restore Hope. With the support of UN-U.S. authorities, Mohammed immediately realized the financial and symbolic benefits of providing his mixed Somali-multinational audience with war movies "made-in-Hollywood." His most popular showings have been *The Good, The Bad and the Ugly, The Dirty Dozen, Rambo,* and of course *Delta Force.*[9] Mohammed insists: "I like American action movies, especially war movies. We compare it [*sic*] with the war here in Somalia." The Somali theater owner continues: "People come here to escape their worries and to dream."[10]

The Somalis are apparently not the only ones who "compare" or confuse these movies with the reality of the UN-U.S. operation in Somalia. Cinema Equatore, the only movie theater still working in Mogadishu, is right in the middle of an area protected by UN forces. Cinema Equatore is like a jewel, preciously preserved by the UN and the United States at the very heart of a city that has fallen prey to, as observers like to put it, "destruction and anarchy." The screen of Cinema Equatore, or what is left of it ("it had to be patched after a mortar hit," says Lorsch),[11] allows the main actors of the post–cold war intervention in Somalia to project their visions and hopes. By means of comparison, or confusion rather, what they see on screen takes precedence over everyday life in occupied Mogadishu. Sylvester Stallone, Clint Eastwood, and Chuck Norris, inside the movie theater, perform more completely and successfully what the Rangers and the Marines vainly try to accomplish outside. And *The Good, the Bad and the Ugly* replays the adventures of Bill Clinton, Boutros Boutros-Ghali and Mohammed Farah Aidid in the sands of Somalia. Cinema Equatore does not provide an escape from the everyday realities of Mogadishu. In fact, it reimmerses all the spectators into the conflict. It reconditions the audience to a heroic Delta Force. Instead of providing a way out, Cinema Equatore provides a way back in as a form of closure for the international diplomatic and military elite present in Somalia. As the film reels to its end, the audience becomes more and more convinced that victory is attainable, that the ugly has been defeated, and that hope has been restored.

This psychological closing process offered by Cinema Equatore, not so much for the Somali population as for the members of the international force of intervention (not many Somalis can actually pay the fifty-cent entrance fee), is perhaps better explained as a process of suture. The notion of "cinematographic suture," introduced by French psychoanalyst Jacques-Alain Miller,[12] works as a constant reactivation of subjectivity. By means of suture, a visual text (painting, photograph, film, computer simulation) reinvests a more positive meaning or identity for the subject/viewer who decides to identify with this type of narrative. The image sutures by adding a missing component deeply felt by the subject in so-called real life. Wholeness of identity and completion of an action are metaphorically and cinematographically rendered by the successful ending (closure) of the film. The technological and imaginary structure of the film adds what is lacking in everyday life.

SUTURE AND FILM

The system of suture is defined as a historical articulation of cinema as discourse.

—STEPHEN HEATH, "NARRATIVE SPACE"

The notion of suture inevitably leads us to investigate the relation between the visual image, its meaning, and identity as both cinema and television assume a dominant role in the production of reality (understood in a Baudrillardian sense as a media-generated mode of cognition) and identity in Somalia. In the 1970s, film theorists influenced by structuralist approaches and by the writings of Jacques Lacan introduced the notion of suture as a basis for critical cinematographic theory. Suture, they claimed, is what turns cinema into a discourse, what makes it a coherent narrative. Starting from a Lacanian model of subject formation (the mirror stage), film theorists affirmed that the visual image provided by a film had a fundamental function in the development of the viewer's subjectivity. To simplify their argument, cinema was in charge of representing and embellishing the subjectivity of the spectator. This is precisely what film theorist Jean-Pierre Oudart thought when he wrote that "suture represents the closure of the cinematic *énoncé* [enunciated] in line with its relationship with its subject (the filmic subject or rather the cinematic subject [s/he who watches the film])."[13] In the overall process of production of meaning and identity, film theorists adopting such a Lacanian perspective viewed cinema as a "second image stage" or a "second mirror stage," thus referring to Lacan's mirror stage as the primal phase of formation of subjectivity.

Lacan's postulate of the mirror stage has often been taken for granted by this critical current of film theory. The notion of the mirror stage now forms a conceptual and psychological dogma that has been all too conveniently left unquestioned in subsequent views on identity and representation in film. Christian Metz's theory of cinematic discourse is symptomatic of such a blind adoption of Lacan's mirror stage as the founding moment of the relationship between subjectivity and the visual.[14] Metz writes that

> the film is like the mirror. But in an essential way, it also differs from this primordial mirror. Although, as in the mirror, everything can be projected, there is one thing, and one only, that is never reflected: the body of the spectator.[15]

In order to better grasp the relationship between the visual and subjectivity as seen by Lacanian film theorists (like Metz), one needs to open a brief theoretical parenthesis that will describe the initial Lacanian moment of the formation of the subject, the mirror stage, taken for granted by film discourses. According to Lacan, the mirror stage corresponds to a phase of infancy (between six and eighteen months) during which the infant in the mother's arms sees his/her image reflected in a mirror. For Lacan, this moment of childhood corresponds to the imaginary. It is crucial to the formation of subjectivity. Lacanian scholar Daniel Dayan explains that "during this stage, the child identifies itself with the visual image of the mother or the person playing the part of the mother."[16] Dayan clarifies the Lacanian mirror stage further by indicating that

> through this identification, the child perceives its own body as a unified whole by analogy with the mother's body. The notion of a unified

body is thus a fantasy before being a reality. It is an image that the child receives from outside. Through the imaginary function, the respective parts of the body are united so as to constitute one body, and therefore to constitute somebody, one self. Identity is thus a formal structure which fundamentally depends upon an identification. Identity is one effect, among others, of the structure through which images are formed: the imaginary.[17]

In the mirror stage, the importance of the visual function for the development of subjectivity is revealed. The mirror stage is, thus, "the threshold of the visible world," as Lacan puts it.[18] From this fundamental phase constitutive of subjectivity, identity is never anything more than an effect of the imaginary, of what the fiction of an image reflected by a mirror/screen reveals. For Lacan, the subject is in representation (imaginary) to the detriment of being in reality (the image of the body takes precedence over the experience of the body).[19] Such a decentralization or disincarnation of the subject is fundamental to many film theorists who see in Lacan's theory of the imaginary a starting point for their own understanding of the relationship between cinema (the moving image) and subjectivity (spectatorship).[20] Dayan demonstrates this position perfectly by stating that "the imaginary constitutes the subject through a 'specular' effect common to the constitution of images."[21]

Having clarified the importance of the mirror stage for psychoanalytic theories of the visual, we can return to Metz's exploration of cinema as a "secondary viewing activity." Metz notes that, differently from the primordial scene of deployment of the imaginary (where the subject is visually present and produced), in a film, the subject-as-spectator is always absent from the mirror/screen. Whereas for Metz the mirror stage is the mark of a presence, the cinema-stage is a constant marker of the absence of self. As Metz puts it, "the reflection of the body has disappeared" in cinema.[22] This so-called absence of self in the film is the postulate (derived from a comparison with the Lacanian mirror stage) from which most of the theorists of suture operate. In order for suture to have any (psychological and technical) relevance in their theories, film scholars need to posit lack or absence as a primary basis. A lack of self, from both the real (as Lacan explained) and the imaginary (the film image) is thus constitutive of suture. For film theorists with a Lacanian background, cinema will necessarily be read as a structure of absence, and suture will be a visual stand-in (or *tenant-lieu*), something that phantasmagorically "takes the place of" lack, and thus allows the filmic narrative to be completed for the subject/spectator.[23]

At this point, a caveat about theory must be introduced. In my reading of the UN-U.S. operation in Somalia, I will insist on the fact that suture does not always have to be read from the perspective of absence or lack. I will suggest that, as much as theories of cinematographic suture can be of tremendous assistance to highlight (my) critical interpretations of the UN's post–cold war operations, the practice of post–cold war peacekeeping symptomatically read in this chapter also has the ability to bring new critical/postmodern dimensions to the often too dogmatic study of visual suture. Specifically, as will be seen later with Althusser's theory of ideology, the postulated use-value of suture as a stand-in for lack is only one of many ways according to which the notion of visual suture can be interpreted. In short, the notion of suture is richer with theoretical implications than what Lacanian scholars, trapped in their dogma of the lack/absence of the subject, suggest.

Keeping this important conceptual caveat in mind, one may return to the classical, even if theoretically restrained, version of suture introduced by film theorists like Metz or psychoanalysts like Lacan. This reading has at least the merit of offering a point of entry into the problem of the use and meaning of cinematographic and visual strategies in questions of identity/subjectivity. Thus, according to Metz, the absence of the body/image of the spectator in the movie has a potentially traumatic effect. Unlike the mirror stage, the subject has a priori no one to identify with here, no already familiar and intuitively recognized bond with another being/image. All of a sudden, faced with a film on screen, the spectator has no mirror stage equivalent in which s/he can truly see himself/herself. The screen on which the (non self-reflecting) images are projected is a potential reversal of the reflection-effect provided by the mirror. The visible absence of the subject (as image of oneself) could, thus, discontinue identification and, having done so, would deprive the subject of the enjoyment of watching movies. Metz, however, finds a solution to this psychological drama. Indeed, Metz finds a way out of this by claiming that subjectivity is, in fact, never truly endangered in cinema. Thanks to the prior constitutive experience of the mirror stage (which overdetermines a subject's being and can never be fully lost), the absence of subjectivity is never total or final. The individual subject always has the cognitive ability (unless s/he experiences some kind of psychic disorder) to realize that there is a "first image stage" (the mirror stage) that predetermines this second visual moment. This is why, according to Metz, one can safely watch movies without the drama and fear of losing one's own image in the process.[24]

It remains, however, that even though the subject-as-spectator maintains a recognition of himself/herself while not being manifestly present in the film, the subject may still allow himself/herself to be visually fooled by the visual apparatus of cinema. The technology of film (a narrated image in movement) gives the visual representation the illusion that it could be real life. As is commonly expressed, in order for the narrative to be understood, the subject/spectator always has to put himself/herself in the hero's shoes. Consciously or not, the spectator chooses to identify at some level with the visual fiction that s/he watches. An experience of absence/lack is, thus, still felt by the subject, not by realizing that s/he is not present on screen, but rather by identifying with a character whose fictive traits of personality may compensate for what the spectator is not or does not have in "real life" (a typical case of identity replication). Cinema facilitates this process of reempowerment by means of image identification because of its own technical structure and, specifically, because of the process of suture. Suture is what gives "life" to the character on screen (the subject by proxy) by not leaving him/her as a frozen sign or picture, but by giving him/her movement, a succession of actions achieved by way of a succession of images. Thus, in cinema, a shot is never isolated. For the narrative to be completed to the satisfaction of the spectator, a following shot must take place until (textual/filmic) closure is achieved (by means of the final sign, "The End"). This process of "shot/countershot" (as film theorists call it) which characterizes films as opposed to other static visual representations is technically what is called suture. The succession of moving images provides the psychological suture as well since it allows the viewing subject to "get the story," and identify with the characters on screen. Silverman summarizes the process by writing that

> the classic cinematic organization depends upon the willingness of the
> subject to become absent itself by permitting a fictional character to
> "stand in" for it, or by allowing a particular point of view to define

what it sees. The operation of suture is successful at the moment that the viewing subject says, "Yes, that's me," or "That's what I see."[25]

The continuity of the film, and that of the imaginary representation achieved by the spectator, are thus guaranteed by a process of suture. Each shot, incomplete as it is, yet complementary to the previous one, gives way to another shot, and this slowly builds the narrative toward its completion, toward a sense of closure. Suture is, technically, nothing more than a constant play between absence and presence (previous/next, shot/countershot). Yet, film theorists believe, it produces for the subject a finished discourse, an impression of wholeness and completion, until the end of the film at least. Suture is a code, technically produced by the cinematic medium, which keeps the fiction (of the story and of the identification of the subject with that story) going. This specific dimension of the notion of cinematographic suture is particularly relevant in the context of the visually mobilized UN mission in Somalia.

SUTURE AND SOMALIA

Suture is a procedure sought by the UN, not only inside Cinema Equatore, but also through the entire Somali operation. The wholeness of a global vision of world affairs, announced by Bush after the revitalizing victory in the Gulf, is what the UN has been mandated to perform in a post–cold war era. As was mentioned above, Somalia, as the first full-fledged post–cold war peacekeeping mission carried out by the UN, is supposed to set an example for future UN interventions. The UN operation in Somalia is supposed to bridge the gap between the visionary abstraction of the New World Order and the reality of an apparently chaotic and disordered world (it is also a matter, as was indicated above, of bridging the gap between panoptic surveillance and the applicability of simulation). Finally, Somalia is supposed to be the "good" example of a successful UN mission in the name of superior humanitarian principles, an example that should be able to cover the soon-to-be-obvious lacunae of the UN's other major post–cold war intervention in Bosnia. In what can be described as a first stage in the Somalia intervention (from 1991 to December 8, 1992, the date of the U.S. landing in Somalia), the UN is, by and large, solely in charge. The support of U.S. troops will only come later. Thus, at the beginning, the UN is directly responsible for the deployment of the above-stated objectives.

The Way They Were: The Early Days of the UN Mission in Somalia

For the UN, it all starts in the early days of 1991. The fall of the Siad Barre dictatorship in Somalia was first seen as one of those many post–cold war welcoming signs. Another ruthless ruler was gone. The end of the cold war no longer allowed dictators to stay in power. As had been affirmed in the post–cold war euphoria, the UN would be willing to lend a helping hand to any society or nation in need of global support. Somalia was one of them, as the post-Barre succession proved to be tumultuous.[26] Yet, the UN and the international community refrain from intervening immediately after Barre's departure (January 1991), even though the clan war is already at its peak.[27] More pressing and mediatically flashy situations need to be addressed in Iraq first. When one has to deal with Saddam Hussein, one does not have time for the yet unknown Somalian clan leaders Ali Mahdi (the leader of the provisional post-Barre government) and Mohammed Farah Aidid (the leader of a rival faction). Things of course will change quickly in the following months as Aidid becomes the world's number one public enemy (in 1992–93). But in the early days of 1991, Somalia is still not on the ideological map of the UN. Somalia does not exist for the UN, as the international community chooses to center its "triumphalist" efforts on the so-called desperate fate of Kuwait. Thus, as the UN is offering moral and legal assistance to the United States and its allies in the Gulf, Somali clan leaders are starting to develop their own visions of political order in the shadow of the international community's visual/mediatic arsenal fully deployed in Kuwait and Iraq. Somalia soon becomes divided into multiple zones of influence controlled by the traditionally powerful regional clans.[28] Somalia is returning to the type of chaos that it had prior to the Barre regime, whose arbitrary political order had at least the merit of "stifling clan conflicts."[29] This is, in fact, not a surprising situation in an area where national identity centered around a judicial state apparatus (the Western model of state-formation) has always been an external and artificial construct.[30] As the attention of the West gradually shifts away from the Persian Gulf to other "disordered" zones of the global landscape, Somalia suddenly emerges as one of the potential theaters of the

UN's new peacekeeping maneuvers. The recognized "anarchy and chaos" taking place between the different clans is an all too painful example of what, for neoliberal scholars and ideologues, becomes the new major force of evil and destruction in international politics: ethnic and regional separatism.[31] In the last months of 1991, as the international community is in search of new sites of post–cold war triumph (the Kurdish zone in Northern Iraq is one of them), the suddenly highly advertised starvation of thousands of Somalis as a result of clan warfare becomes a perfect (humanitarian) alibi for a UN intervention. In traditional UN peacekeeping terms, the situation in Somalia can legitimately call for an intervention. A severe human crisis is developing and, logically, international organizations linked to the UN system (Food and Agriculture Organization, World Health Organization, and United Nations High Commissioner for Refugees) and NGOs may intervene. However, similar humanitarian crises are developing at the same time in other parts of the world (the Sudan, Liberia, Tibet) where the UN has no plan or desire to provide forceful assistance. What really draws the UN into Somalia is the mediatic and visually suturing potential of a large-scale humanitarian mission in a country that offers no obvious international strategic dilemma and whose population, both physically and imaginarily remote from the West, should be easily tamed (after all, the predominance of a clan structure makes Somalia look like a "primitive" society in the eyes of the West). Thus, the crisis in Somalia becomes a perfectly timely excuse for the UN to lead the international community toward disciplinary liberalism by setting an example in the fight against ethnic particularisms.

Boutros-Ghali's Own Agenda: UNOSOM I, the Mission

When Mohammed Sahnoun arrives in Mogadishu in April 1992, heading the United Nations Operation in Somalia (UNOSOM I),[32] his mission is to arrive at a compromise between the two major clan leaders, Ali Mahdi and Mohammed Farah Aidid, and to allow multinational humanitarian missions, conducted by the UN and NGOs, to feed the starving and heal the injured. When Boutros-Ghali decides to send Sahnoun to Somalia, he does more than simply send a UN diplomat of long standing as his special envoy: the UN under the leadership of its secretary-general has mandated the largest peacekeeping operation of the post–cold war era. Somalia becomes a symbol for the new politics of UN interventionism. In a typical post–cold war peacekeeping role, following Boutros-Ghali's recommendations in his *Agenda for Peace,* the humanitarian intervention in Somalia will have to be supported by the deployment of UN blue-helmets. The humanitarian mission comes first, but the blue-helmets are nonetheless dispatched to enforce the good and prompt delivery of relief and medical supplies and to guarantee the safety of the UN's envoys and humanitarian workers.[33] Simultaneously, UN special envoy Mohammed Sahnoun will try to establish a political contact between the rival groups in order not only to facilitate the humanitarian mission, but also to bring the clans to gradually form a centralized and democratic state. The military side of peacekeeping is not considered yet. It will only come later, if needed. In the first months of 1992, a plan for a successful peacekeeping operation (more or less derived from Boutros-Ghali's imprecise new diplomatic reordering presented in his *Agenda for Peace*) is thus deployed in Somalia. The three successive stages of the mission (humanitarian, political, premilitary) are intended to harmoniously complement one another and return Somalia to a (new) world of decency and order.

For the UN and its allies, Boutros-Ghali's redefinition of peacekeeping (as seen in chapter 1) is, once again, the rhetorical, if not practical, bridge between "anarchy in Somalia" and "a liberal-democratic state in Somalia," no matter how subtle and complex the Somali society actually may be. The lag between Boutros-Ghali's visionary optimism and the situation in Somalia will nevertheless gradually lead the UN into a more forceful yet, as it will turn out, fatal operation. In November 1992, Boutros-Ghali announces the inevitable: "the situation in Somalia has deteriorated past the point at which it is susceptible to the peace-keeping treatment."[34] The role of the blue-helmets of UNOSOM I, as guardians of the humanitarian efforts and nation-building negotiations, is not working. This version of peacekeeping is no longer sufficient. The more the UN desperately tries to regain control over Somalia and erase clan separatism by means of (mild) peacekeeping, the larger the initial shortcomings of this operation become, and the further away the UN finds itself from instituting neoliberal governance in this part of Africa.[35] In the last days of 1992, the UN is ready to move to the next stage of peacekeeping and apply a more aggressive mode of peace enforcement in an area that desperately refuses to abide by the laws of reason, justice, and democracy. The peacekeeping mission takes on another dimension. Similar to what happened a few months before in Iraq, it is time for Boutros-Ghali to invite the United States into the conflict as the "peace-makers." After all, as Bush had already affirmed, the United States has an interest in maintaining peace, justice, and democracy in the post–cold war world.[36] Furthermore, the United States possesses the military means to "enforce peacekeeping." As Jonathan Howe, the UN's special envoy to Somalia in 1993 (following Sahnoun), rationalizes:

> alone among nations of the world, the United States had the lift and logistical infrastructure to establish a large force rapidly in a remote area in which civil institutions and services were nonexistent and where violent opposition to even a humanitarian mission could be encountered. Fresh from its Desert Storm successes, the United States was the most likely candidate to deter and, if necessary, to prevent armed interference with humanitarian deliveries. Policymakers believed the mission could be accomplished.[37]

After November 1992, Somalia thus becomes a joint UN-U.S. peace-enforcement operation, with the UN providing the vision and the United States providing the action. At the same time, the UN operation in Somalia undergoes an important strategic and psychological metamorphosis. With his appeal to the United States, Boutros-Ghali allows the deployment of a process of visual suture as a way for the UN to regain prestige and for the New World Order vision to gain a spectacular representation in Somalia. To make up for the UN's early inabilities, and to bridge the gap between the representational reality of humanitarian peacekeeping in Somalia and the vision of its founders, the U.S. Marines have to land in Mogadishu with their high-tech, Hollywood-style production to lend a helping hand to the struggling UN. But before analyzing this new episode in the narrative, I offer a preliminary overview of how suture is at work in Somalia. As already mentioned, suture is a (psychological and cinematographic) subtext that runs throughout the Somalian operation.

Somalia's Suturing Process

The joint UN-U.S. post–cold war operation in Somalia is presented as a movie (a John Ford movie rather than an Oliver Stone movie, perhaps; a modern cinematographic narrative of continuity and recovered identity/stability rather than a postmodern performance of uncertain and proliferated identity) to facilitate the deployment of a process of suture. If the Cinema Equatore story can be taken as an example of what happens in Somalia in the first stages of the conflict, it is because the entire intervention is written for the UN as a fictional narrative. Similar to what happens in films, suture is what allows the Somali narrative of post–cold war interventionism to be perceived as a complete and continuous adventure, thus pushing to the side (beyond the limits of the UN's imaginary) the inherent discontinuities and flaws of this operation. In such a perspective, the absence or lack constitutive of suture in the UN's mission in Somalia is not, properly speaking, provided by an image. Rather, the image is what the UN chooses to refer to in order to solidify its identity, and to suture its peacekeeping intervention. The absence preexists the projection of the film for the UN. Prior to walking into Cinema Equatore, one felt the absence to be there already, as a gap between the noble intentions and the actual realization of the humanitarian mission. In such a context, the UN in the first stage of its Somali operation becomes what in film theory is known as an "absent one," that is to say, a subject-as-spectator whose inability to act is nonetheless felicitously compensated for by the "acting" capacity of the characters on screen.

In Somalia, it is not a succession of shots that allows the viewing/acting subjects (the UN and its member states) to regain meaning (of their mission) and identity (as directly involved actors). Rather, it is the intervention of a cinematographic imagery associated with specific filmic productions (like the movies shown in Cinema Equatore) that play a counterpart to the experience of the UN there, and, as counterparts, allow the deployment of a full, yet fictive, narrative of UN post–cold war interventionism. Put in other terms, even though the New World Order script that the UN tries to follow is already replete with absences and gaps, the filmic performances in Somalia and the display of visual effects patch up this recognized absence with a semblance of presence, with a "reconstitutive image of images."

This visual suture performed by means of cinematographic devices is meaningful to the immediate actors of the conflict, to the bluehelmets who have access to Cinema Equatore. For the other viewers who perceive the Somali mission from an outside perspective (global audiences worldwide), an added dimension of suture is required. This added dimension of suture is provided to worldwide audiences by the onslaught of televisual media that, anticipating the arrival of U.S. Marines (sent to the rescue of UNOSOM I), are dispatched to that region to fully "cover" the humanitarian/peacekeeping spectacle. As the U.S. troops arrive in Somalia, "total television" amplifies the fiction of the UN-U.S. co-venture by expanding suture beyond the confines of Cinema Equatore.[38] The pictures are heroic and glamorous. The world of CNN becomes a world of (global) symbolic and ideological suture. (Tele)visually, disciplinary neoliberalism by means of peacekeeping is realized.

HOPE AND GLORY: A SHOW OF FORCE MADE-IN-HOLLYWOOD

Operation Restore Hope: The Greatest Show on Earth

George Kennan has figured it out: "when I woke up this morning, I found the television screen showing live pictures of the Marines going ashore, in the grey dawn of another African day, in Somalia."[39] In a post–cold war age, former (cold war) heroes of U.S. foreign policy (like Kennan) turn on their TV sets and watch CNN, where foreign policy takes place in "real time" in front of their astonished eyes. On that "grey morning" of December 9, 1992, the show of force of the U.S. Marines in Somalia had already started. TV crews and news anchors (Dan Rather was wearing his Desert Storm uniform) had arrived the day before, waiting on the sand dunes to make sure that they would not miss any single moment of the spectacle. And, all of a sudden, they emerged, "equipped with night-vision goggles, their faces smeared dark green,"[40] weapons in hand, ready to shoot (just in case rebel Somalis would actually be hiding behind the dunes or among the many journalists). It was live, visual, hence real: forceful peacekeeping was disembarking on a Mogadishu beach. The Gulf War, part 2. This made-for-TV show about U.S. forces arriving on the shores of Somalia under the eyes of millions of TV viewers was going to condition the entire UN-U.S. Operation Restore Hope (the second phase of the UN mission in Somalia). Western audiences—who had already been familiarized to this mode of TV-landing thanks to new or rerun science fiction programs such as *Star Trek,* where "away teams" are "beamed down to the surface to clean things up"—would follow the exploits of this next generation of global trekkers in eastern Africa. After all, it is only a short step from the fictive "United Federation of Planets" allegorized by *Star Trek* to the "Global World of the United Nations." Nothing would escape the camera anymore and, as in any good *Star Trek* episode, the "United Federation" would prevail. The U.S. Marines landing followed such a high-tech televisual mode, and it all started very well. As Blumenthal recalls:

> The more demonstrative the invading force, the better the pictures. Television lights were shone into the squinting eyes of the liberators. When the sound of rubber landing craft was heard along the beach, the reporters scrambled across the sands. "Welcome to Somalia!" one yelled. Others called out questions. Assuming a professional posture, the soldiers captured the first Somalis they encountered, forcing them to lie prostrate in a row. Lights, cameras, prisoners! Soon, the conquerors were greeted by Brigadier General Imtiaz Shaheen, the commander of the Pakistani unit assigned to the United Nations. He told the Americans to release their captives who were hapless employees from the airport situated just beyond the beach.[41]

This staged military/televisual landing went on for a few days. The Rangers and Delta Force (the "real" one, this time) soon joined the Marines ashore. By now, the UN multinational force, composed mostly of Malaysian, Pakistani, Italian, Belgian, and French divisions, had accepted letting the Yankees do the peacekeeping work and run the show. The new pictures coming out of Somalia were no doubt more symbolically empowering and more ideologically meaningful than anything that the UN troops had been able to accomplish so far. They erased the images of starving children that initially led to the UN mission.[42] Although it willingly allowed the Marines to take the lead, the UN stayed there to fulfill its humanitarian mission, in the shadow of the U.S. hypervisual production. The official objective for the U.S. troops sent to Somalia, "America's finest" as Bush declared,[43] had been set by the outgoing President. In a declaration of December 4, 1992, Bush explained that "when we see Somalia's children starving, all of America hurts."[44] Bush then continued, summarizing the mission in a few, simple words, as simple perhaps as the New World Order slogan he had coined a few months earlier: "We must help them [the Somali children] live. We must give them hope. America must act."[45] In a strange ethical displacement of U.S. national interest (because America hurts when it sees world suffering, national interest is at stake in a post–cold war era), Bush had justified the U.S. involvement in Somalia. A picture (of starving children) had called for an answer, for a visual cover (a countershot) that would suture the post–cold war world.

Operation Restore Hope was a somewhat unprecedented mission. Even if it sought to recall some of the Gulf War's heroic images, the situation was different in Somalia. There was no a priori figure of evil, no Hitler-like ruthless dictator, who could be directly antagonized. The figure of evil would have to be visually constructed out of Somalia's chaos. Furthermore, the organizers of the mission did not think that it would be necessary to take the time to study the situation and, specifically, to take into account the needs and particularities of the local populations on behalf of whom the intervention was taking place.[46] To fully reevoke the triumphant images of the Gulf War, Operation Restore Hope, the latest model of global interventionism and forceful humanitarian peacekeeping, would have to be swift, precise, powerful, and successful. In fact, if it had not been for its proclaimed ethical and altruistic objectives (or covers), Operation Restore Hope could have looked like a typical colonizing mission, with troops on a political and ideological mission.[47] The only difference from previous colonialist enterprises is that this one had to be put on display by and for the media.

The apparent power display of Operation Restore Hope stood in drastic contrast to UNOSOM I. Whereas UNOSOM's forces looked tired, disillusioned and disorganized, the U.S. troops were bold and beautiful, young and restless. "Operation Restore Hope, it seemed, had all the glamour of a military operation without any of the danger," says Blumenthal.[48] At the United States' request, the UN was now ready to "simplify" the conflict by turning the crisis into the search for "figures of evil," for individuals to be identified as obstacles to the full deployment of peacekeeping. Clan leader Mohammed Farah Aidid, hostile to any Western intervention, and still looking to gain control over rival factions, was thus depicted as a potential threat. The scenario was simple: Aidid stood in the way of the UN–U.S. mission. Everything that could go wrong for the multinational force would have to be attributed to Aidid and his clansmen. Somebody had to pay the price for the previous shortcomings of UNOSOM I. In a typical Hollywood scenario, evil was thus given a name and a face. Aidid became an ideal scapegoat. As for the UN, and for Boutros-Ghali, who after he became Egyptian Ambassador to Somalia in the 1980s had developed a strong dislike for Aidid, the clan leader was a perfect target too. Aidid, like Saddam before him and Milošević in the former Yugoslavia, could easily embody all that the UN in a new world of renewed liberal hopes was against: separatist claims, personal power and greed, political treachery. For the United States and, in particular, its new president, Bill Clinton, Aidid could also replay the role that Saddam Hussein had played for Bush: an incarnated evil, a living antithesis to the most basic of American values, and a catalyst for the president's personal resentments.

The arrival of the U.S. troops and the strategic shift of the operation away from the starving to Mohammed Aidid gave a new life to Operation Restore Hope. This was really what the United States, with the support of the UN, had come here for. It was never certain that the Marines could handle a peacekeeping mission. In Iraq, the U.S. troops had to fight a war. In Somalia, they had to work as interposition forces and security providers. But fighting a designated enemy was definitely within their domain of expertise, at least they believed so. Identifying Aidid as the target also helped to define the entire UN-U.S. mission in Somalia. It offered closure to the mission, replenished it. Instead of wandering in the emptiness of Somalia's sands in search of humanitarians to protect, instead of looking for enemies without names and having to experience unpredictable conditions, the joint UN-U.S. peacekeeping mission would now be able to place a name, an image, and an identity on what it was deployed against. The multinational intervention in Somalia became a whole again with a clearly defined goal and a positively foreseeable end. It is as a determinate action that it would have to be seen by international audiences too. The support of televisual imagery would facilitate the symbolic (suturing) display of the search for Aidid and would allow the mission to become a mediatic success, a success measured not so much for its practical achievements in Somalia as for its mediatized (hyper)reality recognized throughout the global mediascape.

Television Coverage and Suture

Television coverage enlarged the audience of this Somalia operation. It allowed nonactors to take part in the intervention by proxy and conditioned them to the supposedly inevitable success of the UN (with the help of the United States) in Somalia. Television as a mobilizing, identity-suturing, and ideology-interpellating mechanism is not a new concept. In his study on war and television, Bruce Cumings quotes cultural critic John Fiske, who asserts that "[TV] realism's desire to 'get the details right' is an ideological practice, for the believability of its fidelity to the real is transferred to the ideology it embodies."[49] Cumings concludes that "[t]he technology impresses the viewer as unmediated reality, TV people cultivate this notion by presenting themselves as objective bearers of facts, and this practice legitimates the ideology television itself peddles."[50] Television has the technological capacity to reach viewers everywhere and to present its images as objective "reality effects." Television forms its own world order by linking individuals from different areas to a unique visual perspective and to a global media network of images that everyone, no matter who or where they are, can access. Televisual projections thus become a powerful means of suture, as the uniqueness of the images (they possess a monopoly on the instantaneous visual representation of so-called realities) and the authority associated with journalistic comments (the pretense of unmediated truth and objectivity about the real events out there) provide closure for the public. The frantic rhythm of TV pictures does not let the viewer's eyes rest and does not allow for one instant the viewer to ever consider whether what s/he sees is real or not, bound by a frame (that of the screen or the camera) or not. Hooked on to his/her TV, glued to the screen, the viewer's imaginary is constantly sutured by the next image, the next commentary, the next commercial spot, the next sport exploit, the next war film footage. No individual narrative on TV may ever be fully closed (for instance, a news report closes the account of the "real events" visually depicted for the day through a temporary conclusion provided by the news anchor's commentary, but leaves enough open space for the story to be covered again the next day or later). But the entire effect of TV, its contemporary discourse of historical authority and immediacy, and its narrative of truthfulness are always achieved thanks to the same shot/countershot, image/next image, absence/presence suturing play described earlier, a technique that gives the impression of covering everything while never leaving the viewer alone. Mark Crispin Miller summarizes this effect nicely by stating that "while it may confront us with the facts of death, bereavement, mutilation, [TV] immediately cancels out the memory of that suffering, replacing its own pictures of despair with a commercial, upbeat and inexhaustibly bright."[51]

Televisual images thus provide the viewer with what Miller calls "buffers."[52] The notion of "buffers" or the "buffering effect" of TV is conceptually close to the idea of suture in film. Televisual images do not simply provide a sense of objective reality about the world (brought into everyone's living room). More importantly, they provide a way of compensating for reality (including the so-called objective reality showed by the images themselves) by adding another "upbeat" image. In short, on TV, there is always a next shot, a next image, a next cartoon, a next lifelike story of hope, a final positive note, even in news reports.[53] Thus, as much as they supposedly reveal, images on TV also buffer us from the so-called ruthless reality of the world. In Somalia, the highly mediatic landing of the U.S. Marines, and their subsequent deployment in the streets of Mogadishu in the first months of 1993 were also designed to buffer the horror-effect caused in the United States (as Bush noted) by the pictures of starving Somali children. They were also supposed to deflect away the incapacity-effect provided by the images of the UN in Somalia.

Seen from the perspective of what it "buffers," television is a prime example of what Althusser calls an "ideological state apparatus" whose mission is to make sure that the dominant (state) ideology and the dominant social relations are effectively implemented and reproduced.[54] Certainly, television and its endless projection of images are not only about serving a dominant ideology or world vision. Limiting one's analysis of the social, cultural, and political effects of TV to this dimension would be reducing a complex phenomenon to a simplistic ideological function. However, since the point here is not to analyze television but to explore the extent and form of suture, the link between TV's buffering effect and ideology adds a supplementary but necessary commentary to the examination of the role(s) of suture in Somalia.

If television offers a point of entry into the relationship between ideology and suture, it is perhaps because its interpellating capacities, to use an Althusserian terminology, are more obvious than those of cinema (but certainly just as effective). Television, like a certain use of cinema (Cinema Equatore is a prime example of this phenomenon), calls its subjects/viewers and mobilizes them for the sake of more encompassing objectives. Television asks its public to "stay as it is," to enter the "imaginary field" provided by the screen, without ever questioning what may (or may not) be behind it. In this manner, viewers or viewed—the distinction does not matter anymore—are at different levels all victims and accomplices of this visual-ideological system. As Miller reminds us,

> TV loves a good victim; . . . 'Stay as you are!' it tells the oppressed. 'Your battered face has earned you our esteem!' Within this schema, the worst thing that can happen to the underdog is not to die or go on suffering, but to become unpitiable, to stand up strong. . . . any group that does attempt to shed its lowly status zips straight from subjugation into villainy.[55]

Miller identifies the victim as the "underdog," the viewed subject. But TV's intimation to the viewing subject to stay as s/he is is the complementary part of such a control mechanism achieved by means of images. Miller's statement, as will be seen, is remarkably prophetic of what happens in Somalia once the Somalis turn from helpless victims into villains, and once the emphasis of the mission is placed on Aidid's capture. His statement is also indicative of a vicious *naïveté* that accompanies the movement of the camera in Somalia, a vicious and bitter innocence (television is always supposed to be neutral) that nonetheless pushes the UN and the United States to start searching for Aidid. The ambush of a Pakistani patrol on June 5, 1993 (twenty-four soldiers die) gave the UN and the United States an obvious alibi for their decision to turn Aidid into Somalia's most wanted. Shortly after the incident with the Pakistani peacekeepers, Howe, the new UN special envoy in Somalia, "issued a warrant for [Aidid's] arrest and detention, offering a $25,000 reward for his capture."[56] It is at this precise moment, when the United States–led Operation Restore Hope redefined the UN mission as a desperate search for an elusive clan leader, that the suturing process mobilized in Somalia showed most blatantly its ideological ramifications. Thus, before resuming our coverage of the UN-U.S. search for Aidid, it is necessary to clarify the essential link between suture and ideology.

HAVE YOU BEEN INTERPELLATED LATELY? SUTURE AS IDEOLOGY

In order to analyze in greater detail the extent of the work of suture as a (visual/technical/psychological) code in which ideological components are imbricated, an examination of the work of ideology in general (of how ideology works) is of critical importance. Althusser has arguably provided the most compelling and insightful analysis of ideology. Furthermore, the characteristics that Althusser ascribes to ideology are, as will be seen, central to the activity/process of suture. Althusser draws his theoretical insights on the question of ideology from previous Marxist critiques. Yet, in a unique way, Althusser combines the traditional Marxist view on ideology with elements derived from psychoanalysis to thus come up with a theory of ideology that clearly differs from orthodox Marxist interpretations. In his lectures on Althusser, Paul Ricoeur notes that "Althusser introduces some important changes in Marxist theory." Ricoeur continues: "Althusser's main improvement is engendered by his linking ideology to its political function, that is, to the question of the reproduction of the system, the reproduction of the conditions of production."[57] Enriching a classical Marxist analysis, Althusser believes that capitalist (bourgeois) exploitation cannot rely only on the control (by the dominant class) and the coercion (by a state apparatus that represents the interests of the dominant class) of the productive forces. A system of exploitation, coercion, and production must find the means to reproduce itself, to reproduce the means and conditions of production in a self-perpetuating manner. It is the role of ideology to reproduce the conditions of production and to guarantee the perpetual subjection of the labor force to the dominant exploitative system.

Nevertheless, ideology is not simply an abstract or imaginary *assemblage* for Althusser.[58] Rather, Althusser affirms that ideology has a material basis in the state, and specifically in what he calls "Ideological State Apparatuses." Thus, Althusser supplements a more orthodox Marxist analysis of the state as a "repressive apparatus" by adding to it an ideological dimension. Althusser notes: "I shall call Ideological State Apparatuses a certain number of *realities* which present themselves to the immediate observer in the form of distinct specialized institutions."[59] Althusser gives a nonexhaustive list of Ideological State Apparatuses (ISAs): the religious ISA, the family, the legal ISA, the communications ISA, and so on. It is clear that for Althusser some of these ISAs, if not most of them, can be repressive as well. However, says Althusser, it is not enough to study them from the point of view of their coercive capacities since most of these ISAs express their "reality" from another perspective, less visible perhaps, but just as powerful and enduring for the subjected individuals, that of ideology. Althusser affirms: "the Repressive State Apparatus functions 'by violence,' whereas the Ideological State Apparatuses *function 'by ideology.'*"[60]

Althusser, then, turns to an explanation of ideology, its content, and its mode of application. Althusser writes that:

> All ideology represents in its necessarily imaginary distortions not the existing relations of production (and the other relations that derive from them), but above all the (imaginary) relationship of individuals to the relations of production and the relations that derive from them. What is represented in ideology is therefore not the system of the real relations which govern the existence of individuals, but the imaginary relation of those individuals to the real relations in which they live.[61]

Althusser's account of ideology (and of its intervention in individuals' lives) is uncannily reminiscent of Lacan's description of identity formation in the mirror stage (described earlier). Ideology works as a mirror image to the extent that it is in ideology that the imaginary relationship of individual subjects to their relations of production is given. Like a mirror, giving only a visual *aperçu* (intuition) of the real (here, both Lacanian and Althusserian) while foreclosing anything else that does not fit within the visual frame, ideology distorts the individual's perception of the real and introduces the subject to a world of imaginary identifications, references, and allusions.

Althusser, however, immediately supplements this first thesis with a second one. Ideology is not only an imaginary relation to real relations. Rather, "this imaginary relation is itself endowed with a material existence."[62] As was noted above, it is in Ideological State Apparatuses that Althusser finds the "material" (real) expression of ideology. As he puts it, "an ideology always exists in an apparatus, and its practice or practices."[63] Without the material side of ideology, without state apparatuses where the workings of ideology are located, the reproduction of the conditions of production, and the perpetuation of the subjection of the labor force could not be achieved. Put differently, it is because ideology has a "material existence" in ISAs that individual subjects can be "interpellated" by its imaginary relation. Ideological interpellation does not take place in the abstract. Rather, ideological interpellation has to be mobilized in specific (historical) contexts, structures, and institutions.

Interpellation is for Althusser a very important notion since it represents the moment when ideology is effectively implemented, recognized, and internalized by the individual subject. Interpellation is the moment when the individual, recognizing the signs of ideology (that s/he interprets as belonging to him/her), submits his/her subjectivity to the hegemonic order, accepts it as legitimate, and thus allows by his/her acceptance the reproduction of the dominant system. Althusser explains interpellation in the following terms: "ideology 'acts' or 'functions' in such a way that it 'recruits' subjects among the individuals (it recruits them all), or 'transforms' the individuals into subjects (it transforms them all) by that very precise operation which I have called *interpellation* or hailing, and which can be imagined along the lines of the most commonplace everyday police (or other) hailing: 'Hey, you there!'"[64] This interpellative function of ideology is fundamental. Once again, it is not simply imaginary. It is also very material since every ISA contains an interpellating mechanism that mobilizes the subject to the dominant system it represents. In a sense, interpellation is constitutive of both subjection and ideology. Individuals are constituted as subjects within a specific ideological order or framework while ideology is mobilized and reinforced by the subjection of the subjects, that is to say, their recognition as subjects of the existing order. This coconstitution of subjects and ideology, what Althusser calls "the duplicate mirror-structure of ideology," is once again made possible by the work of interpellation.[65] Interpellation, grounded in the material conditions of existence and production of individuals as Althusser indicates, allows the closure of the ideological and subjecting system and contributes to the reproduction of the dominant order. Interpellation is an ideological police that reinforces the existing order while (en)closing the subjects within a self-perpetuating carceral.

Interpellation has rarely been included in critical approaches to international relations.[66] This is all the more surprising since international relations appears to be particularly dependent upon such a mode of ideological hailing. International relations has traditionally relied upon ideological mechanisms to convey (a certain) knowledge about the international system and, perhaps more importantly, to organize the discipline. One may take realist/neorealist theories to be emblematic of the exercise of interpellation in international relations. As was suggested in chapter 1, the realist domestic analogy is a prime example of an (Althusserian) ideological mechanism.

Domestic analogy is the method through which realist/neorealist paradigms of international thought impose anarchy as a common-sensical, conventional, and dogmatic principle of international politics. Domestic analogy is an interpellating device through which realism hails international students, theorists, and practitioners into conforming to its mode of observation and analysis (a mode of thinking that they are also conditioned to reproduce).

Interpellation is not limited to realist circles. It is crucial to the deployment of neoliberal/neoidealist institutionalist discourses too. As was clearly indicated in the previous chapter, ideology-filled notions such as globalization or governance have been mobilized in the 1990s through the work and strategies of international institutions and organizations like the UN. A critique of international ideology derived from Althusser suggests that what these institutions have sought to achieve is to interpellate the international community into adhering to the ideological and procedural dictates of disciplinary liberalism on a global scale (cooperation, interdependence, multilateral security, peacemaking, nation building, etc.). To be sure, this critical analysis is central to the present reading of the relationship between ideology and peacekeeping in Somalia. Althusser's work does not simply compel the critical scholar to finally recognize the importance of interpellation as a material/ideological process that defines many contemporary international relations practices. His critical insight may also make us start developing a new critical language to make sense of key international processes. One may, for example, think in terms of what some have already started to call "IGOs" (Ideological Governmentality Organizations),[67] that is to say, international ideological apparatuses (like the UN, NATO, GATT, Worldwatch, etc.) whose function is to interpellate the international community (of states and individual subjects) into contemporary regimes of global neoliberal governance.

This detour through Althusser's theory of ideology and through his fundamental notion of interpellation has not been fruitless. It has helped us formalize, concretize, and verbalize the nature, problem, and effects of ideology in the abstract and in the concrete practice of contemporary international relations. Replete with these important critical notions derived from Althusser's work, we may resume our initial theoretical course.

Interpellation takes us back to the notion of suture. Indeed, Kaja

Silverman has noted that "the concept of interpellation would seem to be intimately related to that of suture."[68] Of central importance here, and for Althusser's theory of ideology and interpellation as well, is not so much that ideology works by means of imaginary representations. It is rather that it is necessary for ideology, as evidenced in the process of interpellation, to have a material basis that sustains the dominant order. By analogy, theorists of suture have shown that it is necessary for suture to have a material basis in discourse in particular in order to be successful. For Althusser, the subject identifies with the imaginary representations of ideology thanks to the material sociopolitical narrative of interpellation inside the ISAs. In return, in a "duplicate mirror-structure" mode, the response of the subjects to the interpellation allows the perpetuation of the ideological discourse, and the reproduction of this "largely imaginary world outlook."[69] Suture can be seen as having the same effects as interpellation. It facilitates the identification of the subject-as-spectator with an imaginary representation, but necessitates the work of a material/visual text (the film/image) in a real contextual framing (the movie theater/the screen) to take place. Furthermore, and this is precisely where ideology intervenes in the process of suture, suture conditions, through its imposed narrativity, linearity, and order (shot/counter-shot), the viewing subject to accept the discourse it produces. In suture, the viewing subjects allow the cinematic/televisual discourse to take place (the story depicted by the moving images exists only to the extent that someone watches it) while they accept being represented by this discourse. Once again, as Silverman has already mentioned, suture, like interpellation, takes place when the subject, faced with the picture, declares: "Yes, that's me. That's what I see."[70]

When the process of suture is no longer read in the context of individual identification, but in the perspective of a more global ideological operation, a "duplicate mirror-structure" of suture can be evidenced as well. Suture then becomes a system that "functions not only to re-interpellate the viewing subject into the same discursive positions, thereby giving that subject the illusion of a stable and continuous identity, but to re-articulate the existing symbolic order in ideologically orthodox ways."[71]

This suturing system is at play in the UN's peacekeeping mission in Somalia. In Somalia, what both cinematographic and televisual suturing techniques hope to achieve is not only a conditioning of the

UN-U.S. forces present in Somalia and of the global audiences watching the made-in-Hollywood show of force (as was suggested earlier). Beyond a reactivation of both UN and U.S. post–cold war identities in Somalia, a larger ideological enterprise is "re-articulated." Intimations to disciplinary liberalism in Somalia are reinforced and reproduced by the images (the visual narratives) to which both the viewed and viewing subjects of the Somalia operation have to subscribe. More symbolically, it is the New World Order slogan introduced by Bush after the Gulf War, with its globalizing overtones, that is (visually) replayed through, among other things, Somalia's multiple instances of visual interpellation (as a sequel to the Gulf War). New World Order liberalism is an ideology in the Althusserian sense (a world outlook) that offers and represents both for sovereign states (the subjects of international politics) and for individual beings (the subjects of global policies) an imaginary universal relationship to their everyday existences. Yet, and still within an Althusserian critical context, it is also an ideology that necessitates for its application and perpetuation a "material" basis, that, like the ISAs in the case of capitalist state ideologies, could interpellate its subjects. The global mediascape created by the (tele)visual media is the ever changing and ever expanding sphere where the subjects of New World Order international politics/policies are ideologically interpellated and where neoliberal outlooks are visually sutured. Thus, in Somalia, it would be futile to try to disentangle the reactivation of identities performed by the visual sutures from the visual rearticulations of ideology. As Althusser's theory of ideology and various analyses of visual suture have demonstrated, individual identities (subject formations) and global ideologies (the formation of what Althusser calls "the Subject") are intricately embedded both in the imaginary constructions that they require and in the material conditions where they necessarily collide. In this manner, the case of Somalia in the perspective of New World Order politics is only a short step away from Althusser's theory of ideology in the bourgeois-capitalist state. It exemplifies how, in a post–cold war era of international affairs, more general issues of ideology are still imbricated in more specific instances of suture. The last section of this chapter continues the analysis of the question of suture/ideology. It returns to the fiction of UN-U.S. interventionism in Somalia which, slowly, comes to its end. However, as will be made clear, the ending of the

Somalia story is not a "happy" ending. In Somalia, narrative closure cannot be realized, as images no longer suture but, on the contrary, start to disempower (the UN), deactivate (identities), and dearticulate (ideology).

AFTER OPERATION RESTORE HOPE, BEYOND PEACEKEEPING: THE LAST SCENES, SEAMS, AND SIMULATIONS OF SOMALIA

Desperately Searching for Aidid

The UN-U.S. joint venture soon discovered that trying to capture Aidid in Mogadishu was "like going after Brer Rabbit in the briar patch."[72] The desperate search for the elusive Aidid, meant to symbolize Operation Restore Hope, was to prove fatal to the entire enterprise. Despite its highly mediatic emphasis, the U.S. cavalry followed by a few UN troops could not apprehend Aidid.[73] The operational and political complexity of the Somalia mission had become extremely simplistic. It was no longer a matter of peacekeeping, humanitarianism, or relief supply. It was simply about getting Aidid. But the reality of Aidid's capture was not as easy to achieve as the fiction relied on by both the UN and the United States would have liked to suggest. Instead of showing Aidid as a prisoner of the UN and the United States in his jail cell (as had been done a few years before with Noriega), international TV reports kept on showing Aidid as a defiant clan leader rallying his troops or addressing the populace live on CNN. By the end of 1993, the glamorous pictures of the Marines landing had faded. The images from Somalia that circulated through the mediascape were constantly depicting a triumphant Aidid who, after escaping the U.S. Rangers, nevertheless was able to find a way of staying (a)live in the media. This was not the image of triumphalism the West had hoped for. These were not the suturing pictures needed by the actors of the conflict, either. In Somalia, the images were everywhere. But unlike what had been achieved in Iraq, where the military kept a close scrutiny on what was being shown (visual censorship as much as visual display characterized the Gulf War), here in Somalia, the images were beyond (ideological) control. What had looked like a harmless excess of U.S. triumphalism in the Marines landing of December 1992 now turned into an embarrassing excess of visual reports where everything (the good and the bad) was made visible. As for the U.S. public, which had hoped to witness a sequel to the Iraq mission in Somalia, the entire Aidid affair was now beyond comprehension. Why go after Aidid through the maze of Mogadishu streets when he was available for everyone to see, here at home, live on CNN? The shock caused by the image (the absence of buffer) was to become even bigger for Western audiences when, suddenly, instead of seeing "their" troops chasing Somali rebels, the only thing they could see was tortured U.S. soldiers dragged down the streets of Mogadishu. The pictures had obviously betrayed the UN-U.S. coalition.[74] In an ironic twist, but with the same desire for spectacularity, the high-tech images were glaringly showing the failure of multinational peacekeeping in Somalia and were announcing the humiliation of U.S. foreign policy in the region.[75] Once a perfect simulation of technological and military prowess, TV images had now become the strange accomplice of Somalia's cynical desire of vengeance against the UN, its values, and its policies.

Terminal Identity: The Durant Crisis

When you're watching John Wayne movies, you think all you need to do is give your name, rank, and serial number. But if you take a hard line like that, all you do is make it hard on yourself.
— MICHAEL DURANT, OCTOBER 3, 1993

That Michael Durant, the U.S. helicopter pilot shot down and taken hostage during an attack on Aidid's Mogadishu compound, defines his behavior during the eleven days of his detention by referring to John Wayne movies is more than anecdotal. It once again reveals how imbricated fiction and reality are in Somalia. All references, even for the U.S. soldiers of this operation, become fictive. Identifications are made, positively or negatively, against the backdrop of Hollywood productions or other phantasmagoric representations. As a counterexample (like John Wayne for Durant) or as a means of comparison (Clint Eastwood's movies), cinematographic constructions are the standard for what is "real" or not in Somalia. What the intervention in Somalia produced was not political order or humanitarian security, but imaginary heroes like John Wayne (in John Ford movies) or simulated antiheroes like Michael Durant (his story could have been a perfect scenario for an Oliver Stone film).

On October 3, 1993, the screen where the UN-U.S. joint venture had projected its reempowering and suturing images was suddenly torn apart. On that day, a major raid on Aidid's compound had been organized by the U.S. commanding officers in Somalia. This military assault was designed to put an end to Aidid's arrogance and, by the same token, was supposed to guarantee the future safety of UN peacekeepers in the Mogadishu area. What was planned to be a major show of U.S. military might actually turned out to be one of the most appalling and embarrassing mediatic depictions of post–cold war UN-U.S. joint peacekeeping: "Within hours, horrifying pictures materialized on television screens: the corpses of American soldiers dragged through the streets of Mogadishu and burned by jubilant crowds, and a bloodied and bruised American hostage [Michael Durant] reciting his name and job in a monotone terror."[76] The countering (or buffering) effects of TV images or cinematic productions/devices was no longer realized. The shot/countershot technique upon which the code of suture relied no longer performed its task, thus unveiling the absence and impotence of the UN's post–cold war peacekeeping strategies (and those of the United States too). In a Lacanian sense, the Durant crisis marked the "irruption of the real" in the imaginary structure relied upon by the West from the beginning of the intervention in Somalia. Symbolically (if not practically), the Durant crisis terminated the Somalia operation.[77] It was terminal, but it did not bring closure.

Far from closing or suturing identity and ideology, the Durant crisis ripped the suturing process wide open. It suddenly reopened the debate (in the general public, among politicians, among scholars) about the necessity of UN leadership in post–cold war international affairs, a question that the Bosnian conflict would only exacerbate. The failure of UN peacekeeping in Somalia brought the UN and its backers into a crisis of incomprehension where the almost naïve inability to figure out what had gone wrong glaringly conflicted with the graphic reality of the bloody images broadcast by international TV crews.[78] This posttraumatic response was no doubt a sudden change of tone after the exuberant optimism (displayed by Boutros-Ghali and the neoidealists, above all) of the aftermath of the Gulf War. The West, behind the UN, had gone into Somalia with the hope of ideologically suturing a New World Order. The West would now leave Somalia with images of a New World Disorder.

The UN's apparent shortcomings in Somalia affected the image of member states as well, particularly of those that had followed the UN in this ideology-rekindling operation. Somalia, in 1993–94, put into question their foreign policies and their overt reliance on peacekeeping led by international organizations like the UN. After the Durant crisis, the debate over whether or not the United States should continue to follow UN policies became a salient issue in foreign policy circles. This debate was also fueled by what was happening in Bosnia (as will be seen in the next chapter). The prompt withdrawal of U.S. forces from Somalia, announced by Bill Clinton immediately after the October incidents,[79] is certainly to be placed in the context created by the peacekeeping failure in Somalia. In short, as much as the Durant crisis was unexpected and shocking, it was also traumatic for all of the actors involved in the mission, apart perhaps from the Somalis who, once the cameras abandoned the scene, would once again be left alone.[80]

The Residues of Suture: What's Left for the UN after Somalia?

The retelling of the Somalia narrative offered in this chapter has enriched theories of vision and representation in the field of politics and ideology by pushing the notion of suture to its conceptual limits. In the perspective of the failure of the UN-U.S. operation, images continue to display their vivid depictions (Durant's bloodied face, mutilated bodies of U.S. soldiers, triumphant public appearances by Aidid, and jubilant Somali crowds throwing stones at Western observers) despite the fact that suture stops providing the ideological interpellation sought by the UN. If the Durant crisis terminates the UN's attempts at suturing its ideological projections in Somalia, it does not, however, terminate the play of the visual. In short, the film is still running. Images become fatal for the UN and its mobilization of ideology, but they continue to be highly visible. Images do not simply stop with and cannot be limited to suturing and ideological constructs.

Film theorists saw suture as a code aimed at reordering and controlling visual projections. Suture was a (psychoanalytic and cinematographic) construct employed to keep images at a distance by controlling the visual and making it fit with the dominant discourse/ideology. Similarly, theorists of suture hoped to maintain the dogma that images were lack or absence. In such a perspective, suture was a necessary cover for a fundamental absence that required the superimposition of a structural support so that images could become interpretable and intelligible, and could be encoded in a hegemonic discourse. This role was clearly exemplified by the UN's attempts, via visual suturing devices (Cinema Equatore, television projections), at bridging the gap between its neoliberal objectives (its empty visions in need of material substance, in need of action), and the reality of its experience in Somalia.

But, once again, the UN-U.S. debacle in Somalia showed a detachment of images from suture. Whereas suture artificially tried to enforce closure, the last visual scenes out of Somalia announced what Steven Shaviro has called "an uncanny, excessive residue of being that subsists when all *should* be lacking."[81] The last scenes out of Somalia gave way to seams and scars, as suture no longer (en)closed but rather worked as an excessive trace, a residue of uncontrollable images. It is perhaps the case that once the real (of Somalia's refusal of UN ideologies, its nonresponse to New World Order interpellations) catches up with simulation (the neoliberal world order of UN humanitarian peacekeeping as visually mobilized in Somalia),[82] suture is left to look like an imperfect dotted line, a gruesomely scarred tissue that, far from hiding the wound, artificially covers it and, in any case, draws the visual attention to where ruptures take place. It becomes a case of bad plastic surgery.

By emphasizing the residues of the visual, this latest version of suture (suggested by Shaviro's theory) gives a new life to images. Because images flow beyond the control of any ideological apparatus or structural code, the restrictive and reconstitutive processes of cinematographic/ideological suture introduced earlier are doomed to become pointless. Shaviro's theory of images as haunting visual residues operates a reversal in the relationship between images and suture. It is no longer images that are devoid of meaning and, as such, need to be filled with ideological and resymbolizing content. Rather, images are always already full of multiple and complex significations that can potentially transgress efforts aimed at reorganizing and controlling them. Seen at this new critical angle, cinematographic or televisual suture is nothing more than an empty form that reveals its simulacrum and its weak visual construction when, as is doomed to happen, images finally creep through the inherent inconsistencies of suture. Thus, Shaviro intimates that the image "is not the index of something that is missing, but the insistence on something that refuses to disappear."[83]

This understanding of ideology (through visual suture) as an empty form is no doubt different from Althusser's notion of ideology. It is, I believe, too convenient to assume that ideology is nothing more than an imaginary fiction that has only limited bearings on everyday practice. Althusser's theory has the merit of showing that ideology, through its interpellating characteristics, is more than the fictive effect of a visual simulacrum. It has, as Althusser puts it, "material effects" for the interpellated subjects (and, as such, it has subjective and subjecting effects as well), just as the disciplinary (neo)liberal ideology implemented and visually sutured by the United Nations in Somalia has had "real effects," at least for the time being, for both the viewing subjects (member states of the UN, Western audiences, the general public across the mediascape) and the viewed individuals (the Somalis and the soldiers of the UN-U.S. multinational force). In fact, theories of visual suture and their links to ideology, as shown before, cannot be simply discarded by Shaviro's attempt at depicting the visual as an anarchic and disseminated loose ensemble of vengeful images. Shaviro's understanding of the visual gives credence to the apparent turn that occurred in Somalia, once the psychological effects of the Durant crisis were finally integrated in the political/ideological imaginaries of the viewing subjects. Or it is perhaps the opposite: the images from Somalia give credence to Shaviro's theory. But the desire expressed by Shaviro to see images come alive and, like possessed objects, turn against their master simulators is also questionable.

It is not clear, in fact, in the case of the visual depictions/mobilizations in Somalia, whether the capacity of production of images was reappropriated by the viewed subjects themselves (the vengeful Somalis),[84] by self-animated residues of visual projections that stubbornly refuse to be sutured (Shaviro's theory), or simply by an abreaction of hypertechnological media (Western TV networks and their desire for spectacularity) that had projected those images in the first place. The question of the reappropriation/liberation of images from the production of hegemonic fictions is, as was emphasized throughout the reading of the Somalia operation, a complicated one that, in the absence of material justifications, may be better off left undecided. In any case, the three scenarios of liberation of images from ideological reappropriations suggested here (the revenge of the other, the revenge of the live image, the abreaction of the medium) may be so imbricated into one another that it would be pointless, unless one had specific ideological reasons to favor one interpretation over the rest, to try to privilege any one of them. As mentioned before, Shaviro's theory of the visual (unlike film theorists of suture) privileges the view that images are alive, if not in ideology, at least as aesthetic residues whose expressive powers are able to avert controls and appropriations (an aesthetic essentialism of the visual, perhaps).

This notion of "visual residues" is useful, however, if it is interpreted more modestly. Instead of opposing a new visual essentialism to the (ideological) view of a "reconstructive image of images," one may preferably advance a deconstructive mode of interpretation (and of reinterpretation of suture). In a manner that may recall Derrida's treatment of textual traces,[85] one may suggest that images-as-residues are always already present within the ideological visual suture, just as the traces of writing as *différance* are already present within the text. Here, it is no longer a matter of emphasizing the revolutionary character of images that, one day, decide to reject the visual ideological structures/sutures that stifle them. It is rather a matter of giving images a life of their own, their own life, not by granting them vengeful power, but by going along with the images themselves, by respecting their orderings and relations, their own margins, by remaining inside the textual/visual representations (not above them), and by seeing where these residues, in their proliferation of meaning-effects, take us, as readers/viewers. There is no demystification of visual ideology here, no deciphering, no desire to fly over the material realm with visual residues, no will to aesthetic visual purity. In this perspective, the viewing subject who deconstructs images according to their own structures (instead of blindly accepting their reconstructive intimations) is in the position of what critical semiotician Roland Barthes has called the "reader of myths." The "reader of myths" is the one who "consumes" the visual intimations of ideology "according to the very ends built into its structure: the reader [viewer] lives the myth [ideology via suture] as a story at once true and unreal."[86]

Images as residues, the traces of visual suture, may well be interpreted in the perspective of a dominant discourse or ideology. Images may be read as interpellations directed and accepted by the viewing subjects, just as the soldiers of the UN–U.S. multinational force were interpellated by the visual projections of Cinema Equatore, or similar to the general public, which was interpellated by the televisual depictions of the U.S. Marines landing. But one may also reread or re-envision the ideological play of suture by looking at the residues, traces, discontinuities of this attempt at visual closure and by letting its signals proliferate differences, displacements, plays of signification in ideology. After all, the screen of Cinema Equatore was already torn and patched.

In this context, Shaviro's previous statement that the image "is not the index of something that is missing, but the insistence on something that refuses to disappear" offers a different possibility. It can be read as an indication that, all of a sudden, images have come to life and are capable of expressing a will-to-resistance from ideological constructs aimed at controlling them. But it can also suggest that the materiality of images (moving or static), which are often mobilized by a will-to-suture or a will-to-spectacularity, retains through and with ideological intents (and not beyond them) a disseminated capacity to induce surprise, pleasure, anger, fear, violence, love, and so forth, that is, supplementary and differential meanings. There is always already more to the image than what the master code intimates because of what the master code intimates and of how it does so. This is perhaps how the visual residues of suture associated with the Durant crisis in Somalia can be interpreted. The revenge of the visual noted during this incident is perhaps nothing more than the mark of something, some inconstancy, some operational discontinuity in the UN–U.S. intervention expressed through the deployment of the UN's suturing strategy, but suddenly rendered more visible by a simple twist of fate perhaps, an accident, Somalia's resistance at this particular juncture to the United States–led assault on Aidid's compound.

It remains that, after such a theoretical revisiting of the visual, Somalia's suture, as indicated before, may *no longer not only* be read as a hermetic fictional construct. For the United Nations and its post–cold war policies, Somalia is perhaps *no longer not only* a suture, but the indelible trace of the UN's peacekeeping inconstancies and ideological discontinuities. Somalia's suture, as seen through the final moment of the Durant crisis, does not only enclose. It is also a mechanism whose apparent solidity and homogeneity is made up of

multiple and different residual elements, of images. Read as proliferated traces, visual sutures and their hoped-for ideological interpellations disseminate in Somalia the signs of the UN's operational shortcomings, all of a sudden rendered visible. In a sense, Somalia is a
suture that is not one and that draws the eyes of the viewing subjects
(the sovereign states as subjects of international politics, and individuals as subjects of global policies), if they prefer to look at it in its details rather than rely on metavisions, not necessarily to an intimated
ideological closure—that of disciplinary liberalism and global governance discourses in a post–cold war era—but to the ideological ruptures that are intricate parts of such a global vision.

4

Visions of Otherness and Interventionism in Bosnia, or How the West Was Won Again

THE BALKAN STRIPPER

Then a three-piece band took its place on a platform up front and began tootling American jazz standards, and a woman materialized and stood un-smilingly facing the audience. Small and compact, she wore a matching brown skirt and jacket and a shiny white rayon blouse. In a businesslike way, she began undressing, in what I was informed was to be a delightful striptease. The scattered audience of men and their chunky women silently gulped beer and sipped slivovitz as the dancer removed her suit jacket, her shoes, her blouse, and her skirt, until she stood looking out upon us in her pink rayon slip and bra. It was all done rather antiseptically, as if preparing for a medical examination. Each garment was tidily laid out and patted down on the piano bench, there being no pianist. Then she stepped out of her slip, and in her panties did a few routine steps in approximate time to the music. She had very good legs. Things were heating up. From somewhere she picked up a heavy blue terry cloth robe and wrapped in it, she slipped off her bra and flashed one breast. My fellow writers broke off their dying con-versation. I don't know what got into me, but I asked a fatal question; "Can you tell from looking at her what her nationality is?"

— Arthur Miller, "The Parable of the Stripper"

Through this account of what the author feels is a particularly un-arousing striptease scene (a businesslike, antiseptic, medical peep-show that does not fulfill the author's desires), Miller intends to alle-gorize the entire Bosnian conflict. For the Western observer/voyeur that Miller claims to represent (during his trip to Bosnia in 1994), Bosnia has no attractive power anymore. Miller's cultural and libidinal *décalage* (gap) with the Bosnian reality is exemplified by his asking the "fatal" question: which nationality does the stripper belong to? A supposedly fatal question because, in Miller's mind, and despite the overtly nationalistic and ethnic motivations of the Bosnian conflict, national identification does not matter anymore. What Bosnia is left with, and what really matters, are dead and mutilated human bodies on each side of the ethnic divide.

The analysis of the clash of national identities in the former Yugoslavia offered by Miller in this allegorical tale may call for a psychoanalytic reading.[1] From a psychoanalytic perspective, the fatal question asked by the Western observer represents the sudden and unexpected moment of the "irruption of the real" (the basic truth about Bosnia, i.e., its essentially ethnic origins) in the imaginary universe of the Bosnian conflict. The question is fatal to the actors of the conflict (represented in Miller's story by his fellow Serbian, Croatian, and Slovenian writers) since it brings back their current tensions and disputes into the realm of the superego, that is to say, back to a logic of international politics understood and controlled by the West.[2] In a sense, Miller's question puts an end to the Bosnian conflict by breaking its imaginary structure[3] and allowing a more common-sensical interpretation to prevail.[4] Miller's "nationality" question is the superego's response to an imaginary that it (the super-ego, the West) cannot fully penetrate and make sense of. In the context of the conflict, the question is perhaps the best solution the West has been able to find to the situation in Bosnia since it brings a form of rational closure (the nation and history as reasonable explanations) and circumvents the impenetrable Balkan fantasy (that not even Miller can capture).

Even with the assistance of psychoanalytic theory, the brutal interruption of the Balkan stripper's show (a metaphor for the Bosnian imaginary) by the intervention of the Western voyeur is a pathetic scene. The "fatality" that is on display here, in Miller's tale, is above all that of the West and its agents in Bosnia. After all, Miller's fellow writers from the former Yugoslavia do not care whether, from the Western voyeur's point of view, the strip-show is too clean and "antiseptic" to fulfill desire. They apparently still get pleasure out of what they consider to be a delightful distraction. In their singular cultural

VISIONS OF OTHERNESS · 137

and libidinal modes, they enjoy what they see. In contrast, the West has lost all *jouissance* and desperately turns to Bosnia to try to rediscover a pleasure principle. When all is said and done, Miller's "fatal question" is nothing more than the verbal expression of the West's own fatality. Bosnia is the stage on which the West has decided to play out its pathological condition.

Baudrillard declares that the people of Sarajevo are not "the ones in need of compassion" but that, rather, it is they who have "compassion for our wretched destinies."[5] We in the West, Baudrillard continues, have decided to go to Bosnia to "retrieve a reality for ourselves."[6] In the aftermath of the cold war, this is indeed where the fatal condition of the West and its New World Order lies. No longer able to antagonize an Evil Empire, the Western world faces an ideological tabula rasa. It is now, after the cold war and the "end of history," that the ideological values of/in the West, if they are to be meaningful, should prosper. Yet, what was easily affirmed in the context of an ideological struggle (democracy versus autocracy, liberalism versus socialism, capitalism versus collectivism, etc.) is now hard to recognize and preserve in an empty domain of ideological self-referentiality (where the dominant ideology is opposed to nothing else but itself). Tautological justifications are offered: liberal democracy is good because it has won; capitalism is necessary because there is no other available logic of production. It is no wonder, then, in such a state of global ideological poverty, if the institutions created by liberal-democracy and liberal-capitalism and in charge of reproducing these ideological formations have become no-escape mechanisms. Totalitarianism arises from the lack of (ideological) alternatives. The vision of the New World Order, as a mode of social construct and human organization both local and global, is a prime example of such a phenomenon. Since the fall of the Berlin Wall (it is after all one of the direct causes of most of the West's worries today), such a fatal ideological condition has been dealt with through fatal strategies.

It is in the context of such posttraumatic fatal strategies (when fatal questions are asked) that one can understand the West's involvement/investment in the former Yugoslavia, specifically in Bosnia. With the hope that, to mix Miller's parable with another metaphor, the Balkan stripper may give the emperor new clothes to cover his ideological nakedness, the United Nations has been sent to

Bosnia as the missionary of the entire Western world to try to rescue, as Baudrillard would have it, the West's "reality principle." The suffering of Bosnia, its down-to-earth racial and territorial quarrels, its dead bodies, "its bleeding"[7] are taken in Paris, London, or Washington as signs of material physical realities that, supposedly, we in the West can no longer experience. Raw ideology as a material resource is not only supposed to be there, in Bosnia, but also basic human and vital energies. This is why Western leaders have sent their mediatic and humanitarian vampire, the United Nations, there, hoping that it can suck up Bosnia's ideological and vital blood. Like it or not, Miller's "Parable of the Stripper" is not a politico-libidinal allegory for what happens in Bosnia. Rather, it describes, albeit in a figurative fashion, the problems of the West in a post–cold war era. The tale of the stripper is a fatal symptom of what happens once the visual strategies relied upon by Western ideologies cannot recover a reality principle (as was shown in Somalia, for example).

In a context of lost ideological ground and desperate search for new global identity structures, reading the complex and confused intervention of the United Nations in Bosnia could be a rather pointless project. It would be so if one were to stop the critical investigation at the level of the vain quest of the West, via the UN, for a new reality principle. Instead of highlighting only the ideological quest of the West in Bosnia (Baudrillard's position) or lamenting the loss of all ideological/moral contents (Slavoj Žižek's position), a more affirmative approach can be adopted. The so-called ideology/reality gap, which tells the story of the West's intervention in the Balkans, is productive of many different formations and situations, the richness of which needs to be read in detail. To put it another way, behind the mask of a fundamental Western absence (an absence of military intervention, of moral compassion, of ideological purpose, of clear identity) that Bosnia tries to fill, an intricate web of ideological and conceptual positions (a hysteria rather than a hysteresis of ideology and theory) is being woven. It is precisely this plurality of ideological formations, which have emerged in the wake of an apparent global ideological stalemate, that is examined in this chapter by showcasing the Bosnian case of UN peacekeeping. Two ideological exercises, however, stand out when one looks at the recent events in the Balkans. One is a strategy of otherness that the Bosnian conflict helps to redefine. The other is a strategy of institutional interventionism that directly mobilizes international organizations like the UN or NATO.

The present analysis of Bosnia and of the post-Bosnian ideological landscape of global politics (through these two specific strategies) starts from a visual methodological perspective. As the previous chapters have already demonstrated, the practice of vision (as a mode of representation or perception) is a common and necessary component of contemporary epistemologies, theories, and ideologies. It is a component in Bosnia as well.[8] The visual productions/depictions of the Bosnian conflict that are introduced and analyzed in this chapter are more directly related to the question of otherness than those addressed in earlier chapters. The photographic or artistic displays mobilized here are more than simple allegories for how otherness functions as an ideological exercise in Western attempts at making sense and reappropriating Bosnia. They are necessary visual components of such an ideological enterprise. Furthermore, even if such visual displays are obviously tied to the question/strategy of otherness in Bosnia, they also help to foreground the more institutional strategy of Western interventionism achieved by means of international organizations, the UN and NATO in particular.

Strategies of otherness and interventionism have a lot in common. These two ideological strategies are intricately connected. Otherness assumes a degree of intervention, specifically, in the case of Bosnia, a moral intervention by the Western observer (or voyeur) that comes as a response to the "Bosnian gaze," to the gaze of the other. Interventionism is an amplification and materialization of the more abstract, symbolic, and individualized strategy of otherness. Interventionism structures and applies otherness to the so-called reality of the Bosnian conflict by interfering (through peacekeeping and humanitarianism) in the conflict. Thus, otherness and interventionism, although treated separately in the present analysis, are often concomitant and coconstituted. They both partake, at different degrees, of the Western search for ideological substance in Bosnia.

The examination of these two strategies starts with a theoretical and polemical duel that directly pits Baudrillard's notion of the "radical other" to Žižek's "Bosnian victim." These two theories, dialectically opposed, provide an intertextual basis for the analysis of the visual photographic and artistic displays presented in this chapter. More importantly, they represent two different positions according to which one may interpret the impact of both otherness and interventionism in Bosnia. For reasons that will be made clear as the text unfolds, I clearly take position alongside Baudrillard. Specifically, I rely upon the virulence, provocation, and conceptual terrorism of Baudrillard's writing to oppose Žižek's vision of otherness and, by the same token, to denounce the strategy of interventionism deployed by means of UN peacekeeping in Bosnia.

ŽIŽEK'S BOSNIAN VICTIM VERSUS BAUDRILLARD'S RADICAL OTHER

Gazes of Sorrow

Faces of Sorrow: Agony in the Former Yugoslavia is a collection of fifty photographic shots taken by thirty-six renowned photojournalists in the course of the Balkan conflict. With the blessing of the major international photo agencies, the shots—which represent different scenes and situations that took place during the war—were assembled and put on display by Photo Perspectives.[9] In the words of its curators and producers, *Faces of Sorrow* "offers indisputable pictorial witness to the searing effects of man's inhumanity to mankind. . . . [The exhibit] depict[s] unspeakable acts of destruction waged by the warring parties from the beginning of the war in Croatia in 1991 through the recent peace accord in Bosnia and Herzegovina. . . . [Its intention] is to give face to the faceless and voice to the victims of this devastating war."[10] Such a visual mode of moral dedication and compassion finds a theoretical equivalent, albeit in a rather covered fashion, in Slavoj Žižek's writing. Indeed, the pictures shown in *Faces of Sorrow* are a perfect stand-in for Žižek's notion of the Bosnian gaze. In the section of his book *Metastases of Enjoyment* entitled "Bosnia," Žižek declares that

> [t]he traumatic element [the irruption of the real] is thus the gaze of the helpless other—child, animal—who does not know why something so horrifying and senseless is happening to him: not the gaze of a hero willingly sacrificing himself for some Cause, but the gaze of a perplexed victim. And in Sarajevo we are dealing with the same bewildered gaze. It is not sufficient to say that the West only passively observes the slaughter in Sarajevo and does not want to act, or even understand what is actually going on there: the true passive observers are the citizens of Sarajevo themselves, who can only witness the horrors to which they are submitted, without being able to understand how something so horrible is possible. This gaze makes us all guilty.[11]

Žižek's Bosnian helpless, bewildered, and guilt-spreading gaze could be that of the sickly Muslim prisoner in the Dretelj camp in Kevin Frayer's photograph (Photo Perspectives, Sipa Press 1996), or that of the raped Muslim women daringly looking at the camera in Andrée Kaiser's shot (Photo Perspectives, Sipa Press for *Newsday* 1996), or perhaps that of the Croatian child behind barbed wire in the UN refugee camp of Kakanj, Bosnia, shown in Anthony Suau's picture (Photo Perspectives, Gamma for *Time* 1996). All these are apparent denotative representations of what Žižek means by the gaze of the Bosnian victim. It is a gaze that exists only to the extent that we, Western observers or photographers as the case may be, are looking at those faces or, to put it in the way of "Photo Perspectives," to the extent that we are producing a visual testimony of those faceless faces. This gaze of the other is an embarrassing constant reminder of what, in the West, we would rather not see. It is the visual proof of our incompetence, failure, and responsibility in Bosnia. For us, the gaze of the Bosnian other is the traumatic response to our curiosity (mediatic voyeurism of Bosnia's plight) and to our impotence (lack of intervention). The gaze of the Bosnian victim is what gets back right in our face once we step out of our domain of fantasy and immunity and peek in through the hole of the other's reality.

But things are actually more complicated than that for Žižek, or so he would like to claim. Indeed, *Faces of Sorrow* plays into Žižek's theoretical scheme at another level that Žižek identifies as that of compassion and humanitarianism. Interestingly, for Žižek, compassion takes place when one consciously seeks to avoid or deflect "the unbearable pressure of the gaze."[12] Compassion provides a buffering effect. It is what allows us *not* to perceive the other's gaze, to mask it so that we can remain guilt-free. Such an approach offers an interesting critical take on humanitarianism since it implies that humanitarian hyperactivity (one of the West's most publicized responses to the Bosnian crisis) is a way of keeping a pretense of moral responsibility while avoiding having to face the disturbing reality of the other's condition. Through compassion and humanitarian altruism, the other is prevented from entering our somewhat coherent and closed imaginary realm (the West and its liberal-democratic ideological structure conceived as a solid and meaningful world outlook for instance),[13] or, to use Žižek's words, "compassion is the way to maintain the proper distance towards a neighbour in trouble."[14] While we are busy working on our humanitarian missions, we do not have to be destabilized by the victim's gaze.

In such a Žižekian perspective, this is just what *Faces of Sorrow* is. It is a visually buffering effect, a space of compassion made available for the West's consumption. By plunging into this photojournalistic display, the Western observer does not have to bear the supposedly heavy cost of actually looking at Bosnia or of coming to the rescue of the Bosnian victim. As this buffering effect, *Faces of Sorrow* is a photographic fetishistic device. While the Western observer looks at the photographed faces of the Bosnian victims, s/he does not have to "see" them (and face the pressure of their gaze). The West sees only an object of compassion, an alibi for humanitarian action, in those pictures that, as Žižek would have it, distort the real, powerful gaze of the Bosnian victim. Typical of a fetishistic construct, *Faces of Sorrow* offers the West a space of denial (I know but nevertheless . . .), an illusion of the real, and a necessary distance from the war in the former Yugoslavia. As Žižek argues, in such a visual scheme, "the victim is presented so that we like to see ourselves in the position from which we stare at her."[15]

When all is said and done, Žižek's theories about the gaze of the other and about compassion toward the Bosnian victim, as illustrated by the *Faces of Sorrow* exhibit, are nothing more than reassembled Lacanian themes used for remoralizing and sentimentalist purposes.[16] Žižek's pamphlet on the Bosnian victim is dominated by one key sentence, pronounced by Žižek as a moral ultimatum: the "gaze [of the Bosnian victim] makes us all guilty."[17] Žižek does not write that the gaze of the victim makes us *feel* guilty, or produces in us a sentiment or impression of guilt (something that another sentiment or illusion, or another encounter with reality might erase). It definitely brings guilt upon us, as a material inescapable condition. Beyond compassion and other trivial fetishistic representations that try to deflect it, guilt is the bottom-line experience in the relationship between us (the West) and them (Bosnians) as it is expressed by their gaze. This sense of guilt, and our moral responsibility that accompanies it, are both inevitable. The West is doomed to be guilty because it never intervened in the first place, at the beginning of the conflict, when it had the opportunity, the moral duty, in fact, to do so. Such a mode of thinking is perhaps typical of a Lacanian construct whereby the subject carries throughout its existence an unresolvable sense of loss/lack.[18] Just as it is with the Lacanian subject, it is always too late for the West (and its subjects) in Bosnia. From this incomplete beginning, the West goes on to carry the omnipresent burden of its inadequacies toward Bosnia and can only express an insatiable but futile desire to make up for this primal loss. For Žižek, this is what the Bosnian gaze reveals.

Žižek conveniently applies this Lacanian framework to what I consider to be his own moralizing intentions. Lacan's theory of the gaze simply becomes Žižek's excuse to bemoan the West's refusal to forcefully intervene in Bosnia.[19] Žižek finds the blame for such an inability to act in what the West, in a postmodern age, has happily plunged into: hyperreality and visual fictions. Just as compassion was a buffer for the real gaze of the Bosnian victim, vision (from TV media like CNN to photo exhibits like *Faces of Sorrow*) is now a cover for action. As Žižek puts it, "[t]he fantasy-image [of the victim], its immobilizing power of fascination, thwarts our ability to act—as Lacan puts it, we 'traverse the fantasy' by way of an act." Žižek continues: "The 'postmodern' ethics of compassion with the victim legitimizes the avoidance, the endless postponement, of the act. . . . The multitude of particular ethics that thrive today . . . is to be conceived precisely as an endeavour to avoid the true ethics, the ethics of the ACT as real."[20] In other words, visual fictions that mask the gaze distort the "true ethics" of action. As will be seen momentarily, Baudrillard happily pulverizes such a nostalgic construct. For the moment, it is enough to note that, by way of a strange reversal effect, Žižek blames postmodernity (incidentally, it is never clear what he means by postmodernity: A temporal stage of late-capitalism? A specific cultural attitude? A current of thought?)[21] for doing what the Lacanian theory of desire, to which he claims to adhere, actually postulates: endlessly postponing the object of enjoyment.[22] It may well be the case that, ignorant of what the postmodern condition has to offer, and afraid of immersing himself in it, Žižek hysterically ascribes to other theoretical/cultural formations the very symptoms found in Lacanian theory. Žižek indeed enjoys his Lacanian symptom a bit too much.

It remains, however, that in his search for a true ethic of action (hidden behind his Lacanian text) Žižek affirms himself as a retrograde (culturally conservative, even) thinker who, far from actually voicing concern in favor of the Bosnians, is mainly worried about the loss of morality in the West. In this sense, Žižek is very close to fellow Balkan writer Stjepan Meštrović, who wonders whether the "veritable voyeuristic orgy of sadomasochistic themes found on American television in the 1990s, from MTV (Music Television) to soap operas" has not caused the moral failure in Bosnia and, by way of consequence, the present demise of the West and its universal modern values.[23] In their different theoretical traditions (Lacan for Žižek, Durkheim for Meštrović), both Žižek and Meštrović are leaning back toward a glorious modern past, which perhaps never was, to try to rediscover a sense of ethical certainty. In short, Meštrović and Žižek share the same soapbox. With culturally conservative pundits like Meštrović and Žižek (intent on fueling the anti-postmodern hysteria), a crusade to recover moral dignity is launched. One may even suggest that both Žižek and Meštrović are seeking to fight contemporary racial fascism in the Balkans with their own dose of retro moral fascism (whether they recognize it or not).

As for the Bosnian victim (Žižek's other), it is merely an insignificant component in a larger ideological scheme. Žižek's other is reduced to a logic of sameness. They are we and we are they. If the gaze of the Bosnian victim is so unbearable to us, it is because, in the end, it is us we are looking at. Hence the need to shield this gaze away and buffer it through compassion and visual constructions. We do not want to admit that the Bosnians are like us, that their apparent difference from us does not stand the test of universal morality. The difference between us and them that we mark through compassion is merely a way for us to refuse to admit that we are (all) the same. Here, difference, as our relationship with the other, is what destroys the foreignness of alterity (otherness) and turns the Bosnian victim into one of us. When all is said and done, the Bosnian victim is for Žižek an alter-ego, another self. This is exactly what he expresses when he writes that "[t]he unbearable is the fact that in a sense *there is no difference*: there are no exotic bloodthirsty 'Balkanians' in Sarajevo, just normal citizens like us. The moment we take full notice of this fact, the frontier that separates 'us' from 'them' is exposed in all its arbitrariness, and we are forced to renounce the safe distance of the external observers."[24] This arbitrary, artificial frontier between us and them, between the West and Bosnia, is of course, for Žižek, the reality that we are afraid to face.[25] Yet, if one is to restore an ethic of action, such a reality (Bosnia's kernel of truth) must be uncovered and accepted. Rediscovering the other as self (the other as the same) is Žižek's way of forcing moral responsibility. We are necessarily responsible for what happens in Bosnia since they are us, a part of us, a part of what we are. This, no doubt, is also Žižek's way of arbitrarily suturing the primary loss (of Western intervention in Bosnia) that haunts his entire nostalgic project.

This representation of the Bosnian victim as yet another self is well illustrated by Gilles Peress's "travelling photographic exhibition" entitled *Farewell to Bosnia*.[26] Peress's exhibit is a photographic tour of Bosnia's war. As he opens his eyes and the lens of his camera to Bosnia's spectacle of destruction and violence, Peress is reminded of his own personal history, of his father and World War II ("I remembered my father, his amputated arm and his pain, his descriptions of addiction to morphine, of World War II, the German occupation and the concentration camps"[27]). Peress, as he puts it and visually reveals it to us, went to Bosnia to encounter "distant echoes of a recent past."[28] There, he found that the darkest days of the Western civilization's history had been replayed. In Bosnia, it was the West that played its most traumatic scenario (World War II, genocide, fascism, etc.) over and over again. The pains the Bosnians experienced under his eyes were his, as captured by his camera: "A flow of buried images started to come back to me. . . . I began to think that I had come to Bosnia in part to see, almost to relive visions, childhood memories."[29] Finally, Peress had to admit: "One is compelled to actually see them [images] to deal with them."[30]

Peress's image-and-text exhibit is a sacrificial offering. Unlike *Faces of Sorrow* which sought to distort the promiscuity of the Bosnian victim, Peress's *Farewell to Bosnia* acts out the West's greatest fear, at least as Žižek sees it: that Bosnia is us, a part of us, of our ever present history and heritage.[31] There is a blind courage to Peress's work that is absent in the *Faces of Sorrow* exhibit. Peress sacrifices himself, his emotional comfort, to prove to Western observers that there is no such thing as an insuperable distance that protects us from Bosnia. Whereas *Faces of Sorrow* was a visual fetish, Peress's *Farewell to Bosnia* offers a visual catharsis, a photographic emotional release that allows us to cope with the fact that Bosnia is no different from us. The implied (Žižekian) message behind this cathartic construct is that we are guilty if we do not feel responsible for them and do not act. Peress is the messiah the West had been waiting for since the end of communism; *Farewell to Bosnia* is his visual/textual gospel. Peress has come down to earth (back from Bosnia and into the Western world, which he tours, through his photos, as a preacher) to redeem our original sins.[32]

Peress's display is a recognition of Žižek's notion of otherness. For Peress, there is nothing alien (antagonistic, dual) about the Bosnian other. Bosnians are people like us: Peress saw them. Bosnia is about us, about our memories. Saving them is first of all saving us. Catching their image, their gaze is first of all reliving our most deeply repressed collective memories. Such a step, such a gaze may be unbearable, as Žižek would say, but Peress's catharsis exonerates us of our guilt (I did it and so can you). Žižek's and Peress's visions of Bosnia mark an apogee for the Western concepts of consumerism and subjectivity, "virus[es] destructive of otherness [alterity]."[33] For Žižek and Peress, Bosnia is "the literal end of alienation. There is no one on the other side anymore."[34] We are the only ones left and, as the chosen few, we must be saved.

Baudrillard and Pop Art from Sarajevo

Trio, a Sarajevo-based pop art design group, offers an ironic revisiting of the Bosnian conflict and of the West's cannibalistic consumption of the Bosnian victim.[35] Displaying a renewed situationist spirit,[36] Trio recombines everyday multinational cultural objects and symbols, and mutilates them by replacing their original designation/ signification with the sign "Sarajevo." A good example of Trio's work is the "Enjoy Sarajevo" piece. Based on the world-famous Coca-Cola advertisement, Trio replaces the Coke logo (the familiar white logo on a red background, as it appears on Coca-Cola bottles and cans) with a Sarajevo sign that uses the same graphic structure. The revisited ad thus becomes "Enjoy Sarajevo," with the year 1994 at the bottom. Another irreverent intervention by Trio is their "I Want You to Save Sarajevo." "I Want You to Save Sarajevo" is a caricature of Uncle Sam's finger-pointing World War I propaganda poster that was meant to interpellate young American males into joining the army. Here, Trio has left the original picture intact. What has changed is the text, which now reads: "I want you to save Sarajevo: nearest recruiting station."

Trio's mode of artistic expression is direct, obvious, cynical, and loud. Like the punk movement that they also emulate, Trio is a matter-of-factly rebellious antihegemonic group. Their work is a disrespectful reaction to the way Western culture has colonized Bosnia and has turned Bosnians into good victims. Trio does not seek to give voice or face to a large-scale ideology. Simply, their reappropriations/mutilations/situations are a cultural jamming of the West's networks of meaning (capital, history, entertainment, etc.), the expression of a pseudoanarchistic pleasure of breaking Western cultural codes and of rejecting Western ideologies (including the Žižek-type humanistico-moralizing ideology of otherness).

Trio's work introduces another vision of the Bosnian other, one already identified by Baudrillard. In "No Pity for Sarajevo,"[37] Baudrillard reflects on the media event organized by Arte, a French-German TV network. In December 1993, in the midst of the Bosnian conflict, Arte decided to open a "cultural corridor" (a corridor for free speech) between western Europe and Sarajevo, a mediatic way of supposedly giving voice to the people of Sarajevo. As Baudrillard mentions, what was striking about that experiment

> was the absolute superiority, the exceptional status conferred by misfortune, distress, and total disillusionment—that very disillusionment which allowed the people of Sarajevo to treat the "Europeans" with contempt, or at least with an air of sarcastic freedom which contrasted with the hypocritical remorse and contrition of those who were linked up with them. They were not the ones in need of compassion; they had compassion for our wretched destinies. "I spit on Europe," said one of them. Nothing offers greater freedom, in fact, or greater sovereignty, than justified contempt—and not even towards the enemy, but towards those basking their good consciences in the warm sun of solidarity.[38]

What Baudrillard saw on Arte's screens is the same thing Trio expresses: a refusal to be assimilated through the game of Western compassion and solidarity, a stubborn choice on the part of the Sarajevans to stand their own ground, not so much against the Serbs or the Croats, but against western Europeans. Unlike the overt disgust shown by the Bosnians of Arte however, Trio has chosen to adopt an ironic distance. Instead of "spitting on Europe," Trio metaphorically and systematically reverses the codes of Western assimilation and consumption by erasing the conventional signs of Western popular culture and replacing them by an arbitrary "Sarajevo" stamp. And so, by looking at Trio's work, the Western observer has the impression that (s)he is dealing with his/her own popular culture but soon realizes that it has been transgressed and reappropriated. By hitting right into the heart of Western media and consumption culture, Trio forcefully reintegrates a dose of singularity and foreignness in the relation between the West and Bosnia. Although at first glance it looks familiar to the Western eye, Trio's pop art inserts a radically alien element that seeks to reestablish the distance between us and them.

Such a distance between us and them is what Baudrillard calls "radical otherness [alterity]." It is arguably a premodern symbolic notion (it is also a retromove, in this sense) that presupposes a total and irreconcilable foreignness, antagonism, or duality between self and other. Although he never explains where he derives the concept of alterity from[39] and certainly never questions whether such a fatal dyssymmetry may not be a precolonization ideal-form in the first place,[40] Baudrillard convincingly demonstrates that the modern project (the work of modernity toward otherness) has always sought to eradicate singularity. In an elegantly formulated statement, Baudrillard declares that

> [s]tarting with modernity, we have entered an era of production of the Other. It is no longer a question of killing, of devouring or seducing the Other, of facing him, of competing with him, of loving or hating the Other. It is first of all a matter of producing the Other. The Other is no longer an object of passion but an object of production. Maybe it is because the Other, in his radical otherness/alterity, or in his irreducible singularity, has become dangerous or unbearable. And so, we have to conjure up his seduction. Or perhaps, more simply, otherness and dual relationships gradually disappear with the rise of individual values and with the destruction of the symbolic ones. In any case, otherness/alterity is lacking and, since we cannot experience otherness as destiny, we must produce the other as difference.[41]

Baudrillard's point is that the Other (it is capitalized because it becomes a reified, sovereign concept; it has become a proper name) does not exist until the desire to put alienation to good use emerges. To put it in a Hobbesian context, the Other is a consequence of the human species' escape from the state of nature and of Leviathan's emergence as an orderer of society. The passage from passion to reason (and later, with capitalism, to production) requires that a distinction be made between Self and Other. As an object of love, labor, and morality, the Other exists only to the extent that I (the self) exist, something that the presence of the other constantly reinforces (the Cartesian cogito is no doubt at the origin of such a vicious circle).

It remains that, created on such a modern ideological basis, otherness could be expressed in a different way than that of the consumption of the other, the meaning it has today. This is the point where Baudrillard introduces the distinction between the German notions of *Verfremdung* and *Entfremdung*:

> *Verfremdung* means becoming other, becoming estranged from oneself—alienation in the literal sense. *Entfremdung*, by contrast, means to be dispossessed of the other, to lose all otherness [alterity]. Now, it is much more serious to be dispossessed of the other than of oneself.[42]

A typical case of *Entfremdung* is Žižek's remoralization of/through the Bosnian victim. Žižek (and the West in general) destroys the singularity of the Bosnian individual, what makes the people of Sarajevo alien to us, so that his not-so-well-hidden ideology of moral unity and solidarity may prevail. In other words, Žižek has to cling desperately to the Western notions of humanity and individuality in order to have a chance to redeem humankind. In such a Baudrillardian perspective, Western observers like Žižek are not any better than the Serbs when it comes to Bosnia. In fact, at different levels (one is symbolic, the other racial), they all take part in the genocide of the Bosnian population.

An anecdote illustrates this point. In the winter of 1992, another mediatico-humanitarian operation took place between Sarajevo and Paris.[43] World-renowned filmmakers assembled in Paris had decided that Sarajevo should become the focus of their work and artistic creativity. Yet, not having any idea of what was really happening in Sarajevo, the filmmakers sent blank videotapes to the people of Sarajevo (to Bosnian journalists who remained there, artists, public figures, etc.) so that they could film their everyday lives, put them on tape, and send the tapes back to Paris. From these tapes, a video documentary called "Homage to Sarajevo" would be made and, later, "real" movies reproducing the fate of Sarajevo would be shot. The filmmakers even dreamt of starting a new international film festival in Sarajevo where those war movies would be premiered (little did they know that, by late 1992, all the movie theaters in Sarajevo had been destroyed).

This anecdote is a perfect illustration of Baudrillard's claim that it is "we [the West, Europe] who are weak, going over there looking for the means to make up for our weakness and loss of reality."[44] The West's quest for reality, for some meaningful ideology, for a validation of identity in the midst of Sarajevo's war landscape is another way of figuring the theft of Bosnia's singularity. Bosnia's radical alterity, its spectacle of death, torture, massive destruction, its barbarous irrational passions, its raw energies are what is seductive to the West. This seductive alterity is why Bosnia must become an object of Western consumption, as Trio's satirical art so aptly shows. It is why the people of Sarajevo must become Other to us, our alter-egos. Once again, similar to Žižek's project, sending blank videotapes to people in Sarajevo so that they can visually record their everyday experiences is the West's way of coping with alterity. For Westerners it is a way of avoiding frankly admitting that we are really seduced by and attracted to the type of passions that Bosnia displays. But the West is supposedly too "civilized" and "enlightened" to acknowledge such an attraction to raw pulsions. Instead of becoming strangers to ourselves (Verfremdung) and happily transcending our modern subjective qualities to enter a completely foreign and unmastered domain (that is to say, choosing seduction, as Baudrillard would suggest), we, Western subjects, have more conveniently opted for Entfremdung and for the safe but weak ideological formations, like compassion or humanitarianism, that come with it. Baudrillard can be granted the final word on the contemporary meaning of otherness:

> The "victimal" society is the easiest and most trivial form of alterity. It marks the resurrection of the Other as misery, as a victim, as an alibi; and the resurrection of ourselves, with our miserable consciousness, who are drawing our pitiful identities from such a necrological mirror. We are exploring the multiple signs of misery in order to prove the presence of God through Evil, just as we are investigating the misfortunes of others in order to find a proof, albeit a negative one, of our existence. The new identity is that of the victim. Everything is organized around the figure of the despoiled, frustrated, and crippled subject, and the "victimal" strategy consists of recognizing the subject as such. . . . The social becomes a clinic for human rights, a plastic surgery for identity. It is no doubt an effective strategy: claiming one's debt, negotiating one's lack, a blackmail of negativity. Yet, it is also a defective strategy since it is a strategy based on weakness and

dissolution; a minimalist, victimizing, and humanitarian strategy, so characteristic of emotional and promotional societies. Don't touch my difference [*Touche pas à ma différence*]![45]

It is, however, Žižek's "weak and defective" strategy of otherness that is imposed today as the normal and universal dimension of human life. The official and institutional strategies of interventionism deployed by the agents of the West—the United Nations, NATO, the European Union, and the United States—to "help" or "save" Bosnia replicate such an attitude and, as such, may be read in this context. International interventionism in Bosnia, as an ideological strategy, is an expansion and institutionalization of Western strategies of otherness. The supposedly divergent versions of interventionism and peacekeeping that have emerged in the course of the Bosnian conflict and in its aftermath (the UN's vision versus NATO's approach, as we shall see) are nothing more than specific institutional strategies deployed to cope with the singularity/alterity of Bosnia. One, the peacekeeping strategy of the United Nations, is very much reminiscent of the "moral buffering" effects mobilized by the *Faces of Sorrow* exhibit. Based on humanitarian concerns and a simulation of enforcement (called "peacemaking"), the UN's peacekeeping efforts hope to turn Bosnia into a conglomerate of safe areas and humanitarian free zones that would function as identity-reflecting mirrors for the West. The other, the military-enforcement strategy by NATO, is more commensurate with Peress's sacrificial intervention in Bosnia and with Žižek's will to rediscover the power of the ethical "act." NATO's involvement marks the moment when the West finally admits that Bosnia is a part of us, of our history and heritage. Since Bosnia is a part of us, of global society as a universal moral community (Žižek's and the UN's vision return to Kant this way), violence in the Balkans must be purged from the international body of politics ("our body") by any means necessary. This last strategy of interventionism is what I call "Western catharsis." I now turn to a reading of these visions of interventionism that are perhaps nothing more than other ways of envisaging other Bosnias, of figuring Bosnia as Other.

OTHER BOSNIAS

Before analyzing the visions of interventionism (as ways of globally mobilizing otherness) deployed by the UN and NATO in Bosnia, a brief historical overview of the conflict in the former Yugoslavia may be helpful. The Bosnian conflict has its origins in the breakup of the Yugoslav Federation in the late 1980s. The death of Tito and the collapse of his "decentralized communist" system led to a resurgence of nationalist sentiments epitomized by Slovenia and Croatia's decisions to declare their independence on June 25, 1991. Immediately after these declarations, the mostly Serb Yugoslav Federal Army (JNA) entered Slovenia. Faced with a well-organized resistance movement in Slovenia, Slobodan Milošević, the Serb nationalist leader of the Yugoslav Federation (who a year earlier had announced that, in case of a breakup of the Federation, he would be compelled to annex the seceding territories),[46] chose to let Slovenia go (at least for the moment). Milošević preferred to concentrate the efforts of the JNA on Croatia where pockets of Serb population were already under the de facto control of Serbian paramilitary groups such as the "Serbian Volunteer Guard" (controlled by the soon-to-be infamous Arkan). Slovenia gained its independence by June 1991.[47] It would take longer for Croatia to achieve the same status. The explosion of violence in Slovenia and Croatia in June 1991 was a clear prelude of what was to come next. Serbian pockets of population in non-Serb regions of the Federation were now controlled by ultranationalists who pledged their support to Belgrade, not to Zagreb or Sarajevo. They would be the direct instigators of an armed conflict that soon would spread beyond Croatia and Slovenia. With its substantial Serb population, Bosnia was to become the next victim. In the summer of 1991, the conflict had not yet officially spread to Bosnia-Herzegovina. The war between Belgrade and the breakup nationalities had been concentrated on Croatia. This early conflict, however, already displayed a fundamental characteristic of the Balkan conflict: by massively displacing thousands of Serbs within Croatia, the Croatian nationalist government of Franko Tudjman (not yet recognized by the West) triggered a strategy of ethnic cleansing. Such a policy, no doubt, reinforced Belgrade's views in favor of annexation.

In September 1991, it was the Bosnian Serbs' turn to ask Belgrade for assistance. The Serbs of Bosnia felt threatened by Croatia's recent call for independence and by the fate of the Serbs of Croatia. The Bosnian Serbs were organized in a local branch of the SDS, the Serbian Democratic Party, which had most of its support among nationalist Serbs in Croatia. The Bosnian section of the SDS was run by

Radovan Karadžić. Not all of the Bosnian Serbs followed the SDS, but in the fall of 1991 Karadžić had been able to muster enough support to ask Belgrade to intervene. Immediately, Belgrade sent some "Federal" troops (the JNA was mostly composed of Serbs) to Bosnia to control the situation and to protect the recognized "Serb Autonomous Regions."[48] Indeed, a few months prior to his call to Belgrade, Karadžić had unilaterally declared that four parts of the territory of Bosnia-Herzegovina were in fact autonomous Serb zones. Justifying his decision by claiming that the Bosnian Serbs needed to be buffered from the rest of the Bosnian population (mostly Muslims and Croats), Karadžić moved before any call by Bosnia for secession and independence. Despite the fact that it was a blatant violation of the spirit and law of the Yugoslav Federation, Milošević had remained silent. His decision in the fall of 1991 of deploying Federal troops in Bosnia was nonetheless an explicit recognition of the so-called Serb Autonomous Regions of Bosnia. Over the next months, the pressure by Karadžić's party on the regional Bosnian government of Izetbegović became incessant. For the regional Bosnian government in Sarajevo, such a pressure was all the more intolerable as the Federal forces sent by Milošević were in effect already occupying the Bosnian territory. At this point, it was clear to most Bosnians that the situation could not remain unchanged for long.

In the winter of 1991–92, international interventions and pressures exacerbated the tension in Bosnia. The internationalization of the Balkan conflict took place after western European nations, carried by their pro-democratization zeal, declared that they recognized both Slovenia and Croatia as newly independent states in January 1992.[49] This move isolated Belgrade even further and caused an immediate intensification of the conflict. Belgrade's position was fairly simple: if the Serbian-led Yugoslav unity could not be affirmed de jure (Western countries no longer seemed to recognize the legality of Yugoslavia), it would have to take place de facto, after the Serbs got rid of any form of resistance in the region. Such a plan, as we saw, had been initiated by Belgrade prior to Europe's recognition of Slovenia and Croatia. The international recognition simply gave Milošević yet another excuse to tighten the grip on the rest of the Federation, which, in his mind, had to become a Serbian-led (if not cleansed) entity. In the early stages, the West and its blind pro-democratic zeal nonetheless had to share the blame for the mounting ethnic tensions in the Balkans.[50]

In the early months of 1992, the conflict had thus been exacerbated and, as a recognized post–cold war international samaritan, the United Nations started to look more closely at the situation. By September 1991, the UN had already imposed an arms embargo on the entire Yugoslav territory. In February 1992, Resolution 743 mandated the deployment of a United Nations Protection Force (UNPROFOR) for Croatia. UNPROFOR's peacekeeping mandate, per Resolution 743, was to help broker a cease-fire and take care of immediate humanitarian needs.[51] UNPROFOR had not yet been called to intervene in Bosnia (for the conflict had officially not started). Despite concentrating on Croatia, the UN in the winter-spring of 1992 nonetheless took two major decisions that would be of extreme importance for Bosnia. First, UNPROFOR's headquarters were established in Sarajevo. Second, the UN accepted Belgrade's requests to use the Bosnian territory to, as Belgrade put it, "withdraw" its tanks and artillery from Croatia. This move was first seen as a good sign by the UN. It supposedly indicated that the Serbs were willing to pull slowly but surely out of Croatia. In reality, it turned out to be a huge diplomatic mistake, as Belgrade used the "withdrawal" excuse to redeploy its artillery around major Bosnian towns and strategic positions.[52]

Meanwhile, the regional government of the Republic of Bosnia-Herzegovina felt the growing pressure and chose to turn to the European Community (EC) for advice and support. In 1991, the European Community had appointed a special commission (led by French constitutional jurist Robert Badinter) to "consider applications from any Yugoslav Republic seeking independence."[53] The Badinter Commission had already told the Bosnian government that a regional referendum would be required prior to the EC's recognition of Bosnia's independence. Trying perhaps to avoid the effects of the previous blunt recognition of both Slovenia and Croatia, the EC calculated that, through such a procedure, it could less controversially ground its future recognition of the Bosnian state. As for the Bosnians, they had already decided that the results would be used to reinforce the claim of a legitimate secession from the Federation. The referendum took place on February 28 and March 1. The Bosnian Serbs refused to recognize the process and chose not to vote. Only 63 percent of the Bosnian population took part in the referendum. Ninety-nine percent of the votes were in favor of independence.[54] Karadžić's SDS, of course, rejected the results. But Bosnia took the opportunity of the vote to declare its independence. This move was to prove fatal. Far from reconciling, the referendum of early March "reaffirmed the gulf between the minimum position of the SDS, on the one hand, and the republic's other parties, on the other."[55] In the aftermath of the referendum, its results, and the choice for independence, Bosnian Serb paramilitary factions, with the passive encouragements of Belgrade, set up barricades around Sarajevo's parliament.[56] It took a month for the tension to turn into an open war. On April 2, 1992, Arkan's "Serbian Volunteer Guard" killed dozens of Muslims in a village on the border with Serbia. On that same day, Serb gunmen "fired indiscriminately from the top of the Holiday Inn Hotel in Sarajevo at anti-war demonstrators."[57] A few days later, on April 6, the EC officially recognized Bosnia. But the JNA had already taken control of the Bosnian territory.

By April 1992, the JNA, encouraged by Karadžić's party and other paramilitary formations, had started to impose a siege on Sarajevo.[58] The siege of Sarajevo also marked the official beginning of the UN's involvement in Bosnia with the deployment of the large-scale humanitarian mission that was to take place during the next three years.[59] Medical NGOs had already been dispatched in the former Yugoslavia (in Croatia and Bosnia above all) since 1991. But it was not until 1992, when the UN officially claimed to take the lead in the conflict, that a first attempt at a multinational intervention, under the form of humanitarian interventionism, was deployed in Bosnia. In August 1992, UNPROFOR's mandate was expanded to include Bosnia (Resolution 770) and the UN was supposedly "empowered to use all measures necessary to deliver humanitarian assistance."[60] Immediately, Sarajevo became the first scene for the United Nations' operation in Bosnia (now called UNPROFOR II).

On the military side of the conflict, by May 1992, UN Resolution 752 had requested the withdrawal of the JNA from all the former Socialist Federal Republics of Yugoslavia, apart from Serbia and Montenegro.[61] This request was taken by international observers to be a clear affirmation by the international community of who the aggressor was. Threatening to enforce economic sanctions, the UN managed to obtain a JNA pullout from Bosnia.[62] In practice, the pullout never took place. Serbia simply continued its military influence by providing troops and armaments to the Bosnian Serbs.

Furthermore, the siege of Sarajevo was strengthened and the ethnic killings by Serbian paramilitaries multiplied. The persistence of the Serb aggression in Bosnia, and the highly mediatized reports of tortures, rapes, and ethnic killings pushed humanitarian actors to intensify their efforts. Humanitarian NGOs from all over the world started to send their specialized personnel. Meanwhile, the UN kept on bringing more troops in an effort to protect the humanitarian operations performed by specialized UN agencies (the UNHCR in particular). In reality, despite the added number of blue-helmets, UNPROFOR's mission of "humanitarian protection" was rather pointless.[63] Although the so-called humanitarian crisis (in all its gruesome dimensions) continued all through 1992, the UN did not offer any believable threat until April 1993 when it finally declared the beginning of Operation Deny Flight, that is to say, the creation of a "no-fly zone" over Bosnia, and identified six UN-protected "safe areas."[64]

Resolutions 816 (no-fly zone over Bosnia) and 824 (safe areas) also foreshadowed the intervention of NATO into the conflict.[65] NATO became the UN's "hired gun," as Spyros Economides and Paul Taylor suggest,[66] in the Bosnian peacekeeping and humanitarian mission, as it was asked to enforce the "no-fly zone" policy. Slowly but surely, the West tried to shift its interventionist strategy by moving away from humanitarian peacekeeping (of the type that had successfully been implemented a few months before in Northern Iraq to protect the Kurds) and turning to a more novel form of military enforcement. Gradually, the UN's joint humanitarian and peacekeeping venture gave way to NATO's more obvious military structure. At the same time, however, the "safe area" strategy of UN peacekeeping marked the heyday of the UN's policy of deterrence, as will be shown momentarily.

The role of the UN's "safe areas" in Bosnia has been much debated. While some have interpreted the "safe areas" as at least one attempt at buffering civilians from the tortures and crimes inherent to the conflict, others have suggested that the creation of those "areas" was aimed less at protecting Bosnian-Muslim victims than at reducing the flow of Bosnian refugees into the West.[67]

Despite the UN's growing threat of using NATO as a way of implementing its humanitarian policies, the Serbs were not stopped in their plan of attacking the "safe areas." The end of 1993 saw the UN's inability to carry out its threats as its supposedly unattackable humanitarian safe havens were violently invaded.[68] In February 1994, after the highly mediatized bombing of a Sarajevo marketplace, the West's attitude toward Bosnia appeared to change. Western European nations and the United States suddenly decided to shift the strategic focus away from the UN and toward NATO. Indeed, in the spring of 1994, NATO took charge by demanding that all Serb artillery around Sarajevo be dismantled.[69] The Serbs, however, continued to make a mockery of the West's threats by capturing the enclave of Bihac (one of the UN's safe areas).[70] Unlike the previous display of UN impotence, NATO, this time, responded (a late response, however). NATO's response represented the first real attempt at using force in the recognized humanitarian crisis. In the last months of 1994, NATO started to bomb Serbian and Bosnian Serb positions. Interestingly, Serb troops retaliated against NATO's attacks, not by directing their actions at NATO, but by taking hostage dozens of blue-helmets who, just as the civilians whom they were supposed to protect, had simply turned into hapless victims.[71] In spite of the vulnerability of the UN's forces still in charge of protecting the "safe areas," NATO, on Washington's orders, launched a large air-bombing campaign that was to be seen as the direct response to the destruction of the Srebrenica enclave and to the massive killings of the Muslims in this enclave by Bosnian Serb troops (led by General Ratko Mladić).[72] Strategically, this last NATO bombing of Serb positions coincided with a Croatian offensive against Milošević's forces in the formerly Croatian Krajina region.[73] In a rather abrupt fashion, Belgrade pushed Karadžić's troops to accept a cease-fire brokered by U.S. special envoy Richard Holbrooke in October 1995.

The cease-fire paved the way for peace talks, which started in Dayton, Ohio, on November 1, 1995. Since Karadžić did not attend the negotiations (he had been indicted by a UN-sponsored International Criminal Tribunal in charge of prosecuting war crimes in the former Yugoslavia), Milošević ended up being the sole representative of Serbian interests in the Dayton Peace Agreements.[74]

The Dayton Peace Agreements were the culmination of a long, and often futile, process of peace negotiations initiated by the West, behind Lord Carrington's mission, in 1991.[75] Finally, the Dayton Peace Agreements divided Bosnia into two parts: a Bosnian Federation, which was to comprise 51 percent of the prewar Bosnian territory; and a Serb Republic (Republika Srbska), which was granted the

remaining 49 percent of the land. The two components of the former
Bosnia would still be part of a single sovereign state (perhaps the
West's way of trying to legitimate its early recognition of Bosnia's independence), called Bosnia-Herzegovina, a fictional state that would
exist de jure (as a legal principle) if not de facto (as a territorial entity
with a clearly identified population and a univocal source of power).
A free election process was to take place to give this new state a semblance of democratic unity and political authority.[76] The Dayton
Agreements also sanctioned the official transfer of international responsibility from the UN to NATO. In accordance with the agreements, a NATO "peacekeeping" force, IFOR (the Implementation
Force, later called SFOR, the Stabilization Force), took over after
UNPROFOR in Bosnia in December 1995. Its one-year mandate
was designed to guarantee the return of the displaced populations in
Bosnia, the peaceful movements of populations from one zone of the
new Bosnia to the other, the creation of a Bosnia-based police force,
the establishment of livable conditions, and the rebuilding of the destroyed infrastructures, tasks normally reserved to the United Nations (in the context of peacekeeping or peacemaking) in a post–cold
war era (SFOR's mandate has since been extended indefinitely).

UN Peacekeeping as Simulated Enforcement

When the UN's mission in the former Yugoslavia was launched in
the spring of 1992, the procedural limits of the operation were never
clearly defined. UNPROFOR's mission was meant to be a typical
case of post–cold war peacekeeping, that is to say, of interposition by
UN forces between warring parties (derived from chapter 6 of the
UN Charter, which deals with the "peaceful settlement of disputes").
However, in the overall euphoria of the New World Order, it was
also seen as an opportunity to experiment with a new form of interventionism, "peacemaking." From the onset, the UN intervention in
the former Yugoslavia, and in Bosnia-Herzegovina above all, played
within the never clearly specified bounds of Boutros-Ghali's four
areas of peacekeeping as described in chapter 1. Peacemaking, one of
the new notions within UN interventionism,[77] supposedly went beyond peacekeeping by threatening to "actively" engage UN troops in
processes of peaceful settlement.[78] A case of hidden enforcement,
peacemaking was intended to become the mark of the new United
Nations in the 1990s, a United Nations supposedly no longer unable

to use force in order to achieve peace. Peacemaking, however, still operated under the legal assumption that the consent of the warring parties would be required prior to intervention. Nevertheless, as a recognized potential use of military means by UN troops, peacemaking was viewed as a rhetorical if not a practical bridge between traditional UN operations and enforcement strategies (the use of military force to stop conflicts without the consent of the parties).

This unclear distinction between peacekeeping and peacemaking in the Bosnian conflict was a deliberate move.[79] Keeping the initial signification of the UN mission in a state of uncertainty allowed different Western strategies to be played out in Bosnia. Indeed, in the first years of the conflict (1992–94), various strategies, from basic humanitarian policies and food relief operations to more daring no-fly zone resolutions and air-bombing retaliations, were attempted. Yet, more importantly, this definitional ambiguity gave UN peacekeeping (or peacemaking) a semblance of force and authority that the Western world, from the European Community to the United States, feigned to believe in and, in any case, used to its advantage as it tried not to acknowledge the presence of the Bosnian conflict.[80] In short, UNPROFOR offered a simulation of enforcement (through its no-fly zone policies, its ineffective sanctions, its threats of using NATO's fire power, etc.) that, during the first years of the conflict, exonerated the West of any responsibility. UNPROFOR gave the pretense that something was actually being done. Echoing *Faces of Sorrow,* the UN's simulation of force and interventionism, against the Serbs and Bosnian Serbs in particular, created a buffering effect necessary for the West to keep Bosnia at a distance (while claiming that, through the UN, the West was still meeting its moral responsibilities).

The UN's simulation of enforcement (via peacemaking/keeping) could have run for years, producing all sorts of desirable scenarios for the West. But the UN's hyperreal intervention in the Balkans (more real than a real, forceful, military intervention) was a conceptual and mediatic illusion, a trap, and the United Nations (not the Serbs) fell into it. Victim of its own illusion, the UN started to believe in the reality of its peacemaking efforts. Believing that it had the strength to hold its ground against the Serbs, the UN decided that it could reproduce its own ideological universe in Bosnia by imposing violence-free "safe areas" (Resolution 824). Claiming that it had the support of NATO, which, in the spring of 1993, when Resolution 824 was taken, did not have any troops in the region and had not even started to devise a plan of action,[81] the United Nations defied the Serbs to attack its humanitarian safe enclaves, the designated zones of simulated UN authority. Of course, the Serbs, who had never really fallen for the UN's trompe l'oeil games (as Baudrillard tells us), made it a point to prove the UN wrong by destroying the "safe areas" one by one, starting with Bihac in the early days of 1994.

In *Simulations,* Baudrillard provocatively suggests that a state apparatus/political authority may actually react more violently to a simulated holdup than to a real one.[82] The United Nations's strategy of "peacemaking/keeping" is an almost perfect Baudrillardian case of a simulation taken for reality. There is, however, a slight difference with Baudrillard's example of a simulated holdup. Indeed, here, in a more perverse manner perhaps, it is the simulator itself who falls prey to its own construction. The UN, as mentioned above, gets caught in its own web of illusions. Meanwhile, the expected targets of the simulation, the people of the Balkans (the Serbs, but also the Bosnians to whom the UN promised assistance), never found the simulation credible. In a sense, the UN's simulation of enforcement was never able to supersede the basic materiality of Bosnia's daily war experience. The Serbs and the Bosnians always knew that UNPROFOR was a visual illusion, a deterrence machine that deterred nothing but itself: "we tell them what we call them here: Smurfs, or simply the Un-Protection force."[83]

United Nations peacekeeping/making as a simulation of enforcement was meant to be a deterrent. UN peacekeeping hoped to reactivate the images of the Gulf War, the smashing air raids on Baghdad, the crushing of Saddam Hussein's armies, without having to physically intervene. Security Council Resolutions on Bosnia were supposed to recall Resolution 678, the resolution that allowed the use of force against Iraq. Economides and Taylor indeed suggest that "it was hoped that the Serbs would interpret [the resolutions] in the light of the earlier resolution [678]." But they conclude that the resolutions on Bosnia were "never backed with any convincing evidence that [this] was real."[84] For the Serbs it had hoped to scare off, UNPROFOR was a failed simulation, "a passive and minimally credible deterrent."[85]

More importantly, the UN had thought that it could serve as a

deterrent for the West as well. By imposing a semblance of enforcement and humanitarian intervention that, transmitted by the most
popular visual media networks (CNN, ITN, NHK) into the West,
would convince Western audiences that their sense of ethical duty
was being represented by proxy by the UN in Bosnia, the UN hoped
any real and potentially costly military intervention by Western forces
would be prevented. In a larger ideological perspective, the New
World Order proclaimed after the Gulf War would remain an unchallenged vision because the UN had taken (simulated) charge in the
Balkans. In short, the UN's simulated enforcement as a strategy of
Western interventionism was a way, once again, as it was in Somalia,
of suturing the ideology-scape of Western disciplinary liberalism and
giving the West a new post–cold war identity, an artificially induced
raison d'être, by presenting Westerners as the rescuers and enforcers
of human decency. As such a suture, the UN's "safe areas" were
meant to protect Western guilty consciences more than actually offer
an infallible asylum to the Bosnian Muslims. Unfortunately for the
West, the UN mostly deterred itself, and its simulated safety nets
were pulverized.

For the UN, Bosnia is thus a continuation of a phenomenon that
had already been witnessed in Somalia. We may refer to this phenomenon as the failure of the visual, or the fatal attraction to visually simulated techniques. Eager to extend both in Somalia and in
Bosnia the benefits of visually and mediatically enhanced trompe
l'oeil devices (which had proven fairly successful in cases of global
surveillance in Iraq and North Korea), the United Nations rediscov-
ers what happens once these simulated scenarios are no longer effective. One may suggest that, beyond the fact that both Somalis and
Serbs never fell for the simulations deployed by the United Nations,
it is the passage from passivity to activity, that is to say, from global
surveillance from space (panopticism) to global policing in practice
(peacekeeping/making in Somalia and Bosnia) that, in a sense, proves
fatal. Confronted with the immediate reality of the Balkan conflict,
with its deployment of raw energy, pulsion, and violence, the United
Nations's strategies of simulation and visually enhanced mobilization of global governance show its conceptual and practical limits.
When the limits of the United Nations's strategies of simulation are
reached, ideology once again turns to more traditional modes of disciplinarity and coercion to achieve its goals. In the case of Bosnia,

this transition is marked by the West's (fatal) recognition of the presence of Bosnia (after the massacre at the Sarajevo marketplace, above all), and the sudden decision by Western heads of state to send NATO as their redeemer and executioner.

NATO's Intervention as Western Catharsis

After the failure of the UN's simulation of use of force (under the notion of peacemaking), a new approach to interventionism was imposed by NATO.[86] NATO's military intervention (limited at the beginning, in February 1994, but more substantial in the following months) was supposed to underscore the sudden decisiveness of the international community, something that the United Nations had apparently failed to achieve. NATO's involvement in Bosnia marked a transition, albeit a gradual one (it is really not until August 1995 that NATO's air strikes became a deterrent factor),[87] from peacekeeping to peace enforcement, from a simulated display of force to a disciplinary mode of coercion, which all took place without the help of the UN.[88]

NATO's intervention was perhaps the first effective attempt at peace enforcement in Bosnia. But it was much more than a sudden outburst of military force. At a more significant level, NATO's actions operated a role reversal in the Western visions of otherness and interventionism in Bosnia. Whereas until then the UN had used NATO as an alibi, as a harmless "hired gun," it was now the UN that was turned into a pawn, an instrument in NATO's strategy and in the games played by the West. All of a sudden, the UN had to become a key player in a completely different game: no longer a play of simulation but, rather, a strategy of Western catharsis orchestrated by NATO.

In order to precisely understand the role of the UN in the strategy of NATO-imposed catharsis, we need to open a theoretical parenthesis. This theoretical parenthesis is needed to define the contours and explore the limits of the notion of catharsis as it has emerged in religious, medical, and political discourses.

The notion of catharsis has already been employed in critical international relations theory circles. Larry George has shown how post–cold war international politics can be read as an age of global moral and political sacrifice and catharsis. Focusing on the issue of U.S. foreign policy before and after the end of the cold war, George has written that "[t]he collapse of the Cold War has left the United States resembling a society in sacrificial crisis, and recent foreign interventions by American forces can be seen as a reaction more to the danger of a post–Cold War shearing of national ideological values than to any real threat posed by Noriega and Hussein."[89] George's analysis borrows from literary anthropologist René Girard the idea that "sacrificial crisis," a lack of periodic ritualistic collective acts of violence through which a community regenerates itself, accurately depicts the contemporary condition of Western societies (and conditions both their domestic and foreign policies). Without a process of sacrificial regeneration, the ideological coherence of the modern community cannot be achieved. The traditional representation of communal values is lacking and a collective identity crisis arises from the absence of adequate sacrifice or "scapegoating," as Girard puts it (finding a good victim).[90] George aptly shows that the end of the cold war marked a ritualistic crisis in American society because U.S. foreign policy was all of a sudden left without the sacrificial specter of communism. In other words, the cold war had served to perpetuate rituals of violence (nuclear scare, Cuban missile crisis, etc.) that had given America a form of domestic ideological coherence and had allowed the inherent tensions of American society to be dispelled. Desperately searching for new victims, American ideology and hegemony were in a state of disarray until George Bush finally found Saddam Hussein. The Gulf War thus offered a cathartic moment (a cleansing space/time that returned things to a level of normality)[91] for the United States by allowing American ideology to regain a meaningful identity internationally and domestically through the renewed play of ritualistic violence (a military intervention).

George's analysis can be generalized to the Western world and its ideologies of otherness and interventionism in a post–cold war era. This line of thinking applies to the Bosnian conflict too, particularly to the extent that the West, as mentioned above, desperately tries to recover a "reality principle" through its various interventions. NATO's charge in Bosnia was in fact a sacrificial act that, after the recognized failure of the UN's strategy of simulated enforcement, it was hoped, would purge the international body (or the universal moral community) of its violent foreign elements.

But the way catharsis was deployed by NATO in Bosnia is informed by another notion derived from Girard's work, the notion of the *katharma* or *pharmakos*. For Girard, the ritual of catharsis is meaningless without taking into account the central role of the *katharma/pharmakos*, the sacrificial victim who works as a stand-in for an "evil object," as Girard explains.[92] Through its suffering (by means of illness, poison, or torture), the victim must find his/her own cure, his/her own way out of the crisis. The *katharma*'s suffering is equated with the "expulsion of impurities," not only in the human body, but also in the entire community. If the *katharma* survives the crisis, the community, by analogy, will be purged of its evils as well. The *katharma*, formerly representing an evil object or presence, then becomes a symbol of good violence, a redeemer and a savior for the community. If the *katharma* dies, his/her sacrifice is not in vain. All sorts of impure energies converge toward the body of the sacrificial victim and, in return for this absorption of evils, the community is emptied of its potential or actual sufferings. The *katharma* thus functions as a sort of symbolic or physiological vacuum for the entire community. It cleanses while it suffers. Girard notes that "[t]he word *katharsis* refers primarily to the mysterious benefits that accrue to the community upon the death of the human *katharma* or *pharmakos*."[93] Such a symbolic function finds an equivalent in medical practice. In medicine, a catharsis is a form of treatment that aggravates "the symptoms, bringing about a salutary crisis that will lead to recovery."[94]

Whether one interprets it in the context of a religious and symbolic ritual or one prefers to look at it as a medical purgative, catharsis remains a process of expulsion of "evil" that centers around the function of the *katharma*. The *katharma* must be credible and symbolic enough to represent the ailments of the community or the body. Similarly, as the Greek term *pharmakon* suggests, the *katharma/pharmakos* must have the faculty to be transformed into a cure that "possesses a simultaneous potential for good and for bad."[95]

Returning to post–cold war international politics, I suggest that, in Bosnia, the United Nations was used by NATO and the West as an international *katharma*. As mentioned earlier, NATO's arrival in Bosnia created a role reversal for the United Nations, which was now asked to follow NATO's lead. Yet, instead of withdrawing from Bosnia, the UN remained and was still regarded by NATO and its member states as an agency in charge of maintaining the safe areas. The continued presence of the UN was essential to the West's plans and to NATO's strategy. But the UN became essential, not so much as a symbol of authority (which it never really was), but as a sacrificial victim. In the spring of 1994, what NATO performed in Bosnia was the ritual sacrifice of the United Nations as a way of appeasing the guilt of the international community. NATO's interventionism as Western catharsis can be understood in those terms, that is to say, in the need to publicly and violently let the UN be destroyed (let the UN play the role of the scapegoat).

This interpretation finds an obvious anecdotal support in the repeated plight of the blue-helmets (the UN's human bodies) in Bosnia after 1994. Once recognized as signs of hope (at least, they were bringing food relief), the blue-helmets suddenly turned into symbols of impotence and hypocrisy. They started to be rejected by all in Bosnia, the Serbs, the Bosnians, the Croats—and of course the West as well. The Bosnians started to treat them with utmost "resentment and scorn."[96] The Serbs and Croats started to toy with them, taking them hostage on many occasions, stealing their vehicles and weapons, or even killing them.[97] The West, finally, symbolically (or ritualistically) turned its back on the UN, rejecting its politics, its mission, and its secretary-general altogether.[98] These events are still congruent with Girard's analysis of catharsis. Girard indeed suggests that "*katharma* is not limited to the victim or the surrogate object; it also refers to the supreme efforts of a mythic or tragic hero."[99] In other words, the hero—or simulated hero in the case of the UN—must die too, particularly when it no longer performs its heroic functions. A fallen hero thus becomes an ideal scapegoat. The recognized impotence of the UN and its mode of intervention after the February 1994 massacre at the Sarajevo marketplace pushed the West, behind NATO as its executioner, to transform the international organization into a sacrificial victim. After all, *katharma* comes from the greek verb *kathairo,* which among other things means to whip, specifically recalling "the practice of whipping the *pharmakos* on the genitals."[100] This is exactly what NATO's dirty mission was: emasculating the *pharmakos* (which, in a sense, had already emasculated himself), blatantly exposing the UN's failures in this crisis.

The expected result of such a strategy of scapegoating the UN was, once again, just as in ritualistic rites or medical purgative practices, to create a mystical/physiological evacuation of the West's pains in Bosnia, to cleanse Western consciences of their primal guilt (as Žižek would have it). The UN's blue-helmets had to suffer in Bosnia so that the fate of the West could more easily be equated with that of the Bosnian victims. In other words, the sacrifice of the UN was a way of showing the world that the West, too, was a victim of this conflict. The fate of the UN, sacrificed by NATO, was that of Bosnia. Once this was established, what NATO was left to do was to pick up the pieces and finally impose its military might as a way of achieving (Western) closure in the Balkans. One finds here a tempting parallel between NATO's strategy and Peress's *Farewell to Bosnia*. Both NATO's interventionism and Peress's photojournalism are cathartic enterprises that hope to drive violence toward one designated ritualistic center (the UN, Peress's emotional comfort) so that the community can be freed of its sufferings and memories (as with Peress), and guilts (as with the West in Bosnia) can finally fade. But there is still a difference between NATO and Peress: NATO chose to sacrifice another body, the UN, whereas Peress, holding the position of the messiah, simply sacrifices himself. Yet, both enterprises are seemingly concerned with the good of the moral community that they represent and hope to rescue through these sacrifices.

What the Western catharsis in Bosnia sought to achieve was get rid of the UN while keeping the pretense that it was all done for the good of the international community. The strategy of UN-scapegoating initiated by NATO may have been intended to symbolically cleanse the Western sense of moral responsibility of its primal guilt in the Balkans. But NATO's military power could have done that better (and finally did so). UN-scapegoating was also a perverse and almost sadistic move on the part of NATO and the West that was designed to mutilate the UN and enjoy the sight of such a suffering. NATO framed the UN and, through this exercise, sought to get rid of Serbia and Bosnia as well.

As NATO's involvement in Bosnia, even after the Dayton Agreements, continues, one can wonder how NATO itself will be affected by these initial sacrificial activities. Is there a curse for the executioner who shows his face? In the aftermath of the Bosnian crisis, NATO, as the executioner, has positioned itself as the new *pharmakos*, as the West's next potential sacrificial victim. The signing of the Dayton Peace Agreement may have marked the apogee of the West's cathartic project. The UN-as-*katharma* disappeared with the crisis and peace was supposedly found. But NATO has also come out of the Dayton Agreement as the new leading institution of Western policies/ideologies, no longer as the executioner of the West, but as its enforcer.[101] As U.S. Secretary of State Warren Christopher mentioned in December 1995, right after the signing of the peace accords, "[w]ithout NATO's determined use of force, our diplomacy could not have brought the parties to the table. Without the prospect of a NATO implementation force, the parties would not have had the confidence to reach—and to implement—a comprehensive settlement. Without NATO, there would be no peace and no hope in Bosnia."[102]

NATO's troops, IFOR and later SFOR, sent to Bosnia to replace the old UNPROFOR mission, have become the new peacekeeping squadrons. Will they be forgiven if they fall, if they do not manage to bury the all too threatening radical foreignness of the Balkans? Already caught in the web of the West's ritual killings in Bosnia, NATO may no longer have the luxury of sacrificing another body. Then, like Peress perhaps, it may be asked to put its own "body" on the line, for the good of the international community. After all, this would be the logical consequence of what has become one of the main lessons of the Bosnian conflict: global diplomacy and peacekeeping strategies as sacrificial practices.

THE ERA OF SACRIFICIAL VIOLENCE

Sacrificing other bodies (NATO's strategy), sacrificing the body of the Other: this is how the liberal, democratic and supposedly peace-oriented strategies of interventionism deployed by the UN and NATO find their place within the Western visions of otherness in Bosnia. The UN's simulation of forceful intervention sacrificed the real (of Bosnia, of the Serbs, their singular causes, their dual relationships) for the sake of a supposedly more encompassing and safer world order. NATO's cathartic strategy of UN-scapegoating finally sacrificed this global imaginary supported by the UN in the hope that something could be saved for Western nations out of the Bosnian quandary. This is the point, as mentioned above, where direct discipline and physical coercion come to the rescue of and take over for failed simulation strategies. The symbolic killing (even if some blue-helmets actually died in the process) of the UN by NATO might have been a good sign for the Bosnians and the Serbs, who never fell for the simulation in the first place. But it actually marked and coincided with the death of Serbia's ambition and of Bosnia as well, the fatal destruction of their radical alterity, to use Baudrillard's notion. The Dayton Peace Agreement was nothing less than a death warrant for both Bosnia and Serbia, the sign that their foreignness (marked by the violence of their oppositions) was no longer on the ideological map of the Western world. The killing of the radical singularities of Bosnia, Serbia, or Croatia as anachronistic nation-states is what the visions of interventionism by the UN and NATO have finally led to. In their place, pseudoliberal sovereign states (the new Bosnian state) and disciplined nationalist entities (Serbia and Montenegro as the new Yugoslavia) have been created. In a sense, these are almost like the old UN "safe areas" in Bosnia: national enclaves that have been policed and cleansed of their ethnic energies, enervated states.

These sacrificial rites, performed by the West and its agents in the name of liberal democracy (the Balkans) or liberal capital (Eastern Europe), are what the so-called New World Order is made of. It is rather a new victim order, as Baudrillard so rightly points out. And the various interventions in Bosnia by the UN or NATO are the signs of a "victim society," which presents itself as "the easiest, most trivial form of otherness."[103]

Baudrillard also mentions that the Bosnians, the Serbs, the Somalis, all sorts of radical aliens, in other words, all those whose singularity has been sacrificed in the name of human morality, dignity, and justice, have started to deploy their vengeful strategies (what Baudrillard calls "the revenge of the mirror-people"). Baudrillard prophesies:

> Here begins the great revenge of otherness [alterity], of all the forms which, subtly or violently deprived of their singularity, henceforth pose an insoluble problem for the social order, and for the political and biological orders.[104]

Baudrillard believes and proclaims, as an incantation perhaps, the final (fatal?) success of radical alterity, of the radical aliens' negativity as opposed to the Western will to positivity through unanimity. This position echoes Girard's warning that catharsis and sacrificial killings may actually unleash more violence and raw forces than the "protected" community can sustain.[105]

Baudrillard's incantation about the vengeance of radical alterity needs to be tempered. This is where Althusser's lucid understanding of ideology, as was suggested earlier, is once again useful (the point where Baudrillard's postmodern analysis can be blended with Althusser's critical thinking). Ideology often presents itself as a no-escape mechanism, not so much because it is imposed from outside the subject (a superstructure exploiting a substructure), but because it relies on the subjects themselves, as a mode of self-disciplinization perhaps, to reproduce its values and belief systems (as was mentioned in chapter 3). This is the point where the key ideological processes of subjection and interpellation intervene, something that Baudrillard's analysis (or prophesy) tends to ignore here. With the help of Althusser, the question thus remains: what happens to the radical singularity of the people of the Balkans after the West has interpellated them into abiding by its values (peace, democracy), policies (free elections, resettlements), and culture (the sudden outburst of tourism and corporate investment in Croatia and Serbia after the war)? Althusser's notions of ideological interpellation and subjection,[106] as well as the more Foucauldian concepts of disciplinization and carceralization presented in earlier chapters, put a damper on Baudrillard's moment of radical euphoria.

And yet Baudrillard is not altogether incorrect. For, in their subjection to the West's ideological modes, through their reabsorption into the Western codes of otherness and global humanitarianism, the Serbs and the Bosnians have introduced a dose of uncertainty into the policies of the West, something that the Somalis had also done in their specific context. The Serbs and Bosnians have opened a breach in the West's ideological edifice and, in a sense, despite the success of the Dayton peace accords, have left the West with a plethora of questions: Can the democratic process succeed? How long will the West's military forces have to stay to monitor the situation (their mandate is constantly extended as if the West could no longer escape)? Will the Bosnian Serbs abide by the electoral process (in both general and municipal elections)? Will the populations want to be displaced and resettled? How long will NATO remain credible? What can be done with the UN now? Will other "Balkan traumas" emerge—in Kosovo, for example? Despite the imposition of a supra-ideological structure (through Western otherness and interventionism) over Bosnia, these questions are to a large extent beyond the West's or NATO's control. And here perhaps is where radical alterity resurfaces. It may be that the success of radical alterity, of the evil share as Baudrillard claims, resides here, in the continuous mode of uncertainty and questioning that the people of the Balkans, no longer as victims but as disciplined members of the new international community, have triggered.

In fact, this may be the way Baudrillard's radical alterity is still meaningful today in Bosnia, and in the practice of international affairs in general: as a mode of uncertainty, confusion, and insecurity that, after all, the West itself has caused, through its own policies and strategies. Such a mode of inherent uncertainty or internal questioning was perhaps to what Trio's pop art was drawing our attention. Just like Baudrillard's prophesy on the "revenge of the mirror people," Trio's artistic *détournement* caught the irony of the Western ideological project, its accursed share, the fact that by multiplying its own ideological/cultural signs all over the international landscape (to the detriment of local singularities and particularisms) the West was simultaneously multiplying its own cancerous cells, the negations of and oppositions to its own ideological order already contained within. This metastasis is perhaps what was so fatal about the visions of otherness and interventionism of the West in Bosnia. And so, waiting for more to happen in Bosnia or somewhere else, why not sadistically rejoice, with the Bosnians and the Serbs perhaps (or, at least, with Baudrillard and Trio), at the idea that, through its pathetic visions, the West, a certain ideological vision of the West, is slowly self-destructing?

5

A Taste of Their Own Medicine: Medical Assistance and Humanitarianism as Substitutes for UN Peacekeeping

L'action humanitaire ne fonctionne pas seulement comme une ambulance et ses adeptes comme des brancardiers. Il s'agit d'un regard, d'une méthode, d'une morale. (Humanitarian action does not only work like an ambulance, and its followers are not only like medics. It is first of all a gaze, a method, and a morality.)

— BERNARD KOUCHNER, "VIVE L'HUMANITAIRE D'ÉTAT" (LONG LIVE STATE HUMANITARIANISM)

"This emptying out of interiority to the benefit of its exterior signs, this exhaustion of the content by the form," which, according to Roland Barthes, is the very principle of triumphant classical art, is also at the basis of humanitarianism as a spectacle.

— RONY BRAUMAN, *DEVANT LE MAL: RWANDA, UN GÉNOCIDE EN DIRECT* (FACED WITH EVIL: RWANDA, WITNESSING LIVE A GENOCIDE)

Over all [the] endeavours on the part of clinical thought . . . hovers the great myth of a pure Gaze that would be pure Language: a speaking eye [that] would scan the entire hospital field, taking in and gathering together each of the singular events that occurred within it; and as it saw, as it saw even more clearly, it would be turned into speech that states and teaches. . . . This speaking eye would be the servant of things and the master of truth.

— MICHEL FOUCAULT, *THE BIRTH OF THE CLINIC*

BOUNDLESS MEDICINE, UNFRAMED VISIONS

A United States–sponsored operation to bring relief supplies to the Kurds of Northern Iraq, a UN peacekeeping mission in war-torn Somalia, NGOs in Sudan fighting a famine, "safe havens" in Bosnia, French doctors in Goma, Zaire, trying to eradicate a cholera epidemic among Rwanda's refugees: humanitarianism is back with a vengeance! The recent resurrection of humanitarian interventionism, freed from the political polemics of the cold war, would probably have remained unnoticed if Western media had not chosen to highlight those new international hotspots. In a post–cold war era, and in the spirit of disciplinary liberalism, medical catastrophes and civil wars are prized commodities. They give Western states and the UN the opportunity to put their liberal humanistic policies into practice, while, for Western media, humanitarianism simply sells. For these reasons, no humanitarian tragedy can exist nowadays without its visual support, which often enhances it in a most spectacular manner. This is not to say, of course, that the media create the tragedies. Rather, a natural catastrophe or an ethnic conflict become ideally fused with mediatic productions to give rise to post–cold war humanitarianism as a hybrid techno-medical formation.[1]

It is perhaps as a mediatically generated sign, deprived of any ethical or altruistic content, that humanitarianism may best be studied. The many interventions by sovereign states, the United Nations, or NGOs that have proliferated all over the post–cold war international landscape, brandishing the flag of medical assistance, peace, food relief, and so on, may be read as popular sound or video bytes that circulate on a humanitarian orbit that rarely connects with the everyday realities of international life where, as usual, states disappear, governments are overthrown, conflicts develop, and people are killed. The desired effects of the global humanitarian spectacle are for Western audiences which, living in liberal-democratic, and mostly evil-cleansed and anarchy-free societies, are demanding their daily doses of "real-life" drama and "real-time" fear.

As Rony Brauman, former president of Médecins sans Frontières (Doctors without Borders), suggests in the above quotation, international humanitarianism is a *myth*, and the various post–cold war humanitarian scenes are individual *mythologies* that mediatically contribute to the production of such a global fiction. Roland Barthes has theorized that in a myth,

> the most socially inspired nuances of passion (conceit, rightfulness, refined cruelty, a sense of "paying one's debts") always felicitously find the clearest sign which can receive them, express them and triumphantly carry them to the confines [of the international order]. It is obvious that at such a pitch, it no longer matters whether the passion is genuine or not. What the public wants is the image of passion, not passion itself.[2]

It is under this condition of myth that (as mythmakers) medical and humanitarian NGOs, like the Médecins sans Frontières (MSF) organization (whose mythological practice in the recent Rwandan conflict is the guiding line of this chapter), become our last action heroes, our remote-controlled Doctor Schweitzers, so to speak. They simulate heroism, sentiment, and compassion in a global mediascape where the globalizing neoliberal policies of Western states and international organizations (like the UN) have been imposed as the only possible scenario and as our ultimate hope mechanism.

In the perspective of this chapter, analyzing humanitarian and medical interventions as myths is only a first step toward a more critical examination of the ideological roles and functions of the humanitarian industry in a New World Order. Humanitarianism is not only a good media storyline. It also serves an ideological purpose in a global process of governance (order) and normalization (law), and in specific situations where the peacekeeping policies of the UN or the power-enforcing interventions of Western states (through NATO, for example) are less appropriate. Put simply, the medico-humanitarian *gaze* (as Kouchner puts it)[3] of organizations like MSF, and their power of penetration inside territories where the presence of the UN is not desirable or not required, contributes to the reinforcement of neoliberal policies in "pathological" regions of the international landscape. It does so by spreading an ideology of unity and solidarity, a sacred union of all the Enlightenment principles (morality, fairness, human dignity, fraternal assistance, etc.) against the forces of evil and destruction (ethnic separatism, totalitarianism, barbarian customs, etc.), that relies on the mediatic effects of medical interventions and compassion. Here, it is once again a matter of turning to the visual to create "reality-effects." Similar perhaps to the "clinical gaze" of nineteenth-century doctors (analyzed by Michel Foucault in *The Birth of the Clinic*), the ideology of humanitarianism sustained by medical NGOs like MSF redistributes the space of international pathology-anarchy and transforms it into a realm of normality-order. It also contributes to the formation of the New World Order as a purified and de-pathologized environment, a secure and truthful domain of action and transaction.

Given these considerations, I find an ideological analysis of the humanitarian phenomenon particularly interesting in the larger context of the UN's post–cold war peacekeeping operations. As was witnessed in Rwanda, humanitarian organizations like MSF, the Red Cross, Care International, Oxfam, or MDM (Médecins du Monde [Doctors of the World], an offshoot of MSF) served as substitutes for the United Nations, whose agencies did not intervene until the crisis was well advanced. When the myth of UN peacekeeping as an interpellating mechanism is not adequate (an urgent regulatory action, that the UN could not provide, was required in Rwanda), organizations like Doctors without Borders can still transcend territorial boundaries in order to impose an ideology of worldwide unity that, by and large, the United Nations had been in charge of implementing since the early 1990s.

In order to consider the strategic and ideological motivations of global humanitarianism, one needs, however, to become a "reader of myths," as Barthes puts it. Indeed, "if one wishes to connect a [humanitarian] mythical schema to a general history, to explain how it corresponds to the interests of a definite society, in short, to pass from semiology to ideology," it is in the position of the reader of myths that one must place oneself.[4] For the reader of myths "consumes the myth according to the very ends built into its structure" and "lives the myth as a story at once true and unreal."[5] Keeping this method in mind, I initiate the reading of medical humanitarianism with a brief look at the myth of the "French Doctors" in Rwanda. Once again, this reading of the humanitarian mythology of MSF is more than an anecdote or an illustrative adornment of the theoretical argument of this chapter. As indicated above, the notion of myth is essential to the condition of international humanitarianism today.

HUMANITARIAN MYTHOLOGIES

May 5, 1989. The front page of the French weekly news magazine *L'Express* reads: "L'Epopée des Médecins sans Frontières" (Doctors without Borders' epic). A picture is juxtaposed to the headline: a French Doctor is holding a Southeast Asian male child in his arms, in front of a light-blue sea and sky seascape. The child is looking at us, the (myth) readers. He is smiling. But the doctor is turning his back to us. He is wearing a white t-shirt with the red emblem of "Médecins du Monde" (MDM) on it: a red dove holding an olive branch. The humanitarian savior's face does not need to be seen. It does not matter who he is (the haircut indicates that the faceless hero is probably male) or what he looks like. The "French Doctors" have no face. They all are interchangeable. They are sent all over the world, accept their mission, know their duty, and refuse to be considered as the new international-assistance heroes. What truly matters is the cause that they serve. Since the child is Asian and the picture shows a seascape, the reader may assume that the medic is on a humanitarian mission in the Sea of China, probably rescuing Vietnamese or Cambodian "Boat People." In the mid-1970s, the rescue of the "Boat People" was one of the highly mediatic missions of the MSF organization, a mission that gave MSF and other organizations (like MDM) their international reputation. This is where the "French Doctors' epic" truly started. The doctor looks toward the horizon: a world of humanitarian conquests is opening in front of his eyes. The child he is holding is only one of the many victims whom he and his courageous colleagues, a new breed of peacekeepers, will have to save. The front page of *L'Express* marks the birth of a new world, a new mediatized era of international humanitarianism. As Kouchner puts it, "the great adventure of the twenty-first century is just beginning. Its name: humanitarianism."[6]

And here is now another example: I am at the barber's, and a copy of Paris-Match *is offered to me. On the cover, a young Negro in a French uniform is saluting, with his eyes uplifted, probably fixed on a fold of the tricolour. All this is the meaning of the picture. But, whether naïvely or not, I see very well what it signifies to me: that France is a great Empire, that all her sons, without any colour discrimination, faithfully serve under her flag, and that there is no better answer to the detractors of an alleged colonialism than the zeal*

shown by this negro in serving his so-called oppressors. I am there-
fore again faced with a greater semiological system: there is a signi-
fier, itself already formed with a previous system (a black soldier is
giving the French salute); there is a signified (it is here a purposeful
mixture of Frenchness and militariness); finally, there is a presence of
the signified through the signifier.[7]

> The criteria for intervention are never a problem for the doctor, the
> medic, or the rescuer who is called to take care of a person in distress.
> It is simply a matter of saving lives. An emergency, an imminent dan-
> ger: there's no other consideration. What would you say if your local
> paramedics had to question themselves, procrastinate, weigh the pros
> and cons of their actions, check the resume of their patients, ask for a
> special authorization, a mandate, or an official approval prior to res-
> cuing people? Well, humanitarian criteria are not different at all when
> the victims of a natural or political catastrophe can only hope for for-
> eign assistance.[8]

It is on the basis of similar principles that humanitarian organizations
like Médecins sans Frontières intervened in Rwanda in the spring
and summer of 1994.[9] Some of them were present when the massacres started in April. They witnessed the massacres of the Tutsis of
Rwanda by the Hutus in "real time," even though, at that time, the
Western media were not fully aware of the situation. Shortly afterward, hordes of "humanitarians" came along with Western journalists once the first camps of Hutu refugees began to be organized in
Zaire or Tanzania. Having, by and large, missed the first flow of victims (Tutsi victims for the most part), they were nonetheless ready to
assume their emergency medical assistance in the cholera-plagued
refugee camps. Here again, an image says it all. We find it on the
cover of former "French Doctor" turned essayist Alain Destexhe's
book *Rwanda: Essai sur le génocide* (Rwanda: An essay on genocide).[10] A man is dying in the arms of a woman, possibly his wife or
mother. The background has been blurred on purpose. Still, the
reader can see that there are some tents, people waiting in line (for
food, water, medical treatment?), and assistance workers moving
around the refugees. Here again, the focus is directly placed on the
victims, on their obvious agony, their soon-to-be death. The relief
workers (doctors, nurses, logisticians, water-suppliers, etc.) once
again perform their task in the shadows. They do not have time to

have a face or a name. They are here to "save lives." "What brought them here is clear. Only the calls of the victims, their screams, their blood justify their presence," as Kouchner intimates.[11] The picture of this refugee camp on the cover of Destexhe's book is yet another visual mythology in which the ideology of rescuing and saving lives is connoted. The medical worker does not care whether the victim is Hutu or Tutsi. It does not even matter to the "humanitarians" if they have been allowed by the local authorities to work here or not. They simply apply what is now known as their "principle of humanitarian interference" (what the "French Doctors" call their *droit d'ingérence*). This is their mission and their ideology. This is why they are doctors *without borders* (my emphasis). Their presence in this refugee camp is not only explained by their acute sense of medical duty, moral responsibility, or fraternal compassion. It is also the mark of a newly enforced ideology that transcends territorial, racial, and political barriers. With them, humanitarianism becomes a universal doctrine that claims that, in a liberal democratic world order, no life should be lost in vain. Through this picture (from its clear focus on the victim to its blurred background of humanitarian aid), the myth of humanitarianism as an ideology of unity is signified. Kouchner, founder of MSF, had already identified this ideology: "By uniting our responses, we shall create an ethics, give the humanitarian method its own discourse, and forge tomorrow's politics in the face of the emerging struggle of the South against the North and the poor against the rich."[12] But the image of a camp of Rwandan refugees on the cover of Destexhe's book reveals the presence of the humanitarian myth and its ideology just as well as Kouchner's text does. What you need to know about humanitarianism is already there, as an innocent myth that, as Barthes puts it, "transforms history into nature" and hides a "semiological [and ideological] system" behind a taken-for-granted morality.[13]

But what must be firmly established at the start is that myth is a system of communication, that it is a message . . . it is a mode of signification, a form. . . . It can be seen that to purport to discriminate among mythical objects according to their substance would be entirely illusory: since myth is a type of speech, everything can be a myth provided it is conveyed by discourse. Myth is not defined by the object of its message, but by the way in which it utters this message: there are formal limits to myth, there are no "substantial" ones. Everything, then, can be a myth? Yes, I believe this, for the universe is infinitely fertile in suggestions. Every object in the world can pass from a closed, silent existence to an oral state, open to appropriation by society, for there is no law, whether natural or not, which forbids talking about things. . . . Speech of this kind is a message. It is therefore by no means confined to oral speech. It can consist of modes of writing or of representations; not only written discourse, but also photography, cinema, reporting, sport, shows, publicity, all these can serve as a support to mythical speech. . . . [W]e are no longer dealing here with a theoretical mode of representation: we are dealing with this particular image, which is given for this particular signification. Mythical speech is made of a material which has already been worked on so as to make it suitable for communication: it is because all the materials of myth (whether pictorial or written) presuppose a signifying consciousness, that one can reason about them while discounting their substance. This substance is not unimportant: pictures, to be sure, are more imperative than writing, they impose meaning at one stroke, without analysing or diluting it. But this is no longer a constitutive difference. Pictures become a kind of writing as soon as they are meaningful: like writing, they call for a lexis.[14]

What does it mean, then, to read humanitarianism as a myth? For Rony Brauman, former director of MSF, the answer is clear. Humanitarianism today is a myth because it is above all a constructed (visual) message. Humanitarian interventions, like the recent one in Rwanda, are mediatic productions staged on purpose to attract Western audiences and, from time to time, politicians.[15] As what may be called a "humanitarian fundamentalist," Brauman regrets and resents this reappropriation of international medical assistance by other self-interested causes. Because humanitarianism has been "reduced" to a myth,[16] Brauman claims, real humanitarian and moral issues have been overlooked. It is because images have been purged of their content by the media ("an emptying of interiority to the benefit of external signs," as Brauman suggested above) that the genocide of Tutsi populations in Rwanda has not been recognized.[17] Brauman here displays a more radical liberal attitude that consists of claiming that the artificiality of the media and their creations distorts the real conditions of human existence. Interestingly, Brauman combines this position with a basic "humanitarian fundamentalism" that argues for a purity of humanitarian action, cleansed of political (state humanitarianism) and mediatic (tabloid humanitarianism) motivations. From this perspective, myth becomes the enemy of true humanitarianism, which, though difficult to achieve, remains nonetheless feasible (given a reintroduction of the right humanitarian values). For Brauman, as the mythical treatment of humanitarianism in Rwanda reveals, a return to the basic principles of humanitarian action requires denunciation of the presence of myth and an attempt to subvert it by providing written testimonies of what actually happens in the "real world" of humanitarianism. Brauman is, however, totally blind to the fact that his antimythical written testimonies and (re)moralizing pamphlets may themselves be some other forms of myth. For, with his own ideological message, Brauman seeks to make humanitarianism "pass from a closed, silent existence to an oral state" (Barthes) open to his own reappropriations. At this point, Brauman's desire to reappropriate the "humanitarian myth" (to return it to an ideal stage of virgin purity) may be antihegemonic, but it still remains embedded in ideology.

This irony is something that Brauman, and the current of humanitarian thought he supports (which is almost as predominant in humanitarian circles as the ideology of unity promoted by Kouchner), cannot admit to. Brauman is stuck with a limited conception of myth, one that retains from Barthes only the critical media analysis. But, as was mentioned above, myth is also and perhaps more importantly the mark of ideology, its very presence. It is the form (one of the many possible forms) an ideology takes in contemporary societies. To use an Althusserian terminology, myth is an interpellative mechanism: its message suggests a position or a situation for the reader to adopt, discard, accept, reject, and, in any case, become familiar with. As such, myth is perhaps the equivalent in semiological terms of what interpellation is in ideological terms (from Barthes, the "reader of myths" to Althusser, the "reader of ideology"). Caught in his own ideological battle, Brauman cannot appreciate the richness of the semiological and ideological nuances offered by the humanitarian myth. He merely consumes it en bloc and, as Barthes's cynical myth-reader, "finds [himself] before a simple system, where the signification becomes literal again"[18] (the humanitarian myth is merely a media construct that distorts real life). According to this interpretation, the scenes of humanitarian mythology described before simply signify the presence of the media and their desire for spectacularity (media ideology). But, in the meantime, other ideological dimensions, connecting the visual myth to other histories, are not allowed to exist. For instance, the ideology of a "new beginning" (the ontological moment of post–cold war humanitarianism) present in the picture on the cover of *L'Express,* as suggested above, is not recognized because, once again, it is read only as a "media scoop" used to glorify the story of the "French Doctors." Similarly, the ideology of unity and solidarity and its ramifications for New World Order policies, for example, are not seen in the picture on the cover of Destexhe's book because it is simply about the media showing a "good victim." As Brauman puts it, "[w]hat a great opportunity to thus see a genocide transformed into a vast humanitarian theater where everyone, from the survivors and the accomplices to the innocents and the torturers, finally plays what from now on is their only desirable role, that of the victim."[19] There is, to be sure, some truth to Brauman's interpretation. But his vision of the myth is mostly the product of his own resentment (of not having been there when the first massacres took place? of having lost what he considers to be pure humanitarian intervention?), which he directs toward the media and state humanitarianism (his personal conflict with Kouchner, for example).[20]

The humanitarian myth today comes to us as a series of texts (written and pictorial as Barthes puts it) that proliferate bits of meaning about the contemporary ideology of humanitarianism, and other ideologies attached to the international humanitarian enterprise. Sometimes, the meaning of the mythical text (intended by the author, the media, etc.) may be missed by the reader. Sometimes, another meaning may be privileged. Sometimes, the mythical text becomes another text and another ideology, as the reader forms his own myth. This is what Bathes calls the "writerly text." In a later work,[21] Barthes argues that "the goal of literary work (of literature as work) is to make the reader no longer a consumer, but a producer of the text."[22] Barthes continues:

> The writerly text is not a thing, we would have a hard time finding it in a bookstore. . . . [T]o rewrite the writerly text would consist only in disseminating it, in dispersing it within the field of infinite difference. The writerly text is a perpetual present, upon which no *consequent*

language (which would inevitably make it past) can be super-imposed; the writerly text is *ourselves writing,* before the infinite play of the world (the world as function) is traversed, intersected, stopped, plasticized by some singular system (Ideology, Genus, Criticism) which reduces the plurality of entrances, the opening of networks, the infinity of languages.[23]

The field of dispersion and difference that is our own reading/writing of myth is "intersected, stopped, and plasticized" (to use Barthes's terminology) by Brauman's ideological deciphering of the humanitarian spectacle. In contrast to his ideological repositioning, my reading seeks not to close the myth (however risky this enterprise might be) by imposing a dogmatic signature upon it. The images that have been treated earlier as myths may reveal mediatic distortions of the humanitarian ideal (Brauman). Or they may indicate the birth and the presence of an ideology of sacred union in post–cold war international affairs (Kouchner's approach). Finally, those images-as-myths may also mobilize humanitarianism as an ideology of post–cold war international relations that combines the two previous readings. This is the reading of humanitarianism (its writerly text) that I offer in this chapter. One may read the humanitarian myth as the sign/presence of an ideology of global and fraternal unity or solidarity that symptomatically needs an abundance of mediatic overproductions and hyperrealizations in order to display reality effects throughout the international landscape (it is through the mobilization of visual media that such an ideology may interpellate individuals and states worldwide). Such a reading of the humanitarian myth is no doubt commensurate with the readings of disciplinary (neo)liberal ideologies of global governance (through UN peacekeeping or other simulated techniques) performed in the previous chapters. Yet, in suggesting this possible reading (my writerly text of contemporary humanitarian myths), I am in no way intending to impose this vision as a final word on the humanitarian question today. Rather, this reading-as-rewriting offers a visual and textual point of entry into humanitarianism that allows us to openly investigate the myth and assess, in a continued process of reading, whether the ideological postulates posed earlier are adequate (to the myth itself). By privileging the Barthesian "writerly" position, the intent is not to let the analysis fall prey to prepackaged theories and prearranged conclusions. Along the continued investigation of humanitarianism, the myth is rewritten, reworked; it is alive, it evolves. It remains to be seen, however, where the humanitarian myth takes us and how (in what forms? for what specific purposes? etc.) the ideological postulates introduced earlier present themselves in the field of theoretical and textual dispersion that is post–cold war international affairs. I start this enterprise with a comprehensive historical/genealogical survey of the notion of humanitarianism. Understanding where humanitarianism, as a concept, a trope, and an ideology, comes from will help us to read this myth in a less dogmatic fashion than that provided by, among others, humanitarian leaders and thinkers like Brauman and Kouchner.

FROM SOLFERINO TO SARAJEVO, OR HOW INTERNATIONAL PATHOLOGIES FINALLY FIND THEIR HUMANITARIAN CURES

And Jesus answering said, A certain man went down from Jerusalem to Jericho, and fell among thieves, which stripped him of his raiment, and wounded him, and departed, leaving him half dead.

And by chance there came down a certain priest that way; and when he saw him, he passed by on the other side.

And likewise a Levite, when he was at the place, came and looked on him, and passed by on the other side.

But a certain Samaritan, as he journeyed, came as he was; and when he saw him, he had compassion on him.

And went to him, and bound up his wounds, pouring in oil and wine, and set him on his own beast, and brought him to an inn, and took care of him.

And on the morrow when he departed, he took out two pence, and gave them to the host, and said unto him, Take care of him; and whatsoever thou spendest more, when I come again, I will repay thee.

Which now of these three, thinkest thou, was neighbour unto him that fell among the thieves?

And he said, He that shewed mercy on him. Then said Jesus unto him, Go, and do thou likewise.

—Luke 10:25–37

Christian Foundations

In the West, the myth of humanitarianism is intricately tied to the history of Christianity. From Luke's parable of the "Good Samaritan" to the lives of the saints, Christian humanitarianism is above all a matter of religious responsibility. The faith in God and in his precepts leads the Christian faithful to adopt humanitarianism as his/her life strategy. As St. Augustine intimates in his *City of God*, the life of the Christian subject on earth is a life of charity. For Augustine, "the one who proposes to love God and his neighbor as himself, not according to man but according to God, is without doubt said because of this love to be a man of good will. This good will is most commonly called 'charity'."[24] Love of God thus finds its expression and fulfillment in acts of good will.

There is, however, a payoff to such a charitable life: all good deeds on earth will be rewarded by the final ascension to God's Kingdom. Conversely, he who is not interested in pursuing such a life will be the victim of "God's wrath" (Augustine) on Judgment Day. And so, out of love (for the faithful), but more importantly out of fear, Christians have imposed the commandment "Love thy neighbor" as one of the basic tenets of Western civilization. The influence of Christianity on European civilization has propagated this belief system and has perpetuated an ideology of altruism (caring for the other), supposedly exemplified by Jesus' own sacrifice.[25]

The notion of human charity and good will is one of the many ways Christian thought has interpellated its subjects into conforming to the humanitarian norm. Since humanitarian assistance (rewritten by Christians as neighborly love) has its foundations in the holy texts, helping one's fellow creature is no longer (was it ever?) an instinctive act that one individual may undertake (or not) upon seeing another being in need. Rather, human charity becomes the mark of civilization, the sign of an enlightened humanity (enlightened by God, and later by human reason) which is revealed in religious texts and norms. An individual's purely autonomous will to assist or not assist another human being in distress or in need is denied to the benefit of a higher religious and moral principle, which commands that human beings act according to recognized precepts of altruism. Duty takes over preference. And the victim becomes a prized moral commodity, a totemic emblem of pity, instead of being a pathetic and embarrassing burden to society (as it often was the case in ancient tribal or military societies). A good victim now calls for (Christian) love whereas s/he used to evoke disdain.[26] Along with the privileged position given to the victim (as that which allows the Christian ideology to be mobilized), human charity becomes a codified practice, a law that, when transgressed (or overlooked), is accompanied by its just punishment, come Judgment Day. Even prior to the grand codifications of legal texts (with the creation of modern nation-states and the first principles of international law in the seventeenth and eighteenth centuries), humanitarianism and its corollary altruistic ideology are more than life strategies, chosen by compassionate individuals who have decided to dedicate their lives to unfortunate others. Humanitarianism and altruistic ideology also presuppose an acceptance of moral and behavioral norms, an adherence to a standard of action and thinking from the subjects who live by such an ideology. Indeed, as the parable of the "Good Samaritan" demonstrates, the Christian ideology of altruism and charity reinscribes humanitarian action in absolute antagonistic terms such as good and evil (a universal good versus a universal evil, God versus Satan). It is according to such an absolute dichotomy that, in their interactions with their fellow Christian subjects, human beings are now judged.

The Rule of Reason and the Requirements of Civil Society

The demystification of God through the revelation of human reason[27] performed by the moderns does very little to modify the Christian humanitarian motif. Instead of recognizing God as the final judge, civil society becomes the marker for what is moral or not.[28] Contracts are passed among individuals, and laws are written to guarantee the development of human life purged of all the causes of division, namely, "competition, diffidence and glory."[29] To ensure that the laws are enforced, state discipline, based on deterrence and punishment, is "voluntarily" created.[30] For modern man, the belief system may no longer be God. But reason emerges as a substitute belief mechanism. By directing human actions, reason is the ultimate guide to moral life.

Reason teaches that it is to the advantage of every individual to live in a collectivity of interdependent beings where the interests of one single individual are intimately and ultimately connected to the common will (as sustained by contractual and communitarian theories). Helping one's neighbor does not only come out of fondness of heart (or love of God). Rather, since a man's property and security depend upon the solidity of the social compact, it would be irrational for a member of the collective not to assist his neighbor.[31] By failing to do so, man would put his own prerogatives in jeopardy. Humanitarianism in the age of the social contract becomes a duty imposed from outside (the collective, the state, the laws), yet made to look as if it comes from an individual being's most sovereign and personal faculty, reason. Such is the mystifying belief deployed by the Enlightenment. The social-contract philosophers have managed to successfully sacrifice the individual will at the altar of communitarianism, while keeping the pretense of liberty and free choice. Under the dictatorship of reason, humanitarianism looks like a voluntary action, but it is in fact a conditioned, regulated, and (as mentioned before) disciplinary practice. Those in society who decide not to exert their humanitarian faculty when they have the possibility, indeed the duty, to do so must finally be either deterred or punished.[32] In the modern state, under the rule of reason, the humanitarian ideology takes the shape of a communitarian ideal. In a communitarian spirit, the humanitarian standards are clad in a rhetoric of social responsibility, collective morality, and reasonable choice.[33] Humanitarianism in society becomes a "universal imperative," whose transgression results in a punishment (exclusion, incarceration, deprivation of property) that is no longer postponed (as it was with the Christian Judgment Day) but is often immediate (nonassistance to an endangered fellow citizen sends you to jail).

War and Humanitarianism

If the practice of altruistic assistance is codified within the state by the seventeenth and eighteenth centuries, humanitarianism is still largely absent from the international scene until the late nineteenth century. Humanitarianism across nations emerges through the practice of war. The notion of "lawful warfare" (or just war) introduced by sixteenth- and seventeenth-century humanist and scholastic jurists (Erasmus, Vitoria, Grotius) is at the origin of the notion of humanitarian assistance in the international affairs of sovereign states. The principle of "lawful warfare" maintains that "it is not contrary . . . to the nature of society to look out for oneself and advance one's own interests, provided the rights of others are not infringed; and consequently the use of force which does not violate the rights of others is not unjust."[34] This doctrine reconciles the bellicose aspirations of sovereigns with a liberal humanist ideology of respect for one's enemies and recognition of the individual's human dignity. Force, by means of war, is necessary for a nation to protect itself. But humane principles must be included to regulate pure power. Among these principles, the protection of the fallen enemies (sparing their lives) is seen by Grotius as a prerequisite. The injured enemy is no longer to be seen as an opponent but as a victim.

Grotius, among other international thinkers of early modernity, combines Christian precepts with the modern notion of reason[35] to arrive at the creation of a body of doctrines (what will later be called international law) that shall make sure that, in the absence of a social pact between states, human dignity is nonetheless recognized, and human life is not "unjustly" sacrificed. Here, it is a combination of divine law and human reason that gives rise to what Grotius calls the "law of nations." Anticipating some of Hobbes's moves perhaps, Grotius suggests that reason is not inherently altruistic but, rather, drives an individual to consider his protection and survival as a priority. International law, according to Grotius, also offers the guarantee that a nation and its members will survive in case of a conflict with a neighbor state (lawful warfare is placed under the condition that it is natural, as was mentioned above, "to look out for oneself and advance one's own interests"). Formally, international law is deployed to protect the lives of the individuals who have been called to defend the national territory from foreign invasions, and, as a reciprocal principle, the enemy soldiers will have to be protected too. There is a sense, then, in which the regulations imposed by Grotius's "lawful warfare" are designed to preserve and serve the interests of states. It is only a fortuitous consequence if the lives of foreign victims are saved as well. The Christian altruistic principles that Grotius is so eager to perpetuate and combine with a more rational discourse (a discourse of rights) are, in fact, only the side effects of a more strategic project that seeks to protect sovereign states in their international relations. Until the second half of the nineteenth century, humanitarianism is, by and large, confined to the spatial and ideological limits of Western liberal-democratic states and their liberal communitarian ideals. In international politics, humanitarian assistance is merely an ideal whose rare and lucky applications are the result of the need for self-preservation of states.

The Red Cross Principles

I have never claimed that I was a spectator of the battles of San Martino and Solferino. That is something of which no one can boast, for such battles as those can never be seen, but only the din of them heard. What I did see were

the horrors of Solferino at the little town called Castiglione della Pieve, near which the great battle of June 24 began. There it was that I was so overcome with compassion, horror, and pity that I became the "Samaritan of Solferino" as people chose to call me because I tried to be useful.
— HENRY DUNANT, *A MEMORY OF SOLFERINO*

Henry Dunant, the new "Samaritan" of modern warfare, had seen enough (too much, in fact) in Solferino to know what he had to do. Dunant decided that, in the international affairs of states, the focus could no longer be placed on war as a strategy of survival for states, but on the consequences of wars from a humanitarian perspective, and on the fate of the victims. It is after this battle between the French and the Austrians (in 1859), during which he tried to organize first-aid relief for the wounded soldiers, that the "Samaritan of Solferino" found the moral strength to create what, a few years later, would become the Red Cross. With Dunant and his *Memory of Solferino,* a new chapter in the history of humanitarianism is open. Wars can no longer justify human suffering. A neutral force must be created, composed of first-aid volunteers, nurses, doctors, water suppliers, and others, to intervene anytime a human or natural catastrophe takes place. Dunant enunciates the principles of Red Cross humanitarian assistance in the following terms:

> [s]ocieties of this kind, once formed and their permanent existence assured, would naturally remain inactive in peacetime. But they would be always organized and ready for the possibility of war. They would have not only to secure the goodwill of the authorities of the countries in which they had been formed, but also, in case of war, to solicit from the rulers of the belligerent states authorization and facilities enabling them to do effective work. . . . The committees would appeal to everybody who, for sincerely philanthropic motives, would undertake to devote himself for the time to this charitable work. The work itself would consist in bringing aid and relief (in agreement with the military commissaries, i.e., when necessary with their support and under their instructions) onto the battlefield whenever battle was joined, and subsequently to continue to care the wounded in the hospitals until convalescence was complete.[36]

The altruistic and communitarian components of humanitarianism are maintained. But Dunant adds to them a new apolitical dimension by dissociating Red Cross interventionism from the affairs of states. The Red Cross and its members operate on an ideological basis summarized by the slogan "tutti fratelli" (all are brothers),[37] an ideology that refuses to discriminate among victims. It is at this precise historical moment that humanitarianism, turned apolitical and transnational by the work of Henry Dunant, adopts an ideology of international solidarity and unity[38] that it has retained until today (as witnessed by Kouchner's interpretation of the work of Médecins sans Frontières). The Red Cross ideology introduced by Dunant allows individuals to rediscover love for their neighbors (in a so-called politically disinterested manner). It also initiates, as French Christian moralist/jurist Jean Lossier puts it, "the building of a new civilization, which would take over all the previous religious and scientific ones" by being placed under "the idea of service" and the notion of active fraternity.[39]

The battle of Solferino built Dunant's reputation as a "good Samaritan" and initiated a process of international humanitarianism based on treaties and institutions.[40] Yet, as he himself acknowledged, Dunant was nothing more than "a mere tourist" who took the appearance of a Samaritan.[41] Dunant was never able to rid himself of the guilt he felt from witnessing the massacres and not being able to do anything to stop them. As he put it, "[t]he feeling one has of one's own inadequacy in such extraordinary and solemn circumstances is unspeakable."[42] Dunant's inadequacy, and his realization that, after all, he was only a Samaritan of circumstance, caught in a battle that he never thought would turn him into an active protagonist, reveals dimensions of his Red Cross project that a strictly denotative reading may not recognize. Indeed, beyond Dunant's grand philanthropic objectives, his desire to cope with what he saw in northern Italy also plays a major role in the birth of the Red Cross. Seen at this angle (that of Dunant's own psychological response to his felt inadequacy), the Red Cross functions as a support group for guilt-ridden neutral observers like Dunant himself. Dunant's Red Cross becomes a mechanism that seeks to reempower those whose fear of physical injury drove them away from combat by giving them a "moral" justification (and a pretense of involvement) for their neutrality. The Red Cross does not only open up a new era of humanitarian action at a denotative level (new international rules, principles, organizations are created), but, moreover, at a connotative level, the Red Cross and Dunant's work operate a reversal of value by turning neutrality into a valued principle and a humanitarian force.[43] Today, in an age of televisually mediated reality, when scenes of violent battles are no longer reported by a remote observer but are consumed live by Western TV audiences at dinner time, humanitarian organizations and their so-called neutral interventions function as conscience-cleaning mechanisms and hope devices, not so much for the victims that they are helping, but, above all, for the moral, altruistic, and charitable ideologies in liberal societies that they are really trying to save. This is a reality of contemporary international humanitarianism that Dunant's experience, and the creation of the Red Cross as an international safety net, help to understand. In fact, we may have to consider Henry Dunant more as a victim of the humanitarian ideology than as one of its heroes. After all, he too fell prey to the interpellating mechanisms that, in a humanistico-altruistic perspective, Western civilization (from its Judeo-Christian heritage to its liberal-communitarian ideals) mobilizes. It is his conditioned belief in society and his disdain for what he considered to be useless deaths that led to his apparent guilty conscience as an observer of human drama (later transformed into a rescuer) and to the creation of the Red Cross.

The Humanitarian System of the United Nations

Until the creation of the United Nations, international humanitarianism remains, by and large, a monopoly of the Red Cross and its institutional regime. In the twentieth century, the Red Cross becomes a universal emblem of assistance, accepted by most nations and recognized by most people. Still, the humanitarian privilege acquired by the Red Cross causes ideological hostilities, as the Red Cross is confronted with human crises it cannot solve (world wars, genocides, famines, etc.). Challenges to the Red Cross, after World War II in particular, come from two distinct sources: sovereign states and their international organizations such as the UN; and humanitarian purists such as nongovernmental medical organizations.

Humanitarianism through the UN system appears to be a way for states to recuperate international assistance, and rechannel the Red Cross activities through more controllable and bureaucratic networks. The UN's humanitarian machinery is not an alternative to the Red Cross as a transnational ideology of unity.[44] It is rather a process of institutional recolonization of Dunant's humanitarian project, now explicitly placed at the service of some of the UN's member states (the winners of World War II). Put differently, the universalizing ideology of the Red Cross, under a humanitarian alibi, is recycled by the UN, legally perfected, and given the political means to affirm itself in the practice of international affairs. Thus, the UN Charter inaugurates an institutional and legal system of "collective defense . . . for the maintenance of world peace"[45] that not only seeks to put an end to international conflicts but, more importantly, intends to humanize international affairs.

The archetypal illustration of such a normalized system of humanitarian law placed under UN auspices is what is known as the Geneva Conventions of 1949. According to this set of conventions "for the protection of war victims," "persons who are not combatants [must] be treated in a humane manner by the prohibition of such practices as the taking of hostages, illegal executions of certain categories of those involved in armed conflicts, and the use of reprisals against persons who are protected by the Conventions."[46] Unlike Dunant's altruistic principles of intervention, these conventions inaugurate a new mode of humanitarianism based on deterrence and nonintervention. The Geneva Conventions impose a code of good conduct for the sovereign states that have signed them. But, more importantly, they ensure that humanitarian interventions by transnational bodies like the Red Cross will in all likelihood not take place in countries that have accepted the conditions set by the Conventions. Because it is rationally assumed that a state party to the Conventions would not violate the rights of individuals covered by these texts, the possibility for humanitarian interventions by nonstate or foreign actors is now limited. In a sense, these conventions create a "humanitarian intervention-free zone" for all the member states covered and immunized by this new legal order. The transnational effects of the Red Cross principles affirmed by Dunant and expressed by the early conventions are thus minimized, and humanitarian intervention, now repoliticized, becomes a right and prerogative of (certain) states only. After all, as Michael Akehurst emphasizes, "*Any* humanitarian intervention, however limited, constitutes a temporary violation of the target state's political independence and territorial integrity."[47] The potential limitations of state sovereignty that universal humanitarian principles could have caused are now prevented by reinscribing humanitarianism inside a strict system of norms, conventions, treaties, and obligations, all governed by the UN system and, ultimately, by its most political organ, the Security

Council. The reciprocity and national integrity principles that were at the basis of some of Grotius's "laws of war" have been rediscovered by the UN's humanitarian system.[48] The ideology of humanitarianism, revisited by international law and by the will of Western states after the Second World War, is once again framed within a logic and rhetoric of diplomatic relations between states.

It is only after the end of the cold war, when the ideological horizons of Western states suddenly appear to expand, that this strictly delineated practice of humanitarian law seems to display more universal ambitions. Freed from its political gridlock, the UN becomes in the 1990s the rediscovered champion of humanitarian internationalism. In 1992, Resolution 688 of the UN Security Council requests full access by humanitarian organizations "in all parts of Iraq," particularly to help the Kurds (in the context of the United States-led Operation Provide Comfort). As James Ingram has noted, this resolution is an overt move "toward the idea of a right of humanitarian intervention, that is, a right to forcibly deliver assistance to people being deprived of the necessities of life or otherwise abused by their governments."[49] The Bosnian conflict has given UN humanitarian agencies yet another opportunity to apply these newly emphasized principles. As a response to civilian massacres in Sarajevo and the rest of Bosnia, Resolution 808 in February 1993 declared that "an international tribunal shall be established for the prosecution of persons responsible for serious violations of international humanitarian law committed in the territory of the former Yugoslavia since 1991."[50] This Security Council Resolution supposedly represents the culmination of the UN's post–cold war humanitarian regime. Defending the principles affirmed by the Geneva Conventions of 1949, the UN-sponsored war-crime tribunal for Yugoslavia is the most flashy contemporary symbol of a humanitarian ideal that has been reinscribed in legal terms.

This suddenly daring regime of international humanitarian law and protection contradicts the previous post–World War II system. Under the UN's leadership, but with different motivations, member states no longer seek to deter the use of humanitarian intervention (particularly from transnational humanitarian groups). Rather, Western nations are now willing to use the humanitarian machinery promoted by the UN as a way of extending their liberal communitarian ideals across the borders of ideologically antagonistic states (like Iraq, Somalia, Yugoslavia, etc.). In a post–cold war era, the universal reach of international humanitarian law has become a convenient instrument for the propagation of Western states' liberal policies and technologies. In this perspective, the more confident work of the UN's humanitarian agencies is, ideologically, a deliberate strategy of Western liberal states.[51]

NGOs' New Fundamentalist and Medical Humanitarianism

The recent proliferation of nongovernmental humanitarian activism across borders is, in many ways, a reaction to both the Red Cross model (and its reabsorption within state-controlled parameters) and the UN's practice of international assistance. Larry Minear and Thomas G. Weiss have argued that humanitarian NGOs have been able to develop an attitude that is "less bound by constraints of politics and sensitivities of sovereignty, often entering areas where governments and UN agencies fear to tread."[52] In short, humanitarian NGOs are considered to represent a return to the true meaning of charitable assistance. They are not spoiled, so it is believed, by strategies of power and capital. Simply, they are organized forms of international assistance, composed of mostly Western volunteers, true "Good Samaritans," who are ready to abandon their privileged situations (in the West) to help whomever is in need, wherever and whenever it is necessary. Their "nongovernmental" status gives them not only the prerogative of transnational mobility (they cannot be clearly identified with a sovereign, a territory, a population, a race), but also a moral immunity, a stamp of purity, so to speak, since they do not represent any particular strategic interest.[53] If anything, they are the rescuers and the defenders of all of humanity. As humanitarian fundamentalists, they return to the words of Dunant (but not to his Red Cross organization) and to the inspiration of Judeo-Christian altruistic precepts to find there the moral justification for their work.

The will to humanitarian purity displayed by NGOs is well exemplified by the founding charters and principles of medical organizations like Médecins sans Frontières. But medical humanitarian organizations also display particularities of their own that may not be represented in other NGOs. Among those particular traits, the emphasis on "medical treatment" deserves particular attention.

According to its charter, MSF is "a private association with an international vocation" that is "mostly composed of doctors and medical specialists, but is also opened to any member whose work can be useful to MSF's mission."[54] MSF is a loosely fashioned organization. Although medics and doctors are the main protagonists of the association, any individual eager to join the cause is presumably welcome. MSF does not impose a privilege of membership. Once again, the actors do not matter. It is the (just) cause they follow that must remain the fundamental objective of the missions.

The cause pursued by MSF is summarized in four principles contained in its founding charter. Principles 3 and 4 are not specific to MSF. Principle 3 reiterates the need for a humanitarian NGO like MSF to be fully independent from any political, economic, or religious power. Principle 4 is a reminder (as well as a legal disclaimer) that members of the association are volunteers who, before joining, should be aware of the risks that are part of the organization's work.[55] Similar principles, with variants, could be found in the founding texts of other NGOs. However, the considerations contained in principles 1 and 2 are much more specific about the mission deployed by MSF and the cause that it has adopted. For these reasons, and for what they show about the place of MSF in the ideology of humanitarian assistance, it is important to read principles 1 and 2 more closely.

1. "Doctors Without Borders bring their support to populations in distress, to the victims of natural or human catastrophes, and of belligerent situations, without any racial, religious, philosophical or political discrimination."[56] This principle is merely a reprise of the Solferino model of humanitarian organization. The "Committees" of human support that Dunant had in mind are simply replaced by a medical association whose members, or at least most of them, have developed an expertise in the field of first-aid relief. The nondiscrimination and altruistic basis of the humanitarian ideology is fully subscribed to by members of MSF.

2. "Working according to a strict mode of neutrality and impartiality, and in the name of universal medical ethics and the right of humanitarian assistance, the Doctors Without Borders claim total freedom of action in the deployment of their mission."[57] The first part of this tenet is reminiscent of the Red Cross principles. Political neutrality is required in order to save lives and help suffering populations in a totally disinterested manner. Positing neutrality makes it

easier for humanitarian NGOs to be internationally accepted since, it is believed, they do not represent any particular ideology or strategy of power. It remains the case, however, that the postulate of neutrality of the humanitarian activities of NGOs is often untenable in practice, particularly when they intervene in political crises. As humanitarian workers often realize, they find themselves caught in the political struggles and are sometimes accused by one of the warring factions of furthering the cause of the other camp (by simply not letting the victims die, for example). In fact, in the 1990s, the neutrality postulate appears to be so unapplicable that more and more humanitarian activists are now encouraging humanitarian workers to "take a side" when there is, as they put it, a "moral necessity" to do so.[58]

The second part of this principle shows the originality, as well as the ambiguity, of the Médecins sans Frontières organization and of medical humanitarianism in general. Unlike other humanitarian NGOs, MSF does not found its mode of activism directly on a Christian ethic (as the Red Cross does, for instance). But MSF nonetheless finds a universal postulate for its humanitarian cause by referring its actions to a medical ethic that, as it argues, is globally recognized and practiced. The medical ethic does not have its origins in the love of God (as was the case with early forms of altruism), but in the philosophy of Hippocrates.[59] The Hippocratic oath, the ethical principles of medical treatment sworn to by doctors, serves as an atemporal precept that internationally unites the medical profession.[60] The oath is a medical "social" contract. It is designed to create a corporate bond between doctors. Today, in the age of MSF's humanitarian interventions, the Hippocratic oath is also regarded as a universal truth that allows "normal" medical actions (taking care of a patient, bringing basic relief, etc.) to be taken everywhere, no matter what the territorial, cultural, or judicial realities are in the countries where this universal medical ethic is applied. With MSF, the Hippocratic oath not only unites the medical profession worldwide; it also universalizes first-aid interventions (what the "humanitarians" call their right of humanitarian assistance) and the treatments that come with those missions.

Through this principle of action, MSF adds a key component to the ideology of humanitarianism as it is deployed today. By associating the "right of humanitarian assistance" with the medical domain, humanitarianism is not only a reproduction of Christian and, later, liberal ideals in the practice of post–cold war international affairs. The behavioral commandments given to individuals by the supporters of altruism, neighborly love, communitarianism, or human solidarity are now supplemented by a medical ideology that places its focus on finality (saving lives) rather than on method (how to appease suffering). By adding to its arsenal a medical component, humanitarianism in an era of postideological confrontation on a global scale (after communism) gives itself an extremely forceful normalizing instrument by placing the populations in distress under a regime of univocal, univisual (as Kouchner mentions, humanitarianism is "first of all a gaze"), and universal medical treatment. Unlike Dunant, who could only make up for his physical and psychological inadequacies by creating a neutral rescue-effort system (appeasing distress, not getting rid of it), contemporary humanitarian medical organizations now have the ethical foundations and the technical means to prevent destruction and disorder by saving lives.

But medico-humanitarian interventions do much more than simply save lives. For MSF, humanitarian activism is a matter of imposing "normal life." It is a question of maintaining a life that doctors, all over the world, and united by their universal medical ethic, would consider to be normal. This claim to normal life has no doubt a strong Western influence. After all, Hippocratic medicine was developed first and foremost in the Western world. Preserving "normal life" thus emerges as a medical categorical imperative no matter how incongruent it might be with the cultural preferences and particularisms of the countries in which it is applied. In a sense, the Christian belief in eternal life reemerges here, if not biologically, at least as a mode of social organization. If eternal life remains, even today, an organic impossibility, a medical practice that normalizes life (and establishes a norm—with laws to follow and practices to adopt—on how to biologically live well) is as close as humankind can get, even if artificially, to the dream of eternal life. The medical normalizing practice does not give eternal life (biologically). But it ideologically approximates it by imposing a universal way of life, a globally accepted mode of living and dying (a normality reinforced by statistical measures such as birth rate or mortality).

It remains to be seen, however, how such a medico-humanitarian practice, arguably the most dominant current of humanitarianism today, fits in the mostly hegemonic schema of post–cold war disciplinary liberalism. The following section analyzes the relation between medical practice and the formation of political/institutional order that will clarify this point.

THE CLINICAL GAZE OF THE FRENCH DOCTORS

Medical treatment has traditionally been conditioned by the method of clinical observation.[61] According to the clinical method of medical determination and recognition of the disease, the doctor assumes a primordial position. The clinical doctor points to signs/symptoms that matter, deciphers them, and shows how they relate to both the disease and the likely treatment. Through his precise gaze, the clinical observer holds the key to physiological knowledge and indicates how medicine ought to be practiced. Clinical observation is, as Ludmilla Jordanova has indicated, a formalization of knowledge that is affirmed through a "genre of display."[62] Medical knowledge thus displayed is, above all, an exercise in normality and normativity; normality of the body as it ought to be (and obviously is not), and normativity of the appropriate and accurate treatment that comes as a response to the identified symptoms. For Jordanova, the display of normality rendered by clinical observation has five objectives. (1) It displays the authority of the clinician. (2) It reinforces the credibility of the medical institutions that deploy the clinical gaze. (3) It highlights clinical expertise as a form of scientific and objective knowledge. (4) It demonstrates the humanity of the medical profession by focusing on the philanthropic activities of the doctors (toward their patients and their students). (5) Finally, it displays social acceptability by tying the clinically emphasized symptoms to recognized social patterns (this disease is the result of this activity).[63]

The clinical mode of medical display, and the various processes of normality and normativity linked to it, are also an appropriate way of describing the post–cold war humanitarian practice of medical NGOs. Medical humanitarianism is also a mode of knowledge that relies on clinical display, and not only because the actors of medical humanitarian missions are doctors. It is also a mode of clinical display because it relies on a visual approach to signs and symptoms to achieve order and close knowledge.

Knowledge of the human body and the need to create a field of scientific expertise by showing and teaching are probably no longer the types of order and knowledge that the French Doctors hope to achieve.[64] For MSF, knowledge mobilized by clinical display no longer centers on scientific progress and biology. Their clinical knowledge is affirmed, rather, on ideological and political grounds. Yet, the clinical gaze of the French Doctors is still concerned with the relationship between pathology and normality, with the visible transfer of signs from a sick to a healthy body (as in classical clinical observation). But the signs identified by their detailing gaze are attached to a different organism, to a different conception of what constitutes a "pathological body," in short, to a different object. For the body that is pathologically displayed by their clinical expertise is not merely the mutilated, tortured, or dying human body of the hapless victim whom they are trying to save, but rather the more encompassing, yet just as sick and decaying, sociopolitical body of the state or society in/on which they intervene. In a sense, the bodies of the victims clinically displayed through the visions/testimonies of the French Doctors serve a metonymic function for a larger symbolic body, the body politic of post–cold war anarchic societies that, like Rwanda, can be treated by a proper dose of humanitarianism.

This does not mean that humanitarian doctors have only social-order considerations in mind when they intervene to assist people in need. Such a view would be in total contradiction to the humanitarian ideology described above. Rather, I suggest that, consciously or not, organizations like Médecins sans Frontières participate in another healing enterprise that takes place at a political and ideological level. This healing is mainly achieved through processes of clinical observation on which they rely to publicize their actions and that Western media are so eager to spectacularly replicate. Working as the first-aid providers of war-torn and destruction-prone sociopolitical bodies (states and societies in crisis), the clinical gaze of the French Doctors is tightly connected to world order and international governance issues.

Michel Foucault has eloquently shown how the medical gaze is embedded in issues of sovereignty and governmentality. Medical observation facilitates the delineation of geographic and epistemic spaces that are used by sovereign entities (often, state apparatuses) to govern their subjects. Lines of physiological demarcation (ascribing the lepers to specific towns, quarantining the victims of epidemics, creating a social hierarchy of classes that are the most likely to suffer from such and such disease, etc.) are easily mutated into the contours of socially ascribed places that then form an accepted separation between the normal and the pathological, the safe and the hazardous, the tame and the wild. By displaying sociophysiological categorizations, medical knowledge is a support for the formation of sociopolitical orders. Modern medicine, as Foucault indicates, has thoroughly revisited "[t]he medicine of individual perception, of family assistance, of home care" in order to "be based only on a collectively controlled structure, or on one that is integrated into the social space in its entirety." It is at this point, Foucault adds, that "the institutionalization of disease makes its appearance."[65] For Foucault, the relationship between the medical gaze and issues of governance/governmentality explains why, for instance, the field of medical knowledge was at the center of ideological quarrels in revolutionary France, a period when the formation/knowledge of the individual as subject developed.

The clinic is most directly related to issues of sociopolitical spatialization and order. Clinical observation maps on the human body the passage from the sick or injured mode to the healthy or healed stage as an assumed, accepted, necessary, and desirable process. Symptoms play a key role in this mode of observation. As Mary Ann Doane has mentioned, the symptom "makes visible and material invisible forces to which we would otherwise have no access."[66] What Foucault calls a principle of "invisible visibility"[67] is at the very basis of the use of symptoms in clinical practice. The clinical doctor's gaze is able to identify what is assumed to be an "essential kernel of truth"[68] about the body or condition (s)he is examining. More importantly perhaps, clinical observation functions as a progress narrative that relies on the symptoms (and their evolution) as its unit of movement. In this medical/visual configuration, the pathological body is a fixed object upon which the safe, the tame, and the normal gradually appear (from what the doctor sees and interprets) and finally prevail (as a final diagnosis on the particular case). The clinical gaze is, thus, an ordering, stabilizing, and normalizing process as well. What is seen is always guided by the normal outcome. Diagnosis is always a matter for the clinician of determining how much the symptoms discovered on the body deviate from the norm, and of providing a prognosis that will allow the body to return to its normal state. What is privileged is the normal body, not its variations.

Order (physiological, political, or social) is the only desirable assumption that the clinical mapping strives to restore.

Such a process is also at play through the clinical gaze of medico-humanitarian organizations. Using a universal medical ethic as their progress narrative, and isolating places of disorder, war, famine, and natural catastrophe as their clinical objects, medical NGOs like MSF operate a clear delineation between the abnormal and the normal regions of the post–cold war international landscape. As the direct witnesses of international disorders,[69] humanitarian medics are often the first observers and analysts of those situations. The signs/symptoms of chaos that they identify and, later, display to the world (through their testimonies, appeals for logistical and financial support, visual reports, etc.) turn them into the clinicians of the New World Order.[70] Because of their privileged transnational status of doctors *without* borders, they have gained some sort of global physiological and moral authority (how the international community should function) that allows them, even before other international authorities, to discriminate between what is normal and what is not, what is just or not, and, finally, to determine what needs to be kept, replaced, or eradicated in an "unhealthy" body politic. It thus can be said that the "clinical witnessing" of the French Doctors is one of the first instruments of international normalization and interpellation that is used in contemporary international crises. Because of its unusual status (nongovernmental, transnational, moral, and medical), MSF can almost instantaneously enforce a stabilizing and reordering process in the "anarchic" countries where, in fact, they do not even have to be asked to intervene.

This authority was shown clearly in the case of Rwanda. There, the French Doctors were among the first to denounce the massacre of thousands of Tutsis by the Hutu regime in April–May 1994, much before the international community, behind the Security Council of the United Nations, finally admitted the potential presence of genocide in Rwanda.[71] Humanitarian doctors pushed the international community to talk about genocide in the case of Rwanda and helped to identify the so-called torturers and murderers. As MSF put it, the international community was indeed "faced with a genocide, the extent of which had not been seen since the defeat of the Nazi regime."[72] Having clinically identified a "kernel of truth" and clarified the situation in Rwanda (the mass destruction of one ethnic group by another), the French Doctors could no longer perform their disinterested and neutral medical tasks only. Their gaze was now the holder of a sacred knowledge that had to be verbalized under the form of a sociopolitical concept: genocide.[73] As Brauman explained, "[i]n extreme situations . . . when the very idea of humanity is deliberately crushed, [the humanitarian doctors'] first duty is to speak and to denounce."[74] Through their medico-humanitarian gaze, the French Doctors in Rwanda were able to bridge the gap between first-aid medicine and political order by providing the international community with a deciphering key, a normalized concept, that is, genocide, that would allow them to make sense of the situation socially and ideologically.[75] Understood as a case of widespread ethnic cleansing, the Rwandan situation could now be recuperated in the global language of world order politics and international diplomacy. Having been clarified by MSF, Rwanda was now rhetorically and spatially reconceptualized and reordered (a "new ordering of names" based on a "new ordering of the visual" by means of clinical practice had been found, to use a terminology introduced earlier) as, among other possible things, a failed state, an anarchic society, or an abnormal nation. The map of Rwanda was also physically and geographically redrawn by humanitarian organizations that transformed parts of Rwanda and of the neighboring countries into "safe havens," "humanitarian zones," and "refugee areas." Spatialization took place in Rwanda not only at a symbolic level (establishing Rwanda as a "hot zone" on the ideological scale of the post–cold war world order), but also at a basic territorial level, when Rwanda was physiologically redistributed by humanitarian organizations.[76] I note that it is symptomatic of this reconceptualization and reordering that it was only after the "clinical witnessing" of the French Doctors conceptually and physically reshaped Rwanda in an internationally recognizable form that the international community finally showed some interest.[77] Without the clinical gaze of the French Doctors, Rwanda may never have found a place on the mediatic and ideological map of post–cold war humanitarian interventions.

Even if the objectives sought by MSF are apparently different from those of eighteenth-century clinicians, medico-humanitarian observations are still a matter of governmentality and ideological order, of what Foucault calls "the processes and means put into place, in a given society, to ensure the governance of men."[78] Whereas the old clinicians were, often indirectly, serving the political and ideological purpose of the modern institutional apparatuses, MSF's clinical witnessing is placed directly at the service of disciplinary neoliberalism and its current expressions (unity, solidarity, etc.). This, indeed, can easily be reconciled with MSF's own belief in universal medical ethics. Clinical humanitarianism, after all, may also be interpreted as a method of supergovernmentality. It is not only, and simply, an instrument of global medical assistance. It is also, and more importantly, an instrument of knowledge, subjection, and normalization. In the next section, these theoretical insights are further examined as the relationship between medical NGOs and the United Nations is more symptomatically considered. The specific focus on the relationship between medical NGOs and the UN recenters the present reading of humanitarianism in the larger problematic of the place and role of United Nations peacekeeping in post–cold war international relations.

SUBSTITUTE THEORIES OF INTERVENTIONISM, OR THE UN AS VANISHING MEDIATOR

In his essay "Humanitarian Assistance in a Post–Cold War Era," Frederick Cuny develops an "umbrella theory" of UN-NGOs interaction.[79] Cuny's theory can be used as a point of departure for a symptomatic and critical analysis of the relationship between the UN and medical NGOs today. The "umbrella theory" of humanitarian interventionism is simple. It assumes that the United Nations can serve as a protecting and coordinating body for the practice of humanitarian NGOs in a post–cold war era. Under the UN's protective umbrella, NGOs can more easily "operate in conflict zones."[80] Furthermore, the logistical presence of UN agencies (UNHCR, DHA, UNDP, etc.) can facilitate the relationship between organizations with different strategic objectives (food relief NGOs, medical NGOs, human rights groups, etc.).

This model is yet another blatant case of visionary optimism, reminiscent of the thought process and hope mechanism developed by neoidealist/neoliberal scholars (Kegley, Boutros-Ghali, as seen in chapter 1) to establish the United Nations as a core institution in post–cold war international affairs. Cuny's "umbrella theory" is based on the premise that the UN and most humanitarian NGOs have compatible ideological orientations. From this premise, the UN and NGOs may display different modes of action. But as long as they partake of a similar vision (global governance as realized through humanitarianism), their actions will necessarily be harmonious and complementary. In a sense, this vision resolves the ideological tension within humanitarianism between the state-sponsored UN model of humanitarian assistance and the more independent, supposedly neutral and apolitical mode of intervention by NGOs. For Cuny, these two different approaches to humanitarian action, placed under the sign of the umbrella theory, share a same ideal: implementing global humanitarianism as a universal necessity. This has consequences in practice where, to follow Cuny's line of reasoning, the actions of both the UN and NGOs can be felicitously linked. Whereas the United Nations is mainly interested in prevention and deterrence (preventing humanitarian catastrophes from happening), humanitarian NGOs, and medical NGOs in particular, are geared toward finding a pragmatic and immediate solution to the problem at hand.[81] This is what Cuny calls the opposition between the "early-warning" humanitarian system of the UN and its agencies, and the "early-response" system of most NGOs.[82] Idealistically, with such an approach to humanitarian peacekeeping, the two systems are logistically combined to form a perfectly coherent international humanitarian structure. The UN's early-warning system is based on surveillance (as we saw in chapter 2) and deterrence (applied in both Somalia and Bosnia, with little to no success, however). Beyond, the NGOs' mode of first-aid response is still available as a drastic remedy to humanitarian crises in cases where the UN's operation of humanitarian/peacekeeping deterrence is not sufficient.[83]

The Rwandan conflict, however, clearly demonstrated the limits of such a visionary and interactive model. In a sense, what happened in Rwanda was completely antithetical to Cuny's umbrella theory. In Rwanda, NGOs intervened despite the fact that the United Nations and the international community remained passive and willingly impotent. When the UN's agencies finally offered some logistical support,[84] it was long after most NGOs had already started to act. The failure of the umbrella theory of UN-NGO interaction in Rwanda is, of course, not surprising. It can be explained by the peacekeeping paralysis of the UN after its failed missions in Somalia and Bosnia. What has been called the "Somalia syndrome" has pushed the United Nations to be more cautious before intervening in apparently dangerous domestic situations.[85] But, more importantly, as was seen in the case of Bosnia, the United Nations has lost the support of its member states.

Such a change of attitude toward the UN has important practical consequences for medico-humanitarian NGOs as well. From now on, before assuming a protective role for NGOs, the UN may be more likely to let the humanitarian situation develop. After NGOs establish a humanitarian basis for action, the UN may then consider providing some of its logistical and normative support, as long as this takes place in a fairly riskless fashion. This strategy was evidenced again in November 1996 when the humanitarian crisis involving Hutu refugees ignited in eastern Zaire. Instead of using peacekeeping intervention, the United Nations let its own humanitarian agencies and various NGOs assess the situation and provide first-aid relief under the spotlights of Western media. This example shows once again that, in the 1990s, UN peacekeeping has gone from being rashly optimistic and boldly interventionist (Iraq, North Korea, earlier on in Somalia and Bosnia) to finally being impractical, stymied, and often obsolete (Rwanda and Zaire).

Such a configuration is an ironic reversal of the "umbrella" model as well. In this new peacekeeping scenario, NGOs are sent first, and then, judging from the clinical signals that the NGOs display, the UN Security Council decides whether it is appropriate for the UN to intervene.

Normatively, the Rwandan crisis may have contributed to the development of a new conceptual model of UN-NGOs interaction. Instead of an umbrella model of UN-NGOs activities, we may now be witnessing the rise of what can be called a "substitute theory" of nongovernmental humanitarianism. Based, among other things, on the example of MSF's intervention in Rwanda, and on the potential achievements of international medical assistance in general, this approach supposes that, in the absence of an effective and prompt UN response to what is determined to be a severe humanitarian crisis, it is up to specific NGOs, the most appropriate for the specific task at hand, to meet the basic requirements of international humanitarianism. NGOs' humanitarian interventions could, of course, still be commensurate with New World Order policies (and the requirements of disciplinary liberalism), and to some extent, these actions would also push the United Nations to pass resolutions for more forceful intervention (which happened in Rwanda after the Security Council came up with Resolutions 929 and 935).[86] But, unlike what happened in Somalia, for instance, the United Nations would let NGOs assume the majority of the first-aid task. This is precisely what the UN did in Rwanda by letting medical NGOs take care of and report about the situation in the first months (April–May 1994) of the conflict. Making up for the lack of UN involvement, and using their transnational status and medical ethic as a ground for intervention, MSF was indeed one of the first organizations that sought to establish a semblance of medical/social order in the midst of chaos. The "substitute theory" of medical interventionism suggests that, if UN peacekeeping cannot effectively impose order in what have been recognized to be "anarchic" regions, other organizations that are less tied to the politics of sovereign states and are technologically more flexible ("without borders") can perform a similar task more swiftly and often more adequately. In other words, why wait for the heavy, and often useless, diplomatic and legal artillery of the UN when stealthier medical troops can achieve the required humanitarian goals, often at a lower (or at least less obvious) political and financial cost?

But there is more to the "substitute" theory of medical interventionism than a strictly denotative analysis of the normative relationship between NGOs and the UN. Mediatically, medical NGOs are in many ways more satisfying and eye-catching than the UN. Medical NGOs offer a substitute mode of visuality as well. Indeed, medical assistance has become a prized source of humanitarian spectacle and "real time" news. Everywhere, publics are consuming "live" the exploits of these new forces of hope whose mission is to save lives in the most dangerous zones of the international landscape. Visualizing international order through Doctors without Borders, for instance, is for Western audiences, and at least for the time being, an adequate replacement for the apparent diplomatic failure of UN peacekeeping. Before Rwanda, the task of uniting the global landscape behind global (neo)liberal principles had been granted to the UN and its simulated arsenal of peacekeeping activities. Today, it is perhaps more through the visual filter of humanitarian mythologies (like those described above) that the proponents of disciplinary liberalism worldwide are hoping to unite the international landscape.

The intervention of medical NGOs in the process of post–cold war peacekeeping, and the corollary impotence of the UN, may finally allow critical international relations theorists to reconsider the United Nations as what may be called a "vanishing mediator." The notion of "vanishing mediation" is an important one if one seeks to understand the symbolic and strategic position of the UN in the 1990s (particularly after Somalia, Bosnia, and Rwanda), and not only in relation to NGOs, but also in the overall process of peacekeeping and mobilization of ideology. The theme of vanishing mediation as applied to the UN evokes the notion of the "scapegoat" that was introduced in the previous reading of the Bosnian intervention. But whereas the trope of the scapegoat directly signified the symbolic and ritualistic value of the UN (particularly in relation to NATO), the notion of the United Nations as a vanishing mediator adds to a symbolic reading of the UN a necessary political and ideological dimension. It also allows one to refigure the place of the UN in the practice and theory of international relations in a post–cold war era.

The notion of the "vanishing mediator" is a Hegelian concept which has recently been revived by both Fredric Jameson and Slavoj Žižek.[87] The vanishing mediator is a person, institution, or motivated situation whose sole raison d'être is to perform a specific act/intervention, to fulfill a mission. The mission asked of the vanishing mediator is, like the *katharma* mentioned earlier, to operate change, or at least, an "illusion" of change.[88] The vanishing mediator is an agent that guarantees a rite of passage, yet necessarily disappears once the new order it announces is established (hence, its similarity to the sacrificial scapegoat). One of the clear examples of vanishing mediation given by Žižek is the multiplicity of new leftist-democratic movements that, in eastern Europe in the late 1980s, were instrumental to the reform of communism, its final collapse, and the implementation of market liberal economies.[89] Those reformed communists, in the wake of Gorbachev's *perestroika,* for instance, triggered the revolution and forced the adoption of a capitalist mode of production and organization of society. Yet, as Žižek affirms, once the new system was established, the vanishing mediators had to disappear. Once a new hegemon is imposed, and a new ideology is mobilized, "the agent who initially triggered the process must come to be perceived as its main impediment."[90] The notion of vanishing mediation complicates the symbolic rite of scapegoating by showing that, in recent contemporary contexts, the sacrifice of the *katharma* necessarily takes on ideological dimensions.

When all is said and done, the role/place of the UN in the symbolic and ideological landscape of post–cold war international relations was that of a vanishing mediator. Here again, one has to locate the notion of the vanishing mediator in the context of a passage. The passage, made possible by the UN, is from one specific international order (the cold war system of international relations) to another (the New World Order of global governance). As repeatedly mentioned above, the UN's peacekeeping missions were designed to be the selected moments and formations of change, the specifically visible and highly identifiable points where the old anarchic and dualistic system of split hegemony (between the East and the West) would give way to a visible neoliberal order controlled by liberal-capitalist transactions and liberal-democratic policies on a global scale (disciplinary liberal hegemony). In an ideal perspective, once the United Nations' visually mobilized and simulated operations had achieved this goal (that is to say, had facilitated this rite of passage into a new hegemonic order), the UN would then simply operate a "withdrawal into the sphere of privacy."[91] The UN would lose its "charisma" as a "bearer of change" (Jameson) and let the play of ideology that it had made possible run its course.

The United Nations in a post–cold war era is, however, a case of failed mediation. This statement can be read denotatively (as the impossibility of the UN to serve as an effective mediator or peacemaker in contemporary international crises) or connotatively, at the level of ideology (as the inability of the UN, as a vanishing mediator, to serve the correct functions of transition to a new ideological order). As the Somalia and Bosnia episodes have blatantly demonstrated, the United Nations' operations of change were anything but successful cases of vanishing mediation. The disappearance of the United Nations after both Bosnia and Somalia, and its substitution by NATO (in Europe) and medical NGOs (in Rwanda), do not correspond to the fate of the successful vanishing mediator either. Rather, these episodes evoke a different mode of disappearance or vanishing. It is the disappearance of an agent whose presence has become all too visibly painful. Vanishing mediation is based on the principle of the final/fatal invisibility of the mediator that gives way to the high visibility of newly created institutions and formations. In the case of UN peacekeeping, the reverse took place: as the new international order was confronted with the opposition of contingent singularities in regions and societies that the United Nations should have transformed, the UN's failures and operational difficulties became the most mediatic and visible events. The diplomatic and ideological structures that the UN was supposed to establish are, in the late 1990s, far from being the reality of international relations. In fact, peacekeeping and global governance are less assured than ever as the pictures from the UN's failed missions have demonstrated the artificiality and vulnerability of those ideological constructs. The UN, as unsuccessful vanishing mediator, indeed "vanished," but it left indelible traces and fragments that future agents of change, new vanishing mediators (like medical NGOs in the case of Rwanda) will have to deal with.

Paradoxically, the failure of the UN's mediation may have brought relief to the international organization. Decathected from its messianic role and its ideological positioning, the United Nations in the late 1990s is no longer placed at the center of international peacekeeping operations. Boutros-Ghali's vision of a new global diplomacy has taken a back seat to other strategies of compliance and interventionism. Boutros-Ghali himself has been replaced by Kofi Annan, whom some consider to be a more pragmatic secretary-general. If the UN is still used today (periodically against Iraq or North Korea in particular),[92] it is more as a legal and institutional reference than as an effective implementer of peacekeeping policies. In a sense, the UN has returned to a more narrow and less mediatic function, one it had prior to the end of the cold war.

This disentangling of the UN from ideological operations (a backlash from the early 1990s vision) has meant that the strategies of visual simulation of neoliberal ideological governance and order have been displaced to other institutions and organizations (NGOs, for instance). This "liberation" from the fateful function of the vanishing mediator may open up a less exciting future for the international organization. It may mark a disappearance from the domain of international action. In a logic of vanishing mediation, the disappearance of the mediator is equated to a "symbolic death." It is a "death" (loss of agency) that takes place within the ideological realm in which the mediator had been asked to intervene. No doubt, some contemporary scholars would like to interpret such a symbolic death of the UN as the sign of a good riddance, as the return to a more direct mode of international diplomacy in which states take matters into their own hands.[93] Others may look for other institutional configurations to continue the task initiated by the UN. As for the UN itself, it remains to be seen whether the UN can survive outside ideology or, to put it more accurately, whether it can stand not being a central actor in the future ideological strategies of neoliberal governance. After all, when the UN was granted a new life in the early 1990s, it was precisely because it had been ideologically reenergized, remotivated. Practically, the ability of the UN to operate yet another transition, from being a key player in global ideological schemes to being a silent forum of diplomatic activity, may determine whether the UN has a place in future international operations or, simply, whether it is doomed to suffer a slow and long decay (its actual death would then catch up with its symbolic death). Meanwhile, in the shadow of the vanishing mediator's failure, world order ideologues and practitioners are already planning new strategies and disciplinary modes of global governance: world order ideologues and practitioners, "yet another effort!"[94]

6

Theorizing the Visual:
New Critical Horizons

We used to move around the image. Now, we are moving inside it. A mere glance at an image is no longer satisfactory, and neither is a quick peek with the eye. We now have to enter the image, fuse with it, and then it can take us away in its spiralling vertigo and power.

—PHILIPPE QUÉAU, *LE VIRTUEL: VERTUS ET VERTIGES*
(THE VIRTUAL: VIRTUE AND VERTIGO)

We need the pictures, always the pictures.

—UNHCR OFFICIAL

Techniques and strategies of visual simulation are shaping the contemporary landscape of international politics. Placing the interpretive focus of critical/postmodern international relations theory on the UN and its peacekeeping operations allows one to realize that, in a post–cold war era, techniques such as panopticism, visual suture, clinical witnessing, or photojournalistic displays of the other's gaze are crucial international mechanisms. It is through such visually and mediatically enhanced strategies that both reality and ideology (and reality as ideology) are accessed. In the current practice of international affairs, the strategy of simulation seeks to "fool the eye" of the international observer, now turned into a passive viewer.

THE VISUAL AS SIMULATION

Such a late-modern/postmodern line of argumentation is akin to that in Quéau's introductory quotation. Looking at the image, passively enjoying the spectacle, is no longer sufficient. Rather, penetrating the image, being one with the image is what is now required. This move was explained earlier in this book as the passage from visual representation to visual simulation. Such a transfer in our ways of perceiving the "objective" world (reality) is truly revolutionary. It is both a theoretical and a perceptual revolution. Indeed, it suggests that meaning or referentiality can no longer be achieved through modern modes of cognition (reason, science, art, etc.), but, rather, that techniques of simulation, generating highly visible results, are necessary to make sense of contemporary realities. Our identification with the image has reached a point where we can no longer be dissociated from it. We need the image, always the image! Totally interpellated by the image, we are the image, the image is what we are. The image is not simply our representation anymore, or a representation of our modes of existence and experience. The Cartesian cogito has truly been superseded. New relations of perception and knowledge have arisen. If the Cartesian cogito was premised upon a mode of "high-fidelity" (at least, in the visual sphere), encounters with simulated and virtual worlds are based on what may be called "high-definition."[1] With the modern mode of (symbolic) representation, fidelity was indeed the key to deciphering the world. The sign (acoustic, visual, etc.) had to be faithful to the concept. Knowledge was the recognition of the concept by the sign. Representation was a mode of faithfulness, one achieved by convention and law. By contrast, in simulation, visual signs lie. Or, they may tell the truth. In short, it is no longer possible to distinguish between what is real or not, or between what is true or false. Representational reality, as high-fidelity, no longer matters in simulation. Simulated images/signs are no longer faithful, they can no longer be trusted. High-definition takes over as reality becomes what the code or the medium wants it to be. What is real is what, as Baudrillard puts it, is hyperreal, that is to say, what has been processed through highly advanced visual technologies to become more real than reality itself. "Fooling the eye" is not only an aesthetically pleasing enterprise. More importantly, it also allows a different relationship to "reality" to be affirmed. Reality, in short, can be constantly reprocessed, reinvented, or refigured.

THE UN AS SIMULATION

Such a way of theorizing/perceiving/using the visual is also revolutionary for the practice of international relations. Indeed, the reading of the United Nations and its peacekeeping operations offered in this volume must be placed in this same visual/conceptual context. What the UN sought to reprocess or reinvent, through its peacekeeping missions (read as visually mobilized exercises of simulation), was international reality in general, the way the international community traditionally understands/perceives international relations.

As was theorized in the previous chapters, the UN's strategy of simulation was intricately tied to ideology. Reinventing or reorganizing international reality around notions like global order, international governance, multilateral peace, and so forth, involved simulating specific ideological configurations: a surveillance network over Iraq and North Korea, a nation-building and domestic-anarchy cleansing force in Somalia, a peacemaking commando in Bosnia, and, of course, humanitarians pretty much everywhere. These ideological moments or visions accessed through the simulations of UN peacekeeping were directly modeled out of (disciplinary) neoliberalism. Such an ideology, imposed as the only metaphysical and organizational horizon of humankind after the collapse of communism, was precisely what was at stake through the visual simulations deployed by the UN. Imposing a new "referentiality" by means of visual simulations, the new "reality" of governance and surveillance would be marked by the stamp of (a certain) ideology.

Turning to panopticism as a mode of global surveillance in North Korea and Iraq, the UN first sought to impose global governance (or carceralization, if one prefers) by means of visual deterrence. The simulation of a global eye of power, all-seeing and omnipotent, was designed to coerce "rogue states" and force them into abiding by the New World Order dictates at a minimum physical cost. Here, visual simulation was premised on the principle of "visible invisibility" (Foucault), and the modes of worldwide governance mobilized by the UN were meant simply to be felt, not physically enforced. Such a utopian and self-evident mode of visual compliance, however, proved insufficient when more direct interventions were required (Somalia, Bosnia).

Moving from surveillance to peacekeeping, the UN now had to implement neoliberal policies directly. Yet, lacking the physical means to forcefully intervene, United Nations peacekeeping had to, once again, turn to strategies of simulation. Unlike panopticism however, the simulations of UN peacekeeping had to be seen, not simply felt. They had to leave marks on the visual-scape of post–cold war international affairs. In Somalia and Bosnia, coercion became a matter of "invisible visibility,"[2] and peacekeeping fully adopted the trompe l'oeil scenario theorized by Baudrillard. By means of suture (Somalia) or a more direct mode of simulated peace-enforcement (Bosnia), UN peacekeeping sought to impose a semblance of order, strength, and power. Not possessing the logistic or military means to enforce peace or establish domestic order in war-torn societies, the UN chose to rely on plays of appearances and make-believe situations, hoping that both its agents (blue-helmets, UN officials) and the international community (including the victims whom they hoped to save) would fall for such a scheme.

IDEOLOGY AS SIMULATION

All these incidents show the importance of ideology in operations of simulation. If the UN is the agent of simulation, and peacekeeping is its simulated mode of action, disciplinary liberalism is the code or model (the medium) that interpellates the UN into enacting the simulations. Ideology is perhaps the master-simulator. The relationship between the UN and the specific ideology of (disciplinary) neoliberalism diagnosed in this study also advances postmodern understandings of simulation in general. Indeed, it suggests that if simulation is, once again, a way of getting to reality by other means than direct cognition (a modernist dream) or representation (a modern dogma), it is perhaps nothing more than a way of getting to reality, or visually constructing it, by means of ideology.

Ideology was traditionally interpreted as a mode of representation. Althusser, in a post-Marxist fashion, saw it as such too. It was a way of conveying the domination (and of perpetuating the conditions of domination) of the bourgeois capitalist class. By turning to discipline, police hailings, or violence, ideology was perhaps the archetypal formula for representation. It represented the dominant class and institutional structures in a given period of time. But in a postmodern age, when culture is arguably free-flowing and meaning is less easily fixed, it becomes beneficial to any ideological formation to turn to simulation. Turning to simulation, ideology can indeed "play with appearances," and give the pretense that it is in control, that it possesses the instruments of hegemonic control, even if it does not. The way disciplinary liberalism mobilized the United Nations is symptomatic of such a strategy. Modes of visual surveillance and panopticism (under the notion of globalization) are emblematic of ideology's turn toward simulation as well. This does not mean, however, that ideology (and disciplinary liberalism in the present case) has no grounding in reality anymore, or that it has no material support once it enters simulation. In fact, interpellation and ideological apparatuses (even as IGOs, Ideological Governmentality Organizations) still remain. Rather, what this means is that the calls of ideology to which both the subjected individuals (rogue or well-behaved states and rebel or disciplined individuals) and the agents of ideology (like the UN) respond or react are artificial and self-referential. The urgency of interpellation that ideology requires from its subjects and agents is the product of a simulated situation, of the fact that perhaps, just as with the UN itself, nothing really happens or matters anymore. Disciplinary liberalism, left by itself in a global ideological void, has to simulate international threats and enemies.[3] It is precisely because nothing happens or matters anymore (and anything goes) that ideology needs to simulate stakes and command specific tasks to be carried out by both its subjects and agents. Thus, our particular focus on the UN and disciplinary liberalism throughout this study has yielded an extremely important insight for political and sociological studies of ideology. Indeed, it has revealed that an ideology may be at its peak (becomes hegemonic) when it possesses the ability to master simulation and gain control over the play of appearances.

The ability of ideology to master simulation is an advantage. It gives ideology flexibility and allows it to evolve. No longer obligated to a specific concept, belief, or even agent, ideology can always reinvent its own structures of control, hegemony and interpellation. This is assuredly a privilege that comes with stepping out of representation and moving into simulation. Once again, the practice of UN peacekeeping showed this capacity very clearly. Disciplinary liberalism did not get stuck with the UN. After the failure of the UN's visual simulations in both Somalia and Bosnia (when vision turned fatal, as I argued), other modes of visually constructed international reality were nonetheless found. They directly served the ideological purposes of contemporary liberalism on a worldwide scale.

The strategy of otherness highlighted by Žižek's theory of the Bosnian gaze and criticized by Baudrillard was nothing more than a way for the West of rehabilitating the reality of the Bosnian conflict (of repackaging it, making sense of it, cleansing it). Recategorized and reinterpreted through the notions of guilt and ethical responsibility, Bosnia would make much more sense to the West. Bosnia would no longer become a matter of raw pulsions, but a case of dearly needed liberal values (even if perhaps, at a more basic level, it is those pulsions and energies that truly caught the eye of the Western observer). Here again, as Baudrillard intimated, simulation was at play. The Bosnian victim had to be simulated as other, an alter ego (another self). The face of the victim visually enhanced by photographic displays in the West was depicted as if it were our face, or at least the face of a loved one whom we were savagely abandoning to the world's tyranny. An operation of ideological reconditioning of the international community to Bosnia's drama (through the simulation of the gaze of the other) was a specific mode of disciplinary liberal interpellation that was deployed in the shadow of the UN's peacekeeping failure. Subsequently, NATO's forceful intervention and its sacrifice of the UN vehemently reaffirmed the failure of the UN mission as well as established disciplinary liberalism in the former Yugoslavia.

Even more telling than the case of Bosnia is that of Rwanda. There, another visual strategy, one that was directly premised on liberal ideology and sentiments, took over after the UN's shortcomings in both Somalia and Bosnia subverted the earlier strategies. The mode of clinical witnessing deployed by the French humanitarian doctors in Rwanda once again sought to redefine and organize the situation according to neoliberal World Order parameters. Beyond saving lives, the task of the Doctors without Borders was perhaps primarily to simulate governance, peace, and security a posteriori, after the fact, after the human drama had already taken place. Clinically detailing the situation in a discourse recognizable by enlightened Western audiences (their affirmation that it was all a matter of genocide), their gaze on Rwanda became the "kernel of truth" about what had happened in that country in the spring–summer of 1994, the visually identified proof that Rwanda needed to be reorganized, if not by the UN (as an agent of disciplinary liberalism), at least by medico-humanitarian efforts.

Both cases (Bosnia and Rwanda) demonstrate that ideology is versatile, a condition characteristic of an era of visual simulation. Practically, peacekeeping was able to endure even after the demise of the UN's visual enterprises in Somalia and Bosnia. Disciplinary liberalism was able to displace peacekeeping to other apparatuses (NATO, Médecins sans Frontières) that would be granted the task of continuing the UN's efforts at imposing order, surveillance, or governance by means of simulation.

PEACEKEEPING AS IDEOLOGY

UN peacekeeping in an age of simulation is undetermined, imprecise, and perhaps unreal. UN peacekeeping in a post–cold war era is what Bosnian journalist Zlatko Dizdarević has called "Un-protection."[4] I take this not simply to mean that UN peacekeeping denotatively failed to protect lives and maintain the peace in Bosnia and other places. What UN-as-Unprotection further signifies is that peacekeeping is designed to simulate force, intent, intervention, action, and protection. Within simulation, peacekeeping makes sense. But within representation, it does not work. First of all, as was shown with Boutros-Ghali's *Agenda for Peace,* peacekeeping was never referentially defined. Notions like peacekeeping, peacemaking, post-conflict peacebuilding, and multifunctional peacekeeping have all been offered. But none of these has been (can be) clearly defined. The distinctions and delineations between these notions (and between their alleged fields of intervention) have been left unmarked. In short, peacekeeping has entered an era of representational undecidability that conveniently serves strategies of simulation (as was seen in Bosnia). If peacekeeping can mean nothing and everything at the same time, it is because it is only within simulation that it finds a utility, and, specifically, that it makes ideological sense. Peacekeeping is no longer a matter of diplomatic and normative maneuvers in the realist landscape of international politics. It is rather a matter of discursive, rhetorical, and visually simulated maneuvers in the postrealist mediascape of contemporary global affairs.

It is as such that peacekeeping fits the requirements of disciplinary liberalism. Through its visual applications and episodes (suture, clinical witnessing, etc.), peacekeeping was not intended to represent ideology. Once again, it did not offer ideology a clear chain of meaning, but rather a confused and blurred domain of action/intervention. Furthermore, the new interventionism of UN peacekeeping, as some have called it,[5] and its calls to order and governance did not correspond to the international landscape in which peacekeeping was asked to intervene, a global landscape that was, and still is, anarchic and disordered (as Boutros-Ghali has repeatedly mentioned), but that supposedly longs for liberal peace, global security, and international democracy. On the contrary, the readings of the peacekeeping missions in Somalia and Bosnia performed in this volume have demonstrated that, if anything, the Somali and Bosnian populations (not to mention the Serbs) had a vengeful desire to stand alone rather than abide by the globalizing dictates of neoliberal policies.

Peacekeeping does not represent (disciplinary) liberal ideology. Once again, it simulates it. Peacekeeping depicts a fantasy space or dream land of international affairs (where peacekeeping operations are successful, governance is realized, etc.) inside which claims to neoliberalism on a global scale can be made. Returning to Quéau's initial statement, I concur with him that peacekeeping in a post–cold war era allows ideology to "move inside the image," a place where it can be safe and remain unchallenged. The only "reality" of peacekeeping is what is offered through the various visual interventions, through simulation. The "reality" of post–cold war peacekeeping is a visually constructed reality. The ideology of peacekeeping is a simulated ideology.

VIRTUAL PEACEKEEPING

One may thus reinterpret global peacekeeping in the 1990s as a virtual enterprise. Peacekeeping is virtual not only when institutions or formations other than the UN (like NATO or Médecins sans Frontières) take over the peacekeeping task initially ascribed to the UN in the aftermath of the cold war, and try to remedy its shortcomings.[6] Peacekeeping is also virtual in the sense that it offers international observers and neoliberal ideologues a virtual tour through the post–cold war landscape of international relations. A new configuration of the world, with new divisions between "wild and tame zones" of international action,[7] and new categorizations and distinctions between rogue and disciplined states, is provided by peacekeepers (from the UN to the French Doctors). The daunting international realities of the post–cold war era, the once recognized postrealist dilemma of a lack of systemic organization in the international system, are now visually erased by the task of peacekeeping through which a virtual or parallel universe where nations are rebuilt (Somalia), nuclear weapons are destroyed (Iraq and North Korea), war crimes are eradicated (Bosnia), and humanitarian assistance is implemented (Rwanda) emerges.

The notion of virtuality must be taken seriously when one talks about peacekeeping in the 1990s. This notion is also congruent with the perspective on visual simulation. The term virtual does not mean that peacekeeping has no effect whatsoever on the populations who, as this study has shown, are often disciplined, normalized, governed, or remobilized by these policies. What virtual means, rather, is that the vision of global unity or governance that peacekeeping is designed to mobilize is a matter of visual illusion. Virtual, as Quéau has explained, does not mean nonexistent or inoperative. Etymologically, the term virtual is derived from the Latin words *vis* (force, energy), *vir* (man, human), and *virtus* (initial impulse, source),[8] which also gave us the Italian word *virtú,* used by Machiavelli, for example, to designate the force or traits of character that are dependent upon individual will and courage. Thus, the virtual is first of all a force. It is an energy that generates illusions, a source of power whose quality (virtue/virtual has the sense of quality, too), coupled with ideology, is to manipulate reality and representation. The way such a manipulation is effected is above all by means of visual simulation. The virtual is a visual force.

Such characteristics must be mentioned for they apply to peacekeeping as well. Peacekeeping as a virtual strategy is a visual force, a form of visual power. Within representation, it is once again useless, pointless, and powerless. Within simulation, however, it is virtual and, as such, powerful. As simulation, peacekeeping has the power to visually mobilize images and condition individuals or states into believing in these images. This does not mean that it is always successful. As we saw with the UN, simulation and virtuality do not always win. Not all simulations are convincing. Yet, it remains that such a modality of power (the power of the virtual) is all-pervasive and often endures. Indeed, in the post–cold war international landscape, after the UN's peacekeeping simulations failed, neoliberal ideology did not simply return to more traditional representational modes of power and governance. Rather, disciplinary liberalism persevered with simulation and the virtual, looking for other institutions or organizations that could be more appropriate for the specific task at hand (for example, Doctors without Borders in Rwanda).

Looking at peacekeeping from the perspective of simulation (virtuality) rather than representation (referentiality) is very instructive. Indeed, it suggests that one can be wary of theories and interpretations that seek to dismiss the role of peacekeeping in the contemporary practice of international relations on the grounds that, realistically, it has proven to be useless or inefficient. Only if one remains within representation can such a claim be made. Within simulation, by contrast, peacekeeping has been successful, particularly when one recognizes the ideological motivations associated with such a practice. In the postrealist and virtual landscape of international affairs (or the visual-scape of international "virtual-realism" perhaps), peacekeeping is an instrument of power, a force to be reckoned with. It is all the more powerful as such a claim to power is virtual, representationally nonexistent and empty (and nowhere to be found), and merely simulated. After all, as Baudrillard has repeatedly stated, the strength of power, its incommensurable energy, comes from the fact that it can never be materialized (other than through its agents), and that, at its core, it is perhaps nothing more than a play of appearances.[9]

VIRTUAL WORLD VERSUS REAL WORLD

Critical and postmodern analyses have generally tried to problematize representations of politics based on dichotomies and arbitrary divisions.[10] They have sought to highlight and identify power and ideology processes at stake through such normalized or naturalized distinctions. Alfredo Jaar's visual allegory of the black boxes (presented in chapter 1), a visual display meant to symbolize the dichotomous vision of the West when it comes to Rwanda and "other" non-Western places, was emblematic of such a theoretical enterprise.

But in an era of simulation, it is not the arbitrariness of dichotomies that must be questioned, but rather the virtual/visual processes that seek to fuse different events, images, and identities in a single dominant vision. What must be problematized today is not difference but its simulated and virtual erasure. This need is what Baudrillard has clearly demonstrated in his essay on Bosnia. In an era of global peacekeeping that aims at colonizing international realities by means of visual illusions, by the force of the virtual, what must be reestablished is the difference, distinction, and duality (what Baudrillard calls the radical alterity) between us and them, between the virtual world of international peacekeeping in which claims to neoliberal ideology are made and the real world of so-called disorganized, unstable, and unsafe international realities where clans fight wars against each other, leaders are ruthless, violent crimes are committed, and death occurs.[11]

Such a will to re-mark the distinction between the virtual world and the real world of international affairs is perhaps a retromodernist move. However, it does not seek to re-mark difference and duality as a normalized system of identification and knowledge (as is often the case in classical realist interpretations where differences/dichotomies are used to construct the self, the state, the vision of the inside). Rather, difference is remobilized as a *dare*, as a way of letting foreignness express itself as identity, positioning, or authority, even if such a mode of expression (or alterity) becomes threatening to the self or to the "inside." This dare was what Baudrillard had in mind when he referred to the notion of *Verfremdung* (literally, becoming alienated from oneself). There is, to be sure, a romantic side to this notion of "otherness" and difference, to the view of an other-than-self (a non alter-ego) whose materiality resists the virtuality of global ideological constructs. One may remain cautious about such a view which, in a sense, reinvents a new "ideal-type" (the vengeful other). Conceptually, however, Baudrillard's intervention, his will to reaffirm the separation between us and them, the demarcation between the virtual (self) and the real (other) is an important one. Indeed, it suggests that postmodern and critical discourses today will remain pointless and ineffective as long as they continue to focus their challenge on the question of representation. By directing their critical and theoretically subversive energies toward this traditional problem, they are doomed to never again step onto the field where, today, the political and ideological battles are fought. Too concerned about maintaining themselves as modes of critical analysis at a level (that of representation) that has become pointless, they will continue to produce an interesting and entertaining, albeit predictable and safe, discourse that will fail to address the questions of power and ideology at the level of simulation (the level of "reality" where they are deployed today).

This failure means that oppositions to neoliberal policies and to their specific modalities (surveillance, governance, interventionism, humanitarianism) must not only accept stepping away from representation, but also adopt a discourse that antagonizes the construction of virtual worlds. Such a post-postmodern discourse is not hostile to virtuality as such (to the power/force of/in visual illusions).[12] What it is opposed to, rather, is the technological/perceptual ability of such a construct to eradicate difference and alterity in the name of a dictatorship of virtual "sameness." What post-postmodern writings oppose is, as Baudrillard mentions, the disappearance of singularity (of the condition of being different, dual to the dominant discourse) under the appearance of global unity and neoliberal universality.

Thus, when the dominant discourse/vision of (virtual) universalism brings up the specter of interventionism, post-postmodern writings will become anti-interventionist (beyond all possible moral/political justifications for the intervention). When the hegemonic ideology and its virtual world call for humanitarianism, post-postmodern challenges will become manifestly antihumanitarian. When global governance is imposed as a no-escape mechanism of order, local chaos will be the call of the post-postmodernists. There is, however, no grand scheme beyond such antihegemonic critiques of the "virtual world." There is no grand narrative, no *telos* either. It is rather, in a situationist spirit perhaps, a matter of contingent creativity, one that uses the energy of what it opposes to express its virulence, its difference.

To combat the virtual world of global peacekeeping, duality must return. To combat virtuality (and once again, it is not virtuality as such that is opposed, but virtuality as an ideological strategy used to order human societies) and to be able to offer an effective challenge to disciplinary liberal hegemony, a new anti-imperialist spirit must be deployed. This spirit will pay close attention to disciplinary liberalism's own discourse and will take its mobilized visions seriously. And yet, in a festive and affirmative manner (there is no place for resentment here), it will seek to haunt hegemonic ideology and its visions of global order. As for international relations theory (where, as was shown in this volume, such constructs are always already affirmed), this new spirit of criticism reintroduces a healthy dose of uncertainty, instability and, more important, irreverence. This book, it is hoped, has provided a point of departure for such a destabilizing enterprise.

Appendix

CHRONOLOGY OF THE RWANDAN CRISIS

1885	After the Berlin Conference, the eastern part of today's Rwanda is granted to the German Empire.
1908	Establishment of a German military high command in Kigali. Power is in the hands of the King, or Mwami, who comes from a Tutsi dynasty.
1924	Belgium agrees to take over the trusteeship mandate for both Rwanda and Burundi granted by the League of Nations.
1931	Mwami Musinga is overthrown by the Belgian authorities. Late 1940s: The United Nations grants Belgium a new trusteeship over Rwanda and Burundi. The UN also asks Belgium to initiate the "emancipation" of these two nations.
1957	Publication of "The Bahutu Manifesto," which demands Hutu independence from both the Belgians and the Tutsis.
1959	Toussaint Rwandaise: rebellion of Hutu farmers causes the massacre of 20,000 Tutsis. Rwanda is placed under military surveillance. These events cause the first exodus of Tutsis toward Uganda.

1961	A Hutu party, the Parmehutu organization, rises to power. The new government abolishes the monarchy and proclaims the birth of a republic. A few months later, this decision is confirmed by a national referendum.
1962	Rwanda's independence. A Hutu president, Kayibanda, is elected. But Kayibanda refuses to appoint Tutsi ministers in his government.
1963 and 1967	Tutsis living overseas try to return to Rwanda twice. But they are immediately rejected. Anti-Tutsi pogroms spread all over Rwanda.
1973	Kayibanda is deposed by his commander in chief, Habyarimana, who imposes a new quota limiting to 10 percent the Tutsis permitted in any form of employment available in Rwanda.
1988	In Uganda, the Rwandan Patriotic Front (RPF) is created. It is composed of Tutsis who have fled Rwanda or have been expelled by the pogroms.
October 1, 1990	The RPF attacks in the northeast of the country from its bases in Uganda. Thousands of Tutsis are arrested and accused of working for the RPF.
October 4, 1990	Belgium and France decide to send troops to protect their own citizens in Rwanda and facilitate their evacuation.
October 8, 1990	The Rwandan army kills close to 1,000 Himas, a subgroup of the Tutsi ethnic family.
End of October 1990	The RPF is pushed back into Uganda. Guerrilla warfare begins. Belgium withdraws all its troops but a small French army stays.
June 19, 1991	A new constitution that promotes a multiparty system is put into place.
May 1992	The RPF starts a new offensive that causes the displacement of about 350,000 people.
February 8, 1993	A new offensive by the RPF in the north causes the immediate exodus of one million Hutu refugees. Arbitrary executions by the RPF are reported.

France sends more troops and weapons to support the Hutu regime.

March 7, 1993   A cease-fire is signed in Dar-es-Salaam, Tanzania.

August 4, 1993   Peace accords are signed in Arusha between the Rwandan government and the RPF. It is decided that a transition government will be open to RPF members and that the two armies will be fused into one. A United Nations Mission in Rwanda (UNAMIR) will be in charge of basic assistance and demilitarization.

October 5, 1993   Resolution 872 of the UN Security Council creates UNAMIR. It has twenty-five hundred soldiers and military observers from twenty-three different nations.

November 1, 1993   Beginning of UNAMIR's mission.

April 5, 1994   Resolution 909 of the Security Council extends UNAMIR's mission until July 29.

April 6, 1994   President Habyarimana and President Ntariyamira of Burundi die in a plane crash. Beginning of the killings in Kigali, the Rwandan capital.

April 7, 1994   Rwandan prime minister, opposition leaders and ten Belgian blue-helmets are killed.

April 9, 1994   French parachutists land in Kigali to facilitate withdrawal of European citizens.

April 12, 1994   Beginning of the battle of Kigali between the governmental forces and the RPF. Massacres of Tutsis supposedly take place throughout the country.

April 21, 1994   Resolution 912 of Security Council reduces the number of UN blue-helmets in Rwanda to 270.

May 17, 1994   Resolution 918 of Security Council asks for cease-fire and demands that massacres stop. It also authorizes the deployment of UNAMIR II, with a mission similar to UNAMIR I.

June 8, 1994   Resolution 925 of Security Council allows UNAMIR to stay until December 9, 1994.

June 17, 1994	Boutros-Ghali supports a French initiative in favor of military humanitarian intervention.
June 22, 1994	UN Security Council adopts Resolution 929, which authorizes France and other nations willing to help to use "all necessary means" to protect civilians and provide food aid for a duration of two months.
July 1, 1994	Resolution 935 of Security Council asks for a special commission to examine the possibility of genocide in Rwanda.
July 4, 1994	Kigali is controlled by RPF forces.
July 5, 1994	France creates a "safe humanitarian zone" in the southwestern part of Rwanda in the context of Opération Turquoise.
July 14, 1994	RPF takes over Ruhengeri in the north. Massive exodus of Rwandans into Goma, Zaire.
July 18, 1994	RPF proclaims that the war has ended. Bizimungu, a moderate Hutu, is selected by RPF to be the new president of Rwanda. All parties are included in new government except for Hutu rebels.
July 21, 1994	Cases of cholera are detected in refugee camps in Goma, Zaire.
July 26, 1994	The United States, behind President Clinton, launches Operation Support Hope.
July 29, 1994	France starts to withdraw its troops.
July 31, 1994	The United States sends its first troops to Kigali.
August 1994	Tension rises in refugee camps as Hutu leaders try to organize opposition in exile.
Fall 1994	Thousands die of cholera in refugee camps. Massive international aid is sent to the camps.
1995	New Rwandan government launches appeals for displaced Hutus to return home. Fearing reprisals, only a few Hutus return.
May 1995	Anti-UN demonstrations in Kigali. The UN and Boutros-Ghali are accused by new Rwandan government of having ignored Tutsi massacres in April–May 1994.

September 1995   The UN decides to investigate the responsibility of
                Hutus in the ethnic massacres of 1994.

March 1996   Zaire asks Rwandan refugees in Goma to return
                home. UN personnel begins to leave Kigali.

October 1996   Fighting resumes in eastern Zaire between the
                Zairian government forces and the Tutsi minority
                population in the Goma region. The Rwandan
                Tutsi government intervenes to support Tutsi popu-
                lation in Zaire. Cross-border fighting. The refugee
                camps in the Goma area are caught in the middle
                of the new struggle. The remaining Hutu refugees
                try to escape and wander throughout the region.

November 1996   Hutu refugees in Zaire are scattered all over the
                region. Some decide to return to Rwanda with the
                supposed guarantee that they will not be harassed
                by Tutsi authorities. International community be-
                hind France seeks to send an international humani-
                tarian force, but refugee camps in eastern Zaire
                are no longer a problem as refugees are scattered
                about.

Sources: Alain Destexhe's own chronology (modified and revisited)
in *Rwanda: Essai sur le génocide* (Rwanda: An essay on genocide)
(Brussels: Editions Complexe, 1994), pp. 109–14; *Chicago Tribune;*
and *New York Times.*

Notes

INTRODUCTION

1. Adam Bartos and Christopher Hitchens, *International Territory: The United Nations, 1945–95* (New York: Verso, 1994).

2. Ibid., p. 51.

3. Ibid., p. 74.

4. Ibid., p. 96.

5. Secretary of the Publishers Board, *Your United Nations: The Official Guide Book* (New York: United Nations, 1987), p. 13.

6. A traditional interpretation that, as will be seen momentarily, understands the UN as an institutional framework that represents and implements recognized norms and principles of international governance.

7. Jean Baudrillard, *The System of Objects,* trans. James Benedict (New York: Verso, 1996), p. 3.

8. Bartos and Hitchens, *International Territory,* p. 1.

9. Jack Plano and Roy Olton, *The International Relations Dictionary,* 2nd ed. (Kalamazoo, MI: New Issues, 1979), p. 288 (my emphasis). Also quoted in J. Martin Rochester, *Waiting for the Millennium: The United Nations and the Future World Order* (Columbia: University of South Carolina Press, 1993), p. 6. The notion of the UN as a "formal arrangement" or as a framework is also given by Thomas G. Weiss, David P. Forsythe and Roger A. Coate in their study *The United Nations and Changing World Politics,* 2nd ed. (Boulder, CO: Westview, 1997), pp. 12–14.

10. Rochester, *Waiting for the Millennium,* p. 3.

11. To use Boutros-Ghali's formulation. See Boutros Boutros-Ghali, "Empowering the United Nations," *Foreign Affairs* 71 (1992–93): 89–102.

12. See Robert Kaplan, "The Coming Anarchy," *Atlantic Monthly* (February 1994): 44–76.

13. Boutros-Ghali, "Empowering the United Nations," 91.

14. This new sentiment is thus not far removed from Kenneth Waltz's (neo)realist postulate, which affirms that "[d]omestic systems are centralized and hierarchic. . . . International systems are decentralized and anarchic. The ordering principles of the two structures are distinctly different, indeed, contrary to each other. . . . The prominent character of international politics, however, seems to be the lack of order and of organization. . . . The problem is this: how to conceive of an order without an orderer and of organizational effects where formal organization is lacking." See Kenneth Waltz, *Theory of International Politics* (Reading, MA: Addison-Wesley, 1979), pp. 88–93.

15. Timothy W. Luke, "On Post-War: The Significance of Symbolic Action in War and Deterrence," *Alternatives* 14 (1989): 343–62.

16. Ibid., p. 360.

17. To use Hitchens's own formulation. See Christopher Hitchens, introduction to *International Territory*, p. 30.

18. René Descartes, *Discours de la méthode/Discourse on the Method*, trans. George Heffernan (South Bend, IN: University of Notre Dame Press, 1994), p. 53. Cartesian metaphysics seeks to represent knowledge by postulating a creative suspicion toward the senses: "I resolved to feign that all the things that had entered my mind were no more true than the illusions of my dreams." However, this suspicion stops at the point where the thinking subject has to prevail (and cannot be doubted): "I took note that, while I wanted thus to think that everything was false, it necessarily had to be that I, who was thinking this, were something." Thus, by arbitrary convention, the "truth—*I think therefore I am*—was so firm and so assured that all the most extravagant suppositions of the skeptics were not capable of shaking it." The Cartesian cogito was born. See ibid., p. 51.

19. For Rousseau, representation is guaranteed by the principle of the "general will." Each member of the social compact is an embodiment of the common will and represents one portion of the sovereign (popular sovereignty). See Jean-Jacques Rousseau, *The Social Contract and Discourses*, trans. G. D. H. Cole, (Rutland, VT: Everyman's Library, 1973). For Locke, representation is guaranteed by law, which is "not so much the limitation as the direction of *a free and intelligent agent* to his proper interest." See John Locke, *Second Treatise of Government*, ed. Richard Cox, (Wheeling, IL: Harlan Davidson, 1982), p. 34 (Locke's emphasis).

20. The term "symbolic representation" is simply used here as a way of differentiating it from "political representation," a term that is more

commonly used in political theory and international relations discourses. Once again, as I understand it, political representation is but one modality of symbolic representation, of the logic of representation in general.

21. We can also think of Kant's a priori categories of knowledge in this perspective. See Immanuel Kant, *Critique of Pure Reason,* trans. Werner Pluhar (Indianapolis: Hackett, 1996).

22. Ferdinand de Saussure, *Course on General Linguistics,* trans. Roy Harris (La Salle, IL: Open Court Classics, 1972), p. 15.

23. Kaja Silverman, *The Subject of Semiotics* (New York: Oxford University Press, 1983), p. 6.

24. See Charles Sanders Peirce, *Collected Papers,* eds. Charles Hartshorne and Paul Weiss (Cambridge: Harvard University Press, 1931).

25. Roland Barthes, *Mythologies,* trans. Annette Lavers (New York: Noonday Press, 1972), pp. 137–39.

26. Jacques Derrida has argued that the relationship between signifier and signified also serves to maintain a distinction between those two poles of representational signification. Silverman, clarifying Derrida's insight, suggests that this distinction "is congruent with the traditional opposition of matter and spirit, or substance and thought," an opposition that privileges "the second of these categories over the first." Silverman, *The Subject of Semiotics,* p. 33. Derrida adds that maintaining this absolute distinction between signifier and signified, a postulate of semiological analyses, is a way of imposing, consciously or not, a "transcendental signified," a concept or object that is believed to be final, supreme, sovereign, and unchallengeable. As was clearly seen with Descartes, this supreme/sovereign signified, reified by representational logic, is the cogito, the rational thinking subject. For Derrida, the logic of representation is thus an eminently logocentric practice. See Jacques Derrida, *Of Grammatology,* trans. Gayatri Chakravorty Spivak (Baltimore: Johns Hopkins University Press, 1976), p. 20.

27. Jean Baudrillard, *Simulations* (New York: Semiotext(e), 1983), p. 32.

28. Jean Baudrillard, *Selected Writings,* ed. Mark Poster (Stanford: Stanford University Press, 1988), p. 154.

29. Baudrillard, *Simulations,* p. 11 (Baudrillard's emphasis).

30. William Bogard, *The Simulation of Surveillance: Hypercontrol in Telematic Societies* (New York: Cambridge University Press, 1996), p. 9.

31. Baudrillard, *Selected Writings,* pp. 155, 158.

32. James Der Derian, *Antidiplomacy: Spies, Terror, Speed, and War* (Cambridge: Blackwell, 1992).

33. It is often by means of what Der Derian calls a "global swarming" caused by multiple visual media that sovereign states make sense of their contemporary international realities. Der Derian gives the example of the Combat and Maneuver Training Center for the U.S. Army at Hohenfels,

Germany, where he witnessed various technologically simulated scenarios of the Bosnian conflict taking place through what is referred to as a "box" (a sealed zone of on-the-ground virtual reality where simulated situations and machineries and soldiers interact). Inside the "cyber box," international realities are revisited. The protagonists of the Balkan conflict are given newly invented names (Sowenia, Ruritania, etc.), maps are redrawn, weapons are harmless, and death never occurs. It is through such filters, taken to be "at once true and unreal" (Baudrillard), that sovereign states come face to face with international realities (the Bosnian conflict in the present case), and seek to transform "a simulated war [in]to a simulated peace," as Der Derian puts it. See James Der Derian, "Global Swarming, Virtual Security, and Bosnia," *Washington Quarterly* 19 (1996): 56.

34. More generally, recent analyses have shown that the strategy of simulation may be of salient importance in international relations, even when it does not directly involve the use of visual/virtual technologies or models. Cynthia Weber has argued that claims to Central American nations' sovereignty performed through U.S. interventions (in Grenada or Panama) were also to be read in the context of simulation (an absence of referentiality), not representation (referentiality, production of truth). Central to this analysis is the nature of power, no longer inscribed into identifiable or recognizable events (was it ever?), but rather discursively constructed or, as Weber puts it, simulated through discourses of intervention. See Cynthia Weber, *Simulating Sovereignty: Intervention, the State and Symbolic Exchange* (New York: Cambridge University Press, 1995).

35. The UN Charter starts with: "We the Peoples of the United Nations." See Charter of the United Nations. Done at San Francisco, June 26, 1945. Entered into force, Oct. 24, 1945; for the United States, Oct. 24, 1945. 59 *Statutes at Large* 1031, T. S. No. 993, 3 Bevans 1153, 1976 *Yearbook of the United Nations* 1043.

36. Contemporary realists continue to follow this line of analysis. See John Mearsheimer, "The False Promise of International Institutions," *International Security* 19 (1994–95): 5–49.

37. The Independent Working Group on the Future of the United Nations, *The United Nations in Its Second Half-Century*, Report of the Working Group (New York: Ford Foundation, 1995), p. 4.

38. Friedrich Kratochwil and John Gerard Ruggie, "International Organization: A State of the Art on an Art of the State," *International Organization* 40 (1986): 753–75; reprinted in Friedrich Kratochwil and Edward D. Mansfield, eds., *International Organization: A Reader* (New York: Harper Collins, 1994), p. 5.

39. J. Barry Jones, "The United Nations and the International Political System," in *The United Nations in the New World Order: The World*

Organization at Fifty, ed. Dimitris Bourantonis and Jarrod Wiener (New York: St. Martin's Press, 1996), p. 25.

40. See Kratochwil and Ruggie, "International Organization: A State of the Art on the Art of the State," p. 5.

41. Thomas G. Weiss, David P. Forsythe, and Roger A. Coate, *The United Nations and Changing World Politics,* p. 44.

42. As Paul Diehl mentions, the "first true peacekeeping operation" was invented to "meet the challenges of the Suez crisis in 1956." UN peacekeeping was devised during the crisis as a means of interposition between Egypt and Israel. In the Suez crisis as in other (albeit limited) cases of early cold war United Nations interventionism (in Congo in the context of decolonization, for example), UN peacekeeping was "an attempt to fill the void left by collective security." See Paul F. Diehl, *International Peacekeeping* (Baltimore: Johns Hopkins University Press, 1994), pp. 28–29.

43. See Jacques Derrida, *Writing and Difference,* trans. Alan Bass (Chicago: University of Chicago Press, 1978).

44. David Mitrany, "The Functionalist Approach to World Organization," in *The United Nations and a Just World Order,* ed. Richard A. Falk, Samuel S. Kim, and Saul H. Mendlovitz (Boulder, CO: Westview Press, 1991), p. 158.

45. Kratochwil and Ruggie, "International Organization: A State of the Art on the Art of the State," pp. 10–11.

46. For more on the theory of international regimes, see Stephen Krasner, ed., *International Regimes* (Ithaca, NY: Cornell University Press, 1983), and Robert Keohane, *After Hegemony: Cooperation and Discord in the World Political Economy* (Princeton, NJ: Princeton University Press, 1984).

47. Here, I am targeting a specific form of constructivism developed by Alexander Wendt. Wendt clearly seeks to put a social constructivist framework of interpretation to good institution-building use. Although cognizant of more refined constructivist formulations by Nicholas Onuf, Wendtian constructivism intends to turn the co-constitution of agents and structures (a basic assumption of constructivist scholarship) into a new institutionalist/structural theory of international politics. See Alexander Wendt, "Collective Identity Formation and the International State," *American Political Science Review* 88, no. 2 (1994): 384–96. As presented by Nicholas Onuf in his *World of Our Making* (Columbia: University of South Carolina Press, 1989), constructivism had no intention to provide a theoretical paradigm that could be used to rebuild a specific institutional vision of international politics (even though the apparent absence of prescriptive purpose in Onuf's constructivism made such a strategy, among many others, a possible outcome of constructivist work). Unlike Wendt's, Onuf's constructivist task was (and still is) to invite scholars whose work revolves around the encounter

between social agents and structures to partake of the broad descriptive framework constructivism offers. For a distinction between these two different constructivist trends, see Nicholas Greenwood Onuf, "Worlds of Our Making: The Strange Career of Constructivism in IR," in *Visions of IR,* ed. Donald J. Puchala (Columbia: University of South Carolina Press, forthcoming 1999).

48. Alexander Wendt, "Anarchy Is What States Make of It: The Social Construction of Power Politics," *International Organization* 46 (1992): 391–425; reprinted in Kratochwil and Mansfield, *International Organization: A Reader,* p. 78.

49. Ibid., p. 80.

50. Ibid.

51. See James Mayall, *The New Interventionism, 1991–1994: United Nations Experience in Cambodia, Former Yugoslavia, and Somalia* (New York: Cambridge University Press, 1996), p. 2.

52. Weiss, Forsythe, and Coate, *The United Nations and Changing World Politics,* p. 52 (my emphasis).

53. Timothy W. Luke, "Discourses of Disintegration, Texts of Transformation: Re-reading Realism in the New World Order," *Alternatives* 18 (1993): 245.

54. Baudrillard, *Simulations,* p. 2.

55. See James Der Derian, "Simulation: The Highest Stage of Capitalism?" in *Baudrillard: A Critical Reader,* ed. Douglas Kellner (Cambridge: Blackwell, 1994). Der Derian writes: "are we entering an era in which the Marxist, concrete and steel Lenin is to be replaced by the hyperrealist, laser, and microchip Baudrillard?" (p. 197).

56. Stephen Gill, "Globalisation, Market Civilisation, and Disciplinary Neoliberalism," *Millennium* 24 (1995): 399, 400.

57. In *Discipline and Punish,* Foucault notes that the emergence of discipline (or disciplines rather, as Foucault prefers the plural use of the notion) is concomitant with the discovery of what he calls the "docile body" (as opposed to the tortured body of the condemned). For Foucault, discipline has three key components. First, there is the question of the scale of control: a matter of "not treating the body *en masse,* 'wholesale,' as if it were an indissociable unity, but working it 'retail,' individually; of exercising upon it a subtle coercion, of obtaining holds upon it at the level of the mechanism itself—movements, gestures, attitudes, rapidity: an infinitesimal power over the active body." Second, discipline emphasizes the object of control: not "the signifying elements of behaviour, or the language of the body, but the economy, the efficiency of movements, their internal organization." Finally, discipline is a modality: "it implies an uninterrupted, constant coercion, supervising the processes of the activity rather than its result, and it is exercised

according to a codification that partitions as closely as possible time, space and movement." See Michel Foucault, *Discipline and Punish: The Birth of the Prison,* trans. Alan Sheridan (New York: Vintage Books, 1979), pp. 136–37.

58. Rousseau, *Social Contract and Other Discourses,* p. 192.

59. Ibid., p. 195.

60. See Louis Althusser, "Ideology and Ideological State Apparatuses," in *Lenin and Philosophy, and Other Essays,* trans. Ben Brewster (New York: Monthly Review Press, 1971).

61. Gilles Deleuze and Félix Guattari write that "the subject itself is not at the center, which is occupied by the machine, but on the periphery, with no fixed identity, forever decentered, *defined* by the states through which it passes." See Gilles Deleuze and Félix Guattari, *Anti-Oedipus: Capitalism and Schizophrenia,* trans. Robert Hurley, Mark Seem, and Helen Lane (Minneapolis: University of Minnesota Press, 1983), p. 20 (authors' emphasis).

62. Deriving the notion from Hjelmslev's semiological analyses, Barthes indicates that denotation is "a sign or system of primary signification," a first-order relationship between a concept, a referent, and a signifier. Denotation is a "univocal" and often unequivocal text ("this" means "that"). Such a system is no doubt based on representation. See Roland Barthes, *S/Z,* trans. Richard Miller (New York: Noonday Press, 1974), p. 7.

63. As opposed to denotation, "connotation is a secondary meaning, whose signifier is itself constituted . . . by primary signification, which is denotation." Connotation has the ability "to relate itself to anterior, ulterior, or exterior mentions, to other sites of the text (or of another text)." Connotation is a level of signification that, as Barthes indicates, allows one to revisit denotation, or primary signification, and realize that the so-called innocent denotation was always already caught in an ideological system. In other words, connotation rereads denotation as ideology. Barthes writes that "[i]deologically, finally, this game has the advantage of affording the classic text a certain *innocence.* . . . [D]enotation is the first meaning, but pretends to be so; under this illusion, it is ultimately no more than the *last* of the connotations (the one which seems both to establish and to close the reading)." Ibid., pp. 7–9 (Barthes's emphases).

1. DESTABILIZING LEVIATHAN

1. Thomas Hobbes, *Leviathan,* ed. C. B. MacPherson (New York: Penguin Books, 1985).

2. See John J. Mearsheimer, "Why We Will Soon Miss the Cold War," in *Conflict after the Cold War: Arguments on Causes of War and Peace,* ed. Richard Betts, reprinted from *Atlantic* 266, no. 2 (August 1990): 44–61; and

Robert D. Kaplan, "The Coming Anarchy," *Atlantic Monthly* (February 1994): 44–76.

3. Hobbes, *Leviathan,* p. 186.

4. Slovenian critical theorist Slavoj Žižek holds a similar position when he suggests that "[t]he recent deadlocks of the triumphant liberal-democratic 'new world order' seem to endorse fully [the view that] today's world is more and more marked by the frontier separating its 'inside' from its 'outside'—the frontier between those who succeeded in remaining 'within' (the 'developed,' those to whom the rules of human rights, social security, and so forth, apply), and the others, the excluded (apropos of whom the main concern of the 'developed' is to contain their explosive potential, even if the price to be paid is the neglect of elementary democratic principles)." See Slavoj Žižek, "Caught in Another's Dream in Bosnia," in *Why Bosnia? Writings on the Balkan War,* ed. Rabia Ali and Lawrence Lifschultz (Stony Creek, CN: Pamphleteer's Press, 1993), p. 235.

5. R. B. J. Walker, *Inside/Outside: International Relations as Political Theory* (New York: Cambridge University Press, 1993).

6. Woodrow Wilson's understanding of war in international affairs followed a similar logic. For Wilson, the way states were domestically organized (specifically, if they were democracies or not) explained the propensity of states to be aggressive and, thus, cause an international conflict. See Woodrow Wilson, "The World Must Be Made Safe for Democracy," in *Classics of International Relations,* 3rd ed., ed. John Vasquez (Englewood Cliffs, NJ: Prentice Hall, 1996), pp. 35–38.

7. Kenneth Waltz's neorealism is a more blatant assertion of this privileged domestic vision. His structural approach reinforces and dehistoricizes the classical realist claims regarding this question. See Kenneth Waltz, *Theory of International Politics* (Reading, MA: Addison-Wesley, 1979). For a more detailed critical analysis of the neorealist structural effects on the discipline of international relations theory, see Richard Ashley, "The Poverty of Neorealism," in *Neorealism and Its Critics,* ed. Robert Keohane (New York: Columbia University Press, 1986), pp. 255–300.

8. Frederick Dolan, "Hobbes and/or North: The Rhetoric of American National Security," in *Ideology and Power in the Age of Lenin in Ruins,* ed. Arthur and Marilouise Kroker (New York: St. Martin's Press, 1991), pp. 191–209.

9. This is done mainly by replicating the notion of a "domestic analogy" between Hobbes's depiction of the "state of nature" and international politics as realist international relations scholars see it. More will be said later on the role of the "domestic analogy" in realist theory.

10. Dolan, "Hobbes and/or North," p. 192.

11. For Hobbes, upon entering the Commonwealth, human beings ex-

change the "Rights of nature," that is, "the liberty each man has to use his own power, as he will himselfe, for the preservation of his own nature, that is to say his own life" (*Leviathan*, p. 189), for the "Laws of nature," whereby the Rights of an individual to fully enjoy all of his passions and desires are limited by the recognition that other individuals have equal "Rights" which cannot be violated. The "Laws of nature" guarantee that the enjoyment of an individual's Rights end when and where the Rights of other members of the Commonwealth start. As Hobbes puts it, a Law of nature tells the individual subject: "Do not that to another, which thou wouldest not have done to thyselfe" (ibid., p. 214). Whereas "Rights of nature" guarantee a naturally unimpinged individual free will, "Laws of nature" forbid or limit the deployment of human actions for the so-called benefit of a law-abiding community.

12. That is to say, his grounding of sovereignty in material conditions of existence.

13. Dolan, "Hobbes and/or North," p. 192.

14. Hobbes, *Leviathan*, p. 88.

15. Michael Shapiro calls this displacement from individual nature to state sovereignty a move from proto-sovereignty to sovereignty. Shapiro explains that "[t]o avoid [death] and achieve ['commodious living'], persons calculate that it is best to enter into the primary covenant by which they trade obedience for protection and accept the absolute power of the sovereign." He concludes that "[t]his is the mythic tale that links proto-sovereignty [the pieces that later will make the sovereign whole] with sovereignty, subjectivity with the sovereign order." For Shapiro, this exchange of sovereign positions inaugurates the economistic and contractual model later replicated by Adam Smith. See Michael Shapiro, *Reading "Adam Smith": Desire, History, and Value* (Newbury Park, CA: Sage, 1993), p. 3.

16. Hobbes, *Leviathan*, p. 131.

17. Dolan, "Hobbes and/or North," p. 194.

18. Ibid.

19. David Johnston, *The Rhetoric of Leviathan: Thomas Hobbes and the Politics of Cultural Transformation* (Princeton, NJ: Princeton University Press, 1986), p. 70.

20. Dolan, "Hobbes and/or North," p. 194.

21. Ibid., p. 201.

22. William Connolly summarizes Hobbes's "nominalism" in the following terms: "[Hobbes] treats words as human artifacts, fixed by definition. Knowledge does not reach to the essence of the world; it is created by humans and resides in a theory which meets the dictates of logic and strict definition." See William Connolly, *Political Theory and Modernity* (Ithaca, NY: Cornell University Press, 1993), p. 21.

23. Hobbes, *Leviathan,* p. 105.

24. Johnston, *The Rhetoric of Leviathan,* p. 85.

25. Hobbes, *Leviathan,* pp. 109–10.

26. One may wonder how such a common agreement is possible when individuals are not able to agree on a single mode of signification, expression, and communication. The common agreement to form a "Leviathan" supposedly reflects a unique, unequivocal, and constant choice on the part of all concerned individuals.

27. This is exemplified by John Hall and John Ikenberry's analysis that treats Hobbes as a "realist statist thinker." Hobbes, so they claim, is a theorist of the state because he is able to provide a vision of domestic order and stability guaranteed by the sovereign presence of a structure called the state. From Hobbes's work, they conclude that "the presence of the state allows for peace in social relations within societies." See John Hall and John Ikenberry, *The State* (Minneapolis: University of Minnesota Press, 1989), pp. 9–10. Another good example of this stereotype is provided by David Held, who affirms that "Hobbes produced a political philosophy which is a fascinating point of departure for reflection on the modern theory of the state." See David Held, *Political Theory and the Modern State* (Stanford: Stanford University Press, 1989), p. 14. Because Held is eager to interpret Hobbes as a "statist theorist" as well, his analysis of Hobbes remains bound within the terms of a liberal political discourse on order and the question of the security of the civil community.

28. Walker notes that "[g]iven [Hobbes's] current reputation as one of the great figures in an imagined tradition of political realism in the theory of international relations, it is useful to recall once again why he did not offer any account of the international anarchy that is so often invoked in his name." See Walker, *Inside/Outside,* p. 150.

29. John J. Mearsheimer, "Why We Will Soon Miss the Cold War," in *Conflict after the Cold War: Arguments on the Causes of War and Peace,* ed. Richard Betts (New York: MacMillan, 1994), p. 44; reprinted from *Atlantic* 266, no. 2 (August 1990).

30. For international relations theorists, the seminal passages of Hobbes's vision of the "state of nature" are found in chapter 13 of *Leviathan,* "Of the Naturall Condition of Mankind," pp. 183–88.

31. Hans Morgenthau, *Politics among Nations* (New York: Knopf, 1948), p. 39. Contrary to Morgenthau's affirmation, for Hobbes, there is no necessity for domestic politics to be essentially about a struggle for power. It just happens to be this way. What seems to govern "politics" prior to Leviathan for Hobbes is more fear than power. Power (and the power struggle), for Hobbes, is only a consequence of the fear of death. It is not the

essence of life in anarchy, as Morgenthau puts it, but rather the likely consequence of "natural life."

32. David Campbell, *Writing Security: United States Foreign Policy and
the Politics of Identity* (Minneapolis: University of Minnesota Press, 1992).

33. Walker, *Inside/Outside.*

34. Campbell, *Writing Security,* p. 67.

35. Ibid., p. 69.

36. Walker, *Inside/Outside,* p. 150.

37. Martti Koskenniemi suggests that the unequivocal reference to the
notion of "domestic analogy" does not appear until Emerich de Vattel and
his legal treatise *Le Droit des Gens* (The law of nations) written in 1758.
See Martti Koskenniemi, *From Apology to Utopia: The Structure of International Legal Argument* (Helsinki: Lakimiesliiton Kustannus, Finnish
Lawyers' Publishing Company, 1989), p. 7.

38. Here is perhaps the main analogy between the realists and Hobbes,
the one analogy that really matters: there is in both cases a desire, in the face
of difference and anarchy, to impose order and discipline to solve the specific problems at hand.

39. Hedley Bull, "Hobbes and the International Anarchy," *Social Research* 48 (1981): 717.

40. Hobbes, *Leviathan,* pp. 187–88.

41. Niccolo Machiavelli, *The Prince,* trans. Harvey Mansfield (Chicago:
University of Chicago Press, 1985).

42. Walker, *Inside/Outside,* p. 111.

43. Michael C. Williams has offered a similar interpretation of Hobbes.
Locating Hobbes's thought in a larger context of seventeenth-century skep-
ticism, Williams suggests that the characterization of Hobbes as a founding
figure of realist "anarchy" is problematic. Turning against both the traditional realist tenets on Hobbes and the British rationalist school (epitomized by Bull, who faults Hobbes for not having considered the possibility
of a "covenant among sovereigns"), Williams's reading seeks to "compli-
cate the picture of Hobbesian anarchy." Williams contends that *Leviathan*
is not necessarily concerned with the question of the development of rational calculations and self-interested actions in an inherently dangerous and
inimical international system. What *Leviathan* is about is the search for
possible ethical foundations among political communities. This may still be
geared toward reinforcing/protecting the state. But it does so in a larger
context of "interstate society," to use Walker's terminology, not "anarchy."
As such, Williams concludes, "Leviathan solves a series of much more difficult problems concerning epistemology and ethics and their role in the
creation of political communities." See Michael C. Williams, "Hobbes and

International Relations: A Reconsideration," *International Organization* 50, no. 2 (1996): 230.

44. It can be seen, as Mearsheimer nostalgically affirms, that the cold war polarities were able to impose a clear-cut structure of international stability and order. Under a system of balance of power between the West and the East, "anarchy" was easily contained. See John Mearsheimer, "Why We Will Soon Miss the Cold War," or his more recent essay, "The False Promise of International Institutions," *International Security* 19, no. 3 (winter 1994–95): 5–49.

45. Robert Kaplan, "The Coming Anarchy," *Atlantic Monthly* (February 1994): 44–76.

46. The guarantees that supposedly were once offered by the cold war, retrospectively reinterpreted as a "long peace." See John Lewis Gaddis, "The Long Peace," *International Security* 10, no. 4 (spring 1986): 99–142.

47. Timothy W. Luke, "Placing Power/Siting Space: The Politics of Global and Local in the New World Order," *Environment and Planning D: Society and Space* 12 (1994): 624.

48. Campbell, *Writing Security,* p. 64.

49. Boutros-Ghali, *An Agenda for Peace,* 2nd ed. (New York: United Nations Publication, 1995), pp. 45–46.

50. Not so specific in fact since the border between each of these new UN activities is never clearly defined. This imprecise distinction between peacekeeping and peacemaking will play a determining role in the United Nations operation in Bosnia, as will be seen in chapter 4.

51. Ibid., p. 46.

52. Boutros-Ghali reminds his readership of the importance of those values in the last section of *An Agenda for Peace.* Not surprisingly, those values are traditional communitarian liberal principles such as human liberty, political democracy, equality among peoples and nations, global solidarity, national sovereignty, etc. See *An Agenda for Peace,* pp. 69–72.

53. Charles Kegley, "The Neoidealist Moment in International Studies? Realist Myths and the New International Realities," *International Studies Quarterly* 37 (1993): 131–46.

54. I have provided a more detailed analysis of this "neoidealist moment" in "Deploying Vision, Simulating Action: The United Nations and Its Visualization Strategies in a New World Order," *Alternatives* 21, no. 1 (1996): 67–92.

55. See Kegley, "The Neoidealist Moment," pp. 131–32.

56. See Timothy W. Luke, "New World Order or Neo-world Orders: Power, Politics and Ideology in Informationalizing Glocalities," in *Global Modernities,* ed. Mike Featherstone, Scott Lash and Roland Robertson (Thousand Oaks, CA: Sage, 1995), pp. 91–107. See also John Agnew and

Stuart Corbridge, *Mastering Space: Hegemony, Territory, and International Political Economy* (New York: Routledge, 1995).

57. As Kroker and Weinstein put it. See Arthur Kroker and Michael A. Weinstein, *Data Trash: The Theory of the Virtual Class* (New York: St. Martin's Press, 1994).

58. I refer here to the visual representation of Hobbes's sovereign designed on the cover to the 1651 version of *Leviathan*. This image represents a fictional creature, of giant size, rising over the territorial kingdom, and whose body artificially contains the totality of individual subjects in the kingdom.

59. This formulation is borrowed from Timothy W. Luke's "Placing Power/Siting Space."

2. SPACE QUEST

1. See Jeremy Bentham, *The Panopticon Writings,* ed. Miran Božovič (New York: Verso, 1995).

2. See Michel Foucault, *Discipline and Punish: The Birth of the Prison,* trans. Alan Sheridan (New York: Vintage Books, 1979).

3. Nicholas de Cusa, "The Vision of God," in *Unity and Reform,* ed. John Patrick Dolan (South Bend, IN: University of Notre Dame Press, 1962). Nicholas de Cusa is sometimes known under his latinized name, Cusanus.

4. Dolan mentions that Giles Randall provided one of the first authorized English translations of de Cusa's text in 1646 under the title *The Single Eye.*

5. Ibid., p. 129.

6. In his study of de Cusa's philosophy, Jasper Hopkins indicates that de Cusa witnessed during his lifetime the beginning of the Great Schism, the last days of the Inquisition, and the fall of Constantinople to the Muslim armies. These sudden changes, combined with the emergence of early Renaissance artistic and architectural innovations, pushed Christian scholars and thinkers to reconsider the ways to reach God and live in accordance with his word. See Jasper Hopkins, *A Concise Introduction to the Philosophy of Nicholas de Cusa* (Minneapolis: University of Minnesota Press, 1980).

7. In his zeal, Augustine offered the vision of a mode of human organization on earth that would allow individuals to prepare for their passage into God's Kingdom, after Judgment Day. The organization of the earthly City was to fall under the direct command of God and, as such, should constitute the first stage of God's city, at least for Christian subjects (the second stage was after the death of the body and the elevation of the soul). Such a political ideology can be characterized as dominionism, that is to say, the unmediated realization and implementation of God's plans on earth. See

Augustine, *Political Writings,* trans. Michael W. Tkacz and Douglas Kries (Indianapolis: Hackett, 1994).

8. De Cusa, "The Vision of God," p. 134.

9. Ibid. (my inserts).

10. Ibid., p. 136.

11. Miran Božovič, "An Utterly Dark Spot: Introduction to Jeremy Bentham," Introduction to *The Panopticon Writings,* p. 14.

12. See Michael Klare, *Rogue States and Nuclear Outlaws: America's Search for a New Foreign Policy* (New York: Hill and Wang, 1995).

13. Quoted in ibid., p. 108.

14. Created in 1957, the IAEA is part of the "UN family" of international organizations. Former UN Secretary-General Boutros-Ghali defines the IAEA as "an autonomous intergovernmental organization with cooperative links with the United Nations and its relevant organs." The IAEA provides annual reports to the United Nations General Assembly. See Boutros Boutros-Ghali, *The United Nations and Nuclear Non-Proliferation: An Introduction* (New York: United Nations Publication, 1995), p. 14.

15. North Korea's Assembly ratified the safeguards agreement in April 1992. This agreement is part of the NPT (Non-Proliferation Treaty) system and allows international inspectors from the IAEA to periodically verify declared nuclear facilities. To facilitate the inspections, the country party to such an agreement is required to provide a list of its nuclear testing sites. This agreement also entitles the IAEA to monitor a country's nuclear resources and uses by any means deemed appropriate and recognized as such by the NPT. See Boutros-Ghali, ibid., pp. 13–15.

16. See Michael Klare, *Rogue States and Nuclear Outlaws,* p. 139.

17. Han S. Park, "The Conundrum of the Nuclear Program," in *North Korea: Ideology, Politics, Economy,* ed. Han S. Park (Englewood Cliffs, NJ: Prentice Hall, 1996), p. 223.

18. As Park notes, Moscow's influence was primordial to North Korea's signing of the NPT. See ibid., p. 222.

19. Tim Weiner, "Shift on Cameras by North Koreans," *New York Times,* October 30, 1993.

20. Michael Mazarr, *North Korea and the Bomb: A Case Study in Nonproliferation* (New York: St. Martin's Press, 1995), p. 133.

21. Ibid., p. 94.

22. Ibid., p. 95.

23. Klare, *Rogue States and Nuclear Outlaws,* p. 140.

24. Quoted in Valerie Gillen, *IAEA Inspections and Iraq's Nuclear Capabilities* (Vienna: IAEA Publication, 1992), p. 23.

25. Park, "The Nuclear Conundrum," p. 223.

26. Ibid., p. 225.

27. Ibid., p. 228.

28. On a corollary note, North Korea's connection to the world and world order policies presupposes for many authors a reunification between Pyongyang and Seoul that, as they believe, necessarily means the adoption by the North of the culture and way of life of the South. See, for example, Samuel Kim, "The Two Koreas and World Order," in *Korea and the World: Beyond the Cold War,* ed. Young Whan Kihl (Boulder, CO: Westview, 1994), p. 61.

29. There is in fact a small Christian population in North Korea. It is reported that Billy Graham simply asked Kim Il Sung to be invited over, and the "Great Leader," whose mother was Christian, accepted. This religious televangelical connection provided by Billy Graham was used by the U.S. president as a way to get the message across to the North Korean leader.

30. Klare, *Rogue States and Nuclear Outlaws,* p. 140.

31. Park, "The Nuclear Conundrum," p. 231.

32. Mazarr, *North Korea and the Bomb,* pp. 153–54.

33. Ibid., p. 168.

34. Klare, *Rogue States and Nuclear Outlaws,* p. 140.

35. Voted immediately after the Gulf War, on April 3, 1991. For a thorough presentation of this resolution, see U.S. Congress, *U.N. Security Council Resolutions on Iraq: Compliance and Implementation,* House of Representatives, Subcommittee on Europe and the Middle East of the Committee on Foreign Affairs, 102nd Congress, 2nd session (1992).

36. Eric Chauvistre, *The Implications of IAEA Inspections under Security Council Resolution 687,* Research Papers, UN Institute for Disarmament Research (New York: United Nations Publication, 1992), p. 5.

37. Quoted in Klare, *Rogue States and Nuclear Outlaws,* p. 146.

38. Chauvistre, *The Implications of IAEA Inspections,* p. 5.

39. Ibid., p. 7.

40. *Measure* the amount of declared material, *evaluate* the capacity of nuclear plants to produce usable materials, *assess* the industrial capabilities for the creation of future nuclear plants, *identify* weaponization facilities of all kinds, *search* for hidden or secret weapon sites, *supervise* the removal of hazardous armament. See ibid., p. xi.

41. Ibid., pp. 18–19.

42. See, for example, Ian Johnstone, *Aftermath of the Gulf War: An Assessment of UN Action,* International Peace Academy Occasional Paper Series (Boulder, CO: Lynne Rienner, 1994).

43. Klare, *Rogue States and Nuclear Outlaws,* pp. 145–46 (my emphasis).

44. Fouad Ajami, "Saddam and a Sack of Sugar," *US News & World Report,* December 1, 1997, p. 46.

45. Thomas Friedman, "Head Shot," *New York Times,* November 6, 1997, p. A 39.

46. Ronald Steel, "Unbalanced," *New Republic,* December 8, 1997, p. 19.

47. As Gary Milhollin puts it. See Gary Milhollin, "The Iraqi Bomb," *New Yorker,* February 1993. Kathleen Bailey confirms Milhollin's view by stating that "defeated in war, subject to anytime-anywhere inspections, and with the constant threat of renewal of hostilities in event of noncompliance, Iraq nevertheless was defiant and crafty, and avoided giving a full, detailed disclosure of its weapons and capabilities, as required by Resolution 687." See Kathleen Bailey, *The U.N. Inspections in Iraq: Lessons for On-Site Verifications* (Boulder, CO: Westview, 1995), p. 4.

48. Milhollin, "The Iraqi Bomb," p. 47.

49. Recent reports have indicated that "spying on UN inspectors" has become common practice in Iraq. There is even a special unit of Iraqi troops, called Project 858, whose only task is to oversee the actions and movements of the inspectors. Keeping the pressure on the UN, Saddam may have turned to an ironic strategy of "overseeing the overseers." See The Editors, "Notebook: Spy Story," *New Republic,* December 15, 1997, p. 11.

50. Ibid., p. 51.

51. See W. Seth Carus, "Hide and Seek," *New Republic,* November 24, 1997, p. 28.

52. Ibid.

53. In February 1997, traces of botulic toxin, a deadly biological component, were found by UNSCOM on old neutralized bombs that Iraq had claimed had not been used since 1990. This finding fueled UNSCOM's suspicion that dangerous biological elements such as concentrated toxin or anthrax had probably been tested for military purposes by Iraq since after the Gulf War. Similarly, UNSCOM destroyed sixty-nine tons of chemical agents (including sarin gas) between 1992 and 1994. Despite this setback for Iraq, UN inspectors still believed in 1997 that Iraq was trying to rebuild an easy-to-handle neurotoxic chemical component called VX. These findings have been recorded by French political chronicler Jacques Amalric in "Le Dernier Etat des Stocks d'Armes Irakiens: Comment Saddam Hussein Reste d'Attaque," (The latest status on Iraq's weapons: Or how Saddam Hussein remains fit for combat), *Libération,* December 18, 1997.

54. Since 1991, "dozens of standoffs have taken place between UN inspectors and Iraqi officials." These standoffs have often given Saddam Hussein the opportunity to buy time to hide evidence from UN inspectors.

55. I derive the term "overhead imagery" from Johan Molander's study. See Johan Molander, "Mandated Aerial Inspections," in *Open Skies, Arms*

Control, and Cooperative Security, ed. Michael Krepon and Amy Smithson (New York: St. Martin's Press, 1992).

56. Ibid., p. 149.

57. Klare, *Rogue States and Nuclear Outlaws,* p. 115.

58. Milhollin, "The Iraqi Bomb," p. 51.

59. Ibid., p. 52.

60. As Foucault mentions, it is believed that Bentham had been influenced by the architectural infrastructure of the dormitories in the Paris Military School (1751). See Michel Foucault, "L'oeil du pouvoir," (The eye of power), introductory essay to Bentham, *Le panoptique* (The Panopticon), (Paris: Belfond, 1977).

61. Foucault, *Discipline and Punish,* p. 200.

62. Bentham, *The Panopticon Writings,* p. 43 (Bentham's emphasis).

63. Ibid., p. 45 (Bentham's emphasis).

64. David Lyon, *The Electronic Eye: The Rise of Surveillance Society* (Minneapolis: University of Minnesota Press, 1994), p. 62.

65. William Bogard, *The Simulation of Surveillance: Hypercontrol in Telematic Societies* (New York: Cambridge University Press, 1996).

66. This notion is derived from Baudrillard's analysis of the place of power in the Renaissance palaces where "the actual locus of power would perhaps be nothing more than a perspective effect." Jean Baudrillard, *Selected Writings,* ed. Mark Poster (Stanford: Stanford University Press, 1988), p. 158.

67. Bentham, *The Panopticon Writings,* p. 90.

68. Ibid., p. 112.

69. Božovič, "An Utterly Dark Spot," p. 7.

70. Bentham's entire utilitarian philosophy rests on a calculated balance between pleasure and pain. Pleasure is reactively defined by Bentham as the absence of pain. Utility is a principle of action, a motivation, that represents Bentham's primary desire to reject suffering. The principle of utility aims at maximizing pleasure by, conversely, minimizing the "sum total" of pains. Being free from pain is thus the essential motivation behind Bentham's brand of utilitarianism. See Jeremy Bentham, *The Principles of Morals and Legislation* (Amherst, NY: Prometheus Books, 1988), p. 2. Bentham's anxiety over a possible life of pain, and his inclination to turn to imaginary structures to help him transcend his fears (of everyday life) are well documented. See C. K. Ogden, *Bentham's Theory of Fictions* (New York: Harcourt, Brace, 1932).

71. See Božovič, "An Utterly Dark Spot," p. 4.

72. Bentham, *Panopticon Writings,* p. 101.

73. The first international organizations were created at the end of the nineteenth century. The initial international organizations were created to regulate commerce and security on international rivers and other waterways.

74. This notion of the "territoriality trap," the idea that speed (gaining time) has taken over space, is derived from Paul Virilio's work. Virilio has argued that the strategic attitude of the state which, during a battle for example, consisted of "giving up ground in order to gain Time" has lost its meaning. "Nowadays, gaining Time is exclusively a matter of vectors [flux, flows] and the territory has lost its meaning to the benefit of the missile. In fact, the strategic value of placeless speed [le non-lieu de la vitesse] has replaced the value of space, and the question of owning Time has taken over the notion of territorial possession." See Paul Virilio, *Vitesse et politique* (Paris: Galilée, 1977), p. 131 (my translation). On this topic, see also John Agnew, "The Territorial Trap: The Geographical Assumptions of International Relations Theory," *Review of International Political Economy* 1 (1994): 53–80.

75. I am here indebted to Timothy Luke's notions of "international cyborganizations" and "cyborg subjectivity." See Timothy W. Luke, "Liberal Society and Cyborg Subjectivity: The Politics of Environments, Bodies, and Nature," *Alternatives* 21, no. 1 (1996): 1–30.

76. Bogard, *The Simulation of Surveillance*, p. 8.

77. Ibid., pp. 6–8.

78. After all, simulation is the point where "the imaginary and the real coincide, . . . where the gap between virtual control and actual control disappears." Ibid., p. 9.

79. Bruce Poulin, "An Early Warning Apparatus for the United Nations: A Canadian Policy Memorandum Advocating Space Surveillance in the Post–Cold War Era," *Canadian Journal of Strategic Studies: The McNaughton Papers* 6 (1994): 9–14.

80. Ibid., p. 9.

81. Ibid., pp. 9–10.

82. Ibid., p. 10.

83. Ibid.

84. Ibid.

85. For Poulin, the "triad for confidence building" is PHOTINT-HUMINT-aerial surveillance. PHOTINT is, however, the solidifying mechanism that guarantees that the other two inspection regimes can be successful.

86. Poulin, "An Early Warning Apparatus," p. 10.

87. Ibid., p. 11.

88. See Allen Banner, Andrew Young, and Keith Hall, *Aerial Reconnaissance for Verification of Arms Limitation Agreements: An Introduction* (New York: United Nations Publication, 1990); Michael Krepon and Amy Smithson, *Open-Skies, Arms Control, and Cooperative Security* (New York: St. Martin's Press, 1992); William H. Lewis, "Technology and International Peacekeeping Forces," in *Technology and the Limitation of International*

Conflict, ed. Barry Blechman (Washington, DC: The Johns Hopkins Foreign Policy Institute Papers, 1989), pp. 117–36. Of all the above-cited literatures on surveillance, Lewis's intervention is perhaps the most glaringly optimistic and openly visionary. Lewis writes that technology "holds out the hope of solutions to many otherwise intractable problems ranging from declining agricultural growth rates to mounting birth rates, from the trials of nation building to the tribulations of order building, and from the conquest of space to the violent resolution of disputes among nations." See ibid., p. 117.

89. James Der Derian, "The (S)pace of International Relations: Simulation, Surveillance, Speed," *International Studies Quarterly* 34 (1990): 304.

90. To use Mark Poster's formulation. See Mark Poster, *The Mode of Information* (Chicago: University of Chicago Press, 1990), p. 97.

91. Foucault, *Discipline and Punish,* p. 297.

92. Ibid., p. 303.

93. Just as, for Foucault, "visibility is a trap."

94. The ideological objectives of globalization are intricately tied to the notion of disciplinary liberalism. In such a perspective, globalization is a process of realization of disciplinary liberalism. It works by means of a "universalising culture [that preaches] the desirability and/or necessity of political, economic, and social progress defined in terms of . . . democracy, human rights and welfare, and also by technological developments generated in political and economic competition ruled by capitalism and the free market." All these objectives are finalized in the fulfillment of "the very liberal value of freedom: the unconstrained movement of goods, services, capital and people." See Jef Huysmans, "Post–Cold War Implosion and Globalisation: Liberalism Running Past Itself?" *Millennium* 24 (1995): 481.

95. Stephen Gill, "Globalisation, Market Civilisation, and Disciplinary Neoliberalism," *Millennium* 24 (1995): 399.

96. The approach to globalization and neoliberal international structures traditionally privileged by international relations scholars (from Robert Keohane's *After Hegemony* to Stephen Gill's most recent neo-Gramscian critiques of neoliberal globalization regimes).

97. Lawrence Finkelstein, "What Is Global Governance?" *Global Governance* 1, no. 2 (1995): 369.

98. Ibid.

99. Ibid., p. 368.

100. Michel Foucault, "Governmentality," in *The Foucault Effect: Studies in Governmentality,* ed. Graham Burchell, Colin Gordon, and Peter Miller (Chicago: University of Chicago Press, 1991), p. 102.

101. On the question of the new regimes of environmental governmentality, see Thom Kuehls, *Beyond Sovereign Territory: The Space of Ecopolitics* (Minneapolis: University of Minnesota Press, 1996); and Timothy W. Luke,

Ecocritique: Contesting the Politics of Nature, Economy, and Culture (Minneapolis: University of Minnesota Press, 1997).

102. Finkelstein, "What Is Global Governance?," p. 369.

103. James Rosenau, "Governance in the Twenty-First Century," *Global Governance* 1, no. 1 (1995): 13–43.

104. Ibid., p. 13.

105. Ibid., p. 14.

106. Ibid., pp. 14–15.

107. Foucault, *Discipline and Punish*, p. 298.

108. Ibid., p. 299.

109. Rosenau, "Global Governance in the Twenty-First Century," p. 15.

3. FROM A HOPELESS SITUATION TO OPERATION RESTORE HOPE, AND BEYOND

1. Many journalistic and scholarly reports about the Somali conflict have noted the appropriation of this humanitarian/military intervention by Western televisual media. From the landing of U.S. Marines to the withdrawal of UN forces, Somalia has been characterized as a "televised invasion," or, as some have preferred to call it, "a media-driven spectacle of misguided internationalism." See Chester Crocker, "The Lessons of Somalia," *Foreign Affairs* 74 (1995): 2.

2. Tom Englehardt, *The End of Victory Culture: Cold War America and the Disillusioning of a Generation* (New York: Basic Books, 1995), p. 264.

3. Englehardt explains that, from a visual perspective, the offensive against Saddam Hussein had to conjure away the images of Vietnam that were thoroughly impregnated in American minds and had spread into popular culture by way of the many Vietnam "quagmire films" (*Apocalypse Now, Rambo, The Deer Hunter*, etc.) (Englehardt, ibid., p. 277). Finding its referentiality in heroic and sci-fi movies of the 1980s that sought to make war a "feel-good activity" (George Lucas's *Star Wars* trilogy was mostly responsible for this reversal of imagery), the high-tech and image-controlled approach to the Gulf War was to serve as a "screen-cleaning device" (ibid., p. 272).

4. These two notions (a "reconstructive image of images" and an "antidote to discontrol") are borrowed directly from Englehardt's reading. See ibid., p. 280.

5. In this chapter, my understanding of the real or reality is not simply Baudrillardian (in the sense developed in the previous and following chapters). Here, real/reality is more directly linked to a psychoanalytic and Lacanian connotation. The many references made in the following pages to

Lacan's theory of subjectivity and identification (via the visual) are indicative of such a shift. This shift is certainly not a minor one. However, as will be made clear toward the end of the chapter, the Baudrillardian and Lacanian notions of reality are not too far removed from one another, at least in the present analysis. A brief exposition of the Baudrillardian and Lacanian notions of the real/reality is, however, in order. For Baudrillard, the real (or, rather, as he puts it, the "reality principle" or "reality effects") is always already within simulation. Once again, it is "the generation by models of a real without origin or reality: a hyperreal." See Baudrillard, *Simulations*, p. 2. As the product of a medium, living in and for the medium only, the Baudrillardian real is without depth. Yet, it has taken over cognition, our ability of "making sense" of the world. The Lacanian real is different in principle. And yet, it can be as traumatic for the subject as Baudrillard's notion of the real-as-hyperreal. Whereas the real is for Baudrillard the disembodied condition of contemporary life/practice (of the relationship between object and subject, after the object has taken precedence), Lacan keeps the real (his notion of the "real") at the level of individual subjectivity. Lacan identifies three different stages of individual identification: the imaginary, the symbolic, and the real. They form what he calls the "three registers of human reality" (Daniel Leader and Judy Groves, *Introducing Lacan* [New York: Totem Books, 1995], p. 61). The real is, thus, for Lacan one of the three stages of human life (or "reality" as he puts it). The imaginary is a mode of identification (premised on the mirror-stage, as shall be seen later on) that is based on the specular, on the recognition of oneself through visual reflections, through images. The symbolic, a notion introduced by Lacan after the imaginary, complements the mode of identification by means of the visual. The symbolic is what exists prior to the visual, and continues to affect identification even after the visual stage. It is the place of what Lacan calls the "ideal," not so much as an ideated teleological construct, but as the play of sociocultural structures, institutions, psychological traits that an individual consciously or unconsciously inherits through language, mostly from his/her surrounding environment. The notion of the symbolic is very close to the way Althusser understands ideology, for example. Finally, the real is for Lacan what resists both the imaginary and the symbolic. It often manifests itself as an irruption, as an unexpected and shocking encounter with something that no longer fits within the parameters of the symbolic and/or imaginary. There is, thus, something traumatic and violent about the Lacanian real. It is composed of the traces or fragments of a subject's experience that neither the imaginary nor the symbolic can make sense of. The "uncanniness" of the Lacanian real is recognized by the fact that it cannot be expressed either through visual representation or through language. The real is often accessed through the unconscious. See Leader and Groves,

Introducing Lacan, pp. 42–48 and 60–61. The Baudrillardian and Lacanian notions of the real have an important common perspective, one that allows me to treat the two notions as somewhat equivalent (at least, in this chapter). Both notions reflect a dispossession or disattachment, particularly for the individual subject. In both cases, the real operates a desacralization of subjective experience (through the unconscious for Lacan, through the precession of the model, the simulacrum, and the system of objects for Baudrillard). The real is, thus, a shaky ground for the cogito, the thinking subject, in both configurations. There is, however, a major difference between these two experiences of the real/reality. For Baudrillard, it is possible to experience the real-as-hyperreal as a "second nature," as if there were no difference between simulation and representation. In short, for Baudrillard, the real-as-hyperreal is too real not to be true. It fools the eye, but one may never know. For Lacan, the real is "uncanny" and, as such, a foreign element that the subject experiences as change, difference or rupture. The Lacanian real is never too real to be noticed. It never fools the eye. Rather, it has a shock value (unlike the indifference value of the Baudrillardian hyperreal).

6. As Kaja Silverman indicates. See Kaja Silverman, *The Subject of Semiotics* (Oxford: Oxford University Press, 1983), pp. 215–22.

7. This perhaps contradicts Blumenthal's suggestion that Somalia was a John Ford, not an Oliver Stone movie. Instead of being a John Ford–type of production where the good old U.S. (and UN) cavalry comes to the rescue of the hapless victims threatened by evil-intended and amoral hordes of bandits or unenlightened "redskin-like" savages (Aidid and his followers), Somalia will end up looking like an Oliver Stone movie where (as in *Platoon,* for example) the so-called good guys become entangled in the senseless and irrational drama of war and, in the course of the crisis, end up being the victims and, sometimes, the "bad guys." According to this "Stonian" scenario, instead of glorifying war (and victory), the actors end up questioning the justification for the entire enterprise and are left with nothing else but doubt and torn identities.

8. Donatella Lorsch, Special Report for the *New York Times,* March 8, 1994.

9. Movies generally associated with connotations of Western male bravado, chauvinism, and triumphalism.

10. Quoted in Lorsch, *New York Times,* March 8, 1994.

11. This patching of the screen ironically prefigures the theoretical notion of suture.

12. Jacques-Alain Miller, "Suture (Elements of the Logic of the Signifier)," *Screen* 18 (1977–78): 24–34.

13. Jean-Pierre Oudart, "Cinema and Suture," *Screen* 18 (1977–78): 35.

14. See Christian Metz, *Le signifiant imaginaire* (The imaginary signifier) (Paris: Christian Bourgeois, 1984); *Film Language: A Semiotics of the Cinema,* trans. Michael Taylor (Chicago: University of Chicago Press, 1991).

15. See Metz, *Le signifiant imaginaire,* p. 65 (my translation).

16. Daniel Dayan, "The Tutor-Code of Classic Cinema," *Film Quarterly* 28 (1974): 24.

17. Ibid.

18. Jacques Lacan, *Ecrits: A Selection,* trans. Alan Sheridan (New York: Norton, 1977), p. 3.

19. We encounter here again the notion of the real as it is understood by Lacan. The real is the "return of the repressed," so to speak, of that which cannot be expressed through language, which has no place in representation.

20. This decentralization of the subject (it is a decentralization of the subject and not a decentering of subjectivity in the discourse of psychoanalysis: although the subject is now presented as construed by/through external structures, psychoanalytic thinking is still obsessed with such a decentralized subjectivity) is derived from Freud. As Althusser notes, "Freud has discovered for us that the real subject, the individual in his unique essence, has not the form of an ego, centred on the 'ego', on 'consciousness' or on 'existence'— whether this is existence of the for-itself, of the body proper or of 'behavior'— that the human subject is de-centred, constituted by a structure which has no 'centre' either, except in the imaginary misrecognition of the 'ego'." See Louis Althusser, "Freud and Lacan," in *Lenin and Philosophy and Other Essays by Louis Althusser,* trans. Ben Brewster (New York: Monthly Review Press, 1971), pp. 218–19.

21. Dayan, "The Tutor-Code of Classic Cinema," p. 24.

22. Metz, *Le signifiant imaginaire,* p. 66 (my translation).

23. Jacques Alain-Miller, "Suture," p. 24.

24. Metz, *Le signifiant imaginaire,* pp. 66–70.

25. Silverman, *The Subject of Semiotics,* p. 205.

26. Mohammed Sahnoun, UN special representative to Somalia in 1992, notes that after Barre's departure, "the Somali factions were left to themselves, and soon interclan fighting began." See Mohammed Sahnoun, *Somalia: The Missed Opportunities* (Washington, DC: United States Institute of Peace Press, 1994), p. 10.

27. Ibid., pp. 9–10.

28. Ibid., p. 9. See also Samuel Makinda, *Seeking Peace from Chaos: Humanitarian Intervention in Somalia* (Boulder, CO: Lynne Rienner, 1993), pp. 29–36.

29. Sahnoun, *Somalia: The Missed Opportunities,* p. 5.

30. On the question of Somalian national identity, see David Laitin, *Somalia, Nation in Search of a State* (Boulder, CO: Westview, 1986).

31. This is how "ethnic separatism" has been presented in the international literature on post–cold war politics. Ethnic, regional, and clannish divisions have suddenly become the new big scare in a world that, in the eyes of some of the most arrogant neoliberal Western thinkers, has become suddenly unproblematic from an ideological (if not empirical/historical) point of view. The ecstatic vision of the "end of history" (Francis Fukuyama, *The End of History and the Last Man* [New York: Free Press, 1992]) nonetheless gives birth to new nationalist/ethnic scares that, for some, may take the form of a future "clash of civilizations." See Samuel Huntington, "The Clash of Civilizations," *Foreign Affairs* 72 (1993): 22–49.

32. The deployment of UNOSOM was the result of three successive Security Council resolutions on Somalia. The first resolution, Resolution 733, taken on January 23, 1992, called the entire situation "hopeless" and asked for a "total arms embargo" on Somalia. The two subsequent resolutions, on March 17 and April 24, 1992, established the basis for deeper UN involvement. Resolution 751 on April 24 asked the secretary-general "to facilitate an immediate and effective cessation of hostilities and the maintenance of a cease-fire throughout the country in order to promote the process of reconciliation and political settlement in Somalia and to provide urgent humanitarian assistance." It also "called upon the international community to support with financial and other resources, the implementation of the 90-day Plan of Action for Emergency Humanitarian Assistance to Somalia." See Sahnoun, *Somalia: The Missed Opportunities,* pp. 15–17.

33. See Boutros Boutros-Ghali, *Report of the Secretary General Pursuant of the Statement Adopted by the Summit Meeting of the Security Council on 31 January, 1992* (New York: United Nations Publication, 1995).

34. Sahnoun, *Somalia: The Missed Opportunities,* p. 54.

35. Mohammed Sahnoun gives several reasons for the failure of UNOSOM I. Despite the apparent improvement of the humanitarian condition during the initial period of UN intervention (first part of 1992), the political situation was just as disorderly as before the UN got there. The partial success of the humanitarian mission faded away behind the persistence of clan warfare and a lack of valid state structures. See Sahnoun, ibid., p. 53. The UN's observation in the fall of 1992 that UNOSOM I had not been successful was very indicative of what the UN mission was about in Somalia. The humanitarian mission was only an alibi for a more politically and ideologically advantageous operation: bringing Somalia back into the fold of neoliberal world politics.

36. See Fred Barnes, "Brave New Gimmick," *New Republic,* February 1991, p. 15.

37. Jonathan Howe, "The United States and the United Nations in Somalia: The Limits of Involvement," *Washington Quarterly* 18 (1995): 51.

38. The term is borrowed from Engelhardt. See Engelhardt, *The End of Victory Culture,* p. 292.

39. George Kennan, "Somalia, Through a Glass Darkly," *New York Times,* September 30, 1993.

40. Sidney Blumenthal, "Why Are We in Somalia?" *New Yorker,* October 25, 1993, p. 51.

41. Ibid., pp. 51–52.

42. Blumenthal writes that "[t]he picture of the American arrival was intended to cancel the heartrending pictures of the starving Somali children." Ibid., p. 52.

43. George Bush, "Conditions in Somalia: Creating a Secure Environment," *Vital Speeches of the Day* 59 (January 1993): 163.

44. Ibid.

45. Ibid.

46. As Jonathan Stevenson notes, "American insensitivity to cultural differences was also to blame for the increasing friction [between the multinational force and the Somalis]. The U.S. soldiers were not well briefed about Somali peculiarities." See Jonathan Stevenson, "Hope Restored in Somalia?" *Foreign Policy* 91 (1993): 140.

47. As Blumenthal suggests. See Blumenthal, "Why Are We In Somalia?" p. 53.

48. Ibid., p. 52.

49. John Fiske, *Television Culture* (London: Methuen, 1987), p. 36.

50. Bruce Cumings, *War and Television* (New York: Verso, 1992), p. 21.

51. Mark Crispin Miller, *Boxed In: The Culture of TV* (Evanston, IL: Northwestern University Press, 1988), p. 157.

52. Ibid.

53. As Miller puts it, "the TV newsman comforts us as John Wayne comforted our grandparents, by seeming to have the whole affair in hand." Ibid.

54. Althusser, "Ideology and Ideological State Apparatuses," pp. 170–86.

55. Miller, *Boxed In,* pp. 160–61.

56. John L. Hirsch and Robert B. Oakley, *Somalia and Operation Restore Hope: Reflections on Peacemaking and Peacekeeping* (Washington, DC: United States Institute of Peace Press, 1995), p. 120.

57. Paul Ricoeur, "Althusser's Theory of Ideology," in *Althusser: A Critical Reader,* ed. Gregory Elliott (Cambridge, MA: Blackwell, 1994), p. 51.

58. It is worth noting that this approach to ideology by Althusser operates a shift in traditional Marxist analyses and offers new directions for a criticism of ideology from a Marxist perspective. Althusser reads Marx's *The German Ideology* and notes that "[i]deology, then, is for Marx an

imaginary *assemblage (bricolage)*, a pure dream, empty and vain, constituted by the 'day's residues' from the only full and positive reality, that of the concrete history of concrete material individuals materially producing their existence." See Althusser, "Ideology and Ideological State Apparatuses," p. 160. Althusser's theory of ideology differs from Marx's. Whereas Marx can only see one materiality, that of the real conditions of existence of subjected beings in the system of capitalist production (outside this, everything is pure imagination, dreamwork, fantasy), Althusser sees many other "materialities": those of ideological state apparatuses that produce ideologies as materially experienced conditions from which the reproduction of the system is assured.

59. Ibid., p. 143 (my emphasis). One may note that there is here yet another level of interpretation of the real/reality. It is not necessarily commensurate with either the Baudrillardian or the Lacanian interpretations suggested above. It is the (Marxist) Althusserian reading of reality, one that tends to equate reality with material experience, lived conditions of existence. Yet, unlike Marx, Althusser includes in reality-as-material experience the work/presence of ideology.

60. Ibid., p. 145 (Althusser's emphasis).

61. Ibid., p. 165.

62. Ibid., p. 167.

63. Ibid., p. 166.

64. Ibid., p. 174 (Althusser's emphasis).

65. Ibid., p. 181.

66. Indeed, the role of ideology in international relations has generally been limited to critiques of hegemony. As such, the critical post-Marxist work of Antonio Gramsci (and his theory of hegemony) has been privileged over Althusserian interpretations. See for example Robert Cox, "Social Forces, States, and World Orders: Beyond International Relations Theory," *Millennium* 10, no. 2 (1981): 128–37; and Enrico Augelli and Craig Murphy, *America's Quest for Supremacy and the Third World: A Gramscian Analysis* (London: Francis Pinter, 1988).

67. See Timothy W. Luke and Geróid Ó Tuathail, "On Videocameralistics: The Geopolitics of Failed States, the CNN International, and (UN) Governmentality" *Review of International Political Economy* 4, no. 4 (1997): 709–33.

68. Silverman, *The Subject of Semiotics*, p. 219.

69. Althusser, "Ideology and Ideological State Apparatuses," p. 181.

70. Silverman, *The Subject of Semiotics*, p. 205.

71. Ibid., p. 221.

72. As U.S. Senator Sam Nunn put it. See Sam Nunn, *Meet the Press,* Transcripts, October 10, 1993.

73. One of the most impressive, yet fruitless, efforts of the multinational

force to capture Aidid occurred on June 17, 1993. UN troops decided to storm what was believed to be Aidid's compound. Once they got inside, international troops discovered that Aidid and his supporters had already gone. This type of pointless action was going to be reproduced many times in the following months, as Aidid would continue to frustrate the efforts of the UN-U.S. coalition.

74. Another way of seeing things is to suggest, as Keenan does, that the UN "had set the threshold of the media agenda too high (wanted: Aidid) and then failed to provide adequate photo opportunities." In Keenan's perspective, the problem was not that the UN-U.S. coalition was overreliant on images, but that, after the photo-op landing of U.S. Marines in December 1992, the actors of the operation had forgotten that it was all about images and, instead, started to take their (military/peacekeeping) mission too seriously. Both the UN and the United States forgot that it was all done for the show and, in a sense, took the fiction for the reality. As the mission (chasing Aidid) took a more serious turn (achieving order militarily), the UN-U.S. coalition lost control over the events and allowed the Somalis to "set the agenda." When the media returned to Somalia in the fall of 1993, hoping for another photo-op episode, the tone had now been set by the Somalis, who provided international TV networks with their own version of the fiction: dead and mutilated soldiers, hostages, and a vengeful Aidid. By then, "the UNOSOM media operation [had] lost track of its own operation." See Keenan, "Live from . . . ," p. 155. Keenan's interpretation is very close (in its symptomatic treatment of Somalia as a visually-staged intervention) to mine. The divergence between his reading and mine is simply the result of a different inflection on the question of visual motivation. Whereas Keenan sees an autonomy of will (to vision and spectacularity) on the part of global media networks (they follow their own logic, their own ideology), I tend to look at global televisual productions and their buffering effects as accomplices of the UN-U.S. suturing strategy in Somalia.

75. Blumenthal recalls: "Overnight, the images from Somalia suspended politics in a freeze-frame. The appearance of a hostage turned Clinton into one himself: it was the picture of impotence and defeat, recalling, without any commentary necessary, the fate of the last Democratic President." Blumenthal, "Why Are We in Somalia?" p. 51.

76. Ibid., p. 50.

77. The Somalia operation was only officially terminated in the spring of 1995 when the last forces of UNOSOM II, the subsequent UN humanitarian mission that took over in 1993 after the departure of the U.S. soldiers, eventually left the country. As they left, and despite the feel-good attitude of UN officials claiming that the entire operation had not been useless (they

still affirmed that the UN saved lives and stopped starvation), the UN's lofty peacekeeping objectives in Somalia were far from being realized.

78. This crisis of incomprehension was to become the famous "Somalia syndrome." As Thomas Weiss explains, "the apparent failures of agonizing U.S. and UN efforts in this hapless country have led to the Somalia Syndrome." This marks the recognition that "multilateral interventions to thwart starvation, genocide, the forced movements of peoples, and massive violations of fundamental rights are no longer politically or operationally feasible." See Thomas G. Weiss, "Overcoming the Somalia Syndrome: 'Operation Rekindle Hope'?" *Global Governance* 1, no. 2 (1995): 171.

79. In an October 7, 1993, televised speech, a few days after the Durant episode, Clinton announced the withdrawal of U.S. forces set for March 31, 1994. In the meantime, however, Clinton chose to send more troops to allow the safe withdrawal of the forces already there. See Hirsch and Oakley, *Somalia and Operation Restore Hope*, p. 129.

80. On the trauma of the mission in Somalia, see Brett Litz, Susan Orsillo, Matthew Friedman, Peter Ehlich, and Alfonso Batres, "Posttraumatic Stress Disorder Associated with Peacekeeping Duty in Somalia for U.S. Military Personnel," *American Journal of Psychiatry* 154, no. 2 (1997): 178–84. Among other things, Litz et al. suggest that the "inherently contradictory experiences of the mission as both humanitarian and dangerous" is responsible for the PTSD (Posttraumatic Stress Disorder). The work of visual suture was perhaps designed to cover these "inherently contradictory experiences" and thus avoid this type of traumatic response.

81. Steven Shaviro, *The Cinematic Body* (Minneapolis: University of Minnesota Press, 1993), p. 16 (Shaviro's emphasis).

82. Or, in Lacanian terms, when the real reemerges in the imaginary construct of the subject.

83. Shaviro, *The Cinematic Body*, p. 16.

84. Many testimonies reported that the Somalis, in the last months of the UN mission, often tried to ambush Western journalists and TV crews to take their cameras away, a gesture perhaps designed to show that they regained the capacity of their own visual representation.

85. See Jacques Derrida, *Of Grammatology*, trans. Gayatri Chakravorty Spivak (Baltimore: Johns Hopkins University Press, 1976); *Positions*, trans. Alan Bass (Chicago: The University of Chicago Press, 1981).

86. Roland Barthes, *Mythologies*, trans. Annette Lavers (New York: Noonday Press, 1972), p. 128. Barthes's theory of "myths" is more thoroughly exposed in chapter 5.

4. VISIONS OF OTHERNESS AND INTERVENTIONISM IN BOSNIA, OR HOW THE WEST WAS WON AGAIN

1. Slovenian thinker and critic Slavoj Žižek has provided several such analyses. See for example his essay "Caught in Another's Dream in Bosnia," in *Why Bosnia? Writings on the Balkan War*, eds. Rabia Ali and Lawrence Lifschultz (Stony Creek, CN: Pamphleteer's Press, 1993). Later on in this chapter, I provide a more detailed reading of another essay by Žižek called "Bosnia." This essay is in a larger volume in which Žižek applies Lacanian psychoanalysis to questions of contemporary ideology. See Slavoj Žižek, *The Metastases of Enjoyment: Six Essays on Woman and Causality* (New York: Verso, 1994).

2. The fatal question, from the perspective of the West as superego (as that in relation to which identity is formed), could be reworded as follows: "Hey guys, remember that no matter what you're doing, your fighting is nothing more than a classical post–cold war case of ethnic conflict and national self-determination that has gone real bad!" This is the way the Bosnian conflict has to be understood in/by the West.

3. For the ex-Yugoslavian actors of this war, the imaginary core of Bosnia-as-conflict is composed of a blend of myths and realities created over centuries of common and divided history.

4. This is a point that Renata Salecl notes as well. Salecl writes that in the West, with the help of the media, "traumas hundreds of years old are being replayed and acted out, so that, in order to understand the roots of the conflict, one has to know not only the history of Yugoslavia, but the entire history of the Balkans. . . . [o]ne can only patiently try to grasp the background of the savage spectacle, alien to our civilized system of values." See Renata Salecl, *The Spoils of Freedom* (New York: Routledge, 1994), p. 13.

5. Jean Baudrillard, *The Perfect Crime*, trans. Chris Turner (New York: Verso, 1996), p. 133.

6. Ibid., p. 134.

7. As Baudrillard puts it. See ibid.

8. Stjepan Meštrović has noted the importance of vision in the Western configuration of the Bosnian conflict and human crisis. Eager to blame the West for its so-called lack of responsibility and communitarian sense in the Bosnian crisis, Meštrović has chosen to find fault with what he calls the apathetic condition of "postmodern voyeurism." Meštrović bemoans the fact that what he sees as being a dominant global context of postmodern fictions and visions has led humankind astray and away from a necessary sense of moral duty and ethical responsibility. See Stjepan Meštrović, *The Balkanization of the West: The Confluence of Postmodernism and Postcommunism* (New York: Routledge, 1994).

9. The photographic exhibit could be seen at the Harold Washington Library Center in Chicago in June–July 1994. Photo Perspectives, a web site that functions as a virtual art gallery by exhibiting several photo displays on the internet, has been showcasing *Faces of Sorrow* for the past three years. One may access the site at www.i3tele.com/photoperspectivesmuseum/facesofsorrow.html.

10. Ibid., at web site address.

11. Slavoj Žižek, *Metastases of Enjoyment*, pp. 210–11.

12. Ibid., p. 211.

13. Or, as Žižek puts it, the other is prevented from entering our space of enjoyment. Or, vice versa, we remain blind to the potential presence of the other's enjoyment, a notion that recent immigration issues in Western states, for instance, have given more credence to. See Slavoj Žižek, *Tarrying with the Negative: Kant, Hegel, and the Critique of Ideology* (Durham, NC: Duke University Press, 1993).

14. Slavoj Žižek, *Metastases of Enjoyment*, p. 211.

15. Ibid.

16. I am aware of the fact that my reading of Žižek is provocative, polemical, and controversial and that, as such, it may differ from the way Žižek has recently been used in critical international relations circles. Nevertheless, my reading is motivated by Žižek's own text. I do not claim that my reading is the only adequate interpretation of Žižek's text, that it is the right way of reading Žižek. Simply, it is one of many possible and textually based readings that his text offers. For a different interpretation of Žižek on the question of humanitarianism, see Jenny Edkins, "Legality with a Vengeance: Famines and Humanitarian Relief in 'Complex Emergencies,'" *Millennium: Journal of International Studies* 25, no. 3 (winter 1996): 547–75.

17. Žižek, *Metastases*, p. 211.

18. I have already reflected on this Lacanian tenet in chapter 3.

19. As Žižek mentions in an earlier essay, "[t]he principal obstacle to peace in the former Yugoslavia is not 'archaic ethnic passions,' but the innocent gaze of Europe fascinated by the spectacle of these passions." See Slavoj Žižek, "Caught in Another's Dream in Bosnia," pp. 238–39.

20. Žižek, *Metastases*, p. 214 (Žižek's emphasis).

21. In *Looking Awry: An Introduction to Jacques Lacan through Popular Culture* (Cambridge, MA: MIT Press, 1992), Žižek defines postmodernism as "the 'deconstruction' of [the] claim to universality, from Nietzsche to 'poststructuralism'; the endeavor to prove that this claim to universality is necessarily, constitutively 'false,' that it masks a particular network of power relations; that universal reason is as such, in its very form, 'repressive' and 'totalitarian'; that its truth claim is nothing but an effect of a series of rhetorical figures." See *Looking Awry*, p. 141. This definition is, no doubt,

everything you wanted to know about postmodernism but were afraid to ask Foucault, Derrida, Deleuze, Lyotard, or Baudrillard. Unwilling to read each of these contemporary thinkers in their particular textual contexts, Žižek operates an ideological weld (which in his vocabulary is rephrased as postmodernism or postmodernity) that is nothing more than a bad caricature of the epistemological moment marked by these key thinkers. All the catchy postmodern terms are there (deconstruction, Nietzsche, poststructuralism, network of power relations, etc.) but Žižek does not appear to show any clear understanding of what these terms signify and what precise role they play in the so-called postmodern episteme. Thus, postmodernism is reduced to an anti-Enlightenment project that seeks to "prove" that universal reason is a "false truth." It is of course not clear who Žižek has in mind when he offers such a statement but, as was shown in the postmodern readings performed in the previous chapters, there is no such thing as an obvious will to uncover or unmask false meanings in postmodernism. Not bound by reason, science, and positivism, postmodern thinkers have nothing to prove. In this sense, their works are not only critical but, more importantly, open up a vast field of cultural, political, philosophical, and literary dispersion in the margins of criticism but still within everyday culture, politics, philosophy, and writing. Žižek's definition (but, once again, it is a weld not a definition) is all the more dubious as, later, he identifies Habermas—a contemporary thinker who himself seeks to demarcate his thought from the postmodern trend—as the archetypal postmodern philosopher.

22. Postmodernism can rather be seen, in my opinion, as a context of imminent and immanent enjoyment. Culture is free, available, and ripe for the picking from whatever subject/object position you select, and, to some degree, even when it has been selected for you.

23. Stjepan Meštrović, *The Balkanization of the West*, p. 96.

24. Žižek, *Metastases*, p. 2 (Žižek's emphasis).

25. The term "reality" used here is very close to the Lacanian/Žižekian notion of the "real." As Jenny Edkins reminds us, the "real" is for Žižek "what cannot be symbolised or spoken of; it is in moments of terror and violence that we confront the real." See Jenny Edkins, "Legality with a Vengeance," p. 561, n. 79.

26. Peress's *Farewell to Bosnia* started as a photo exhibit tour that stopped in Washington, D.C.'s Corcoran Gallery; the Photomuseum Winterthur in Switzerland; the Museum of Contemporary Photography in Chicago; P.S. 1 Queens, New York City; the Rhode Island College Art Center; and New Langton Arts in San Francisco. Later, the exhibition was turned into a book. See Gilles Peress, *Farewell to Bosnia* (New York: Scalo, 1994). Peress's photographic collection on Bosnia was also made available by the "Picture Projects" group (a showcase for documentary photography)

on the Internet. There, curators Alison Cornyn, Sue Johnson, and Chris Vail juxtaposed some of Peress's photos with his text, which, in the book, appears at the end under the form of a diary or letters sent from Bosnia by Peress himself to some of his friends back in western European countries. In this exhibit/book/Internet interactive display, Peress tours Bosnia and its spectacle of destruction, displacement, misery, and death through the lens of his camera. His shots are at once realistically brutal and eerily shocking and unexpected.

27. Gilles Peress, *Farewell to Bosnia*, p. 161.

28. Ibid.

29. Ibid.

30. Ibid.

31. When *Farewell to Bosnia* came to the Museum of Contemporary Photography in Chicago in July 1994, Peress organized the shots by theme (refugees, mutilated bodies, etc.) as they now appear in the book, tacked the unframed pictures directly on the wall, and insisted on giving an appearance of density. Peress's installation sought to convey a message of pain and responsibility, one that was supposed to show the West that, in Bosnia, "its old traumas [were] being replayed again and again," as Žižek puts it. See "Caught in Another's Dream in Bosnia," p. 238.

32. I recently came across Peress's more recent photojournalistic account of the 1994 humanitarian crisis in Rwanda. As in *Farewell to Bosnia*, Peress's images from Rwanda (in a volume entitled *The Silence*) are a frank, blunt, and honest depiction of the massacres. The redeeming aspect of the pictures is emphasized too. The messianic/sacrificial posture of Peress's (photographic) gaze in *The Silence* is even more forceful than it is in *Farewell to Bosnia*. To underline the messianic effect, the pictures have been organized in three subsections (which according to Peress represent the three main stages of the Rwandan crisis) that are titled "The Sin," "Purgatory," and "The Judgment." In Rwanda, as in Bosnia, Peress is at once the messiah, the redeemer, and, perhaps, the final judge. See Gilles Peress, *The Silence* (New York: Scalo, 1995).

33. Baudrillard, *The Perfect Crime*, p. 111. Chris Turner, who translated Baudrillard's *Perfect Crime*, uses the term "otherness" every time Baudrillard refers to "altérité." I believe that it is more accurate, both to the original French text and to the English translation of the notion, to use the term "alterity." As such, I will continue to refer to Turner's translation but add alterity in brackets every time "otherness" is used.

34. Ibid., p. 112.

35. Trio's work has been shown in Western capitals over the past five years. As many other photographic or artistic representations of the Bosnian conflict, Trio's display called *Pop Art from Sarajevo* was available on the

Internet in several sites. One can still access their work at www.wmin.ac.uk/ media/sarajevo, or through Goran Sipek's web-page at www.geocities.com/ sunsetstrip/9414/trio.html, where Trio's work appears under the rubric "Trio: Postcards from War." To my knowledge, Trio's work has not been published in any other print form.

36. Situationism is a critical moment/movement derived from the thought and work of 1960s intellectuals like Guy Debord, Giuseppe Pinot-Gallizio, and Asger Jorn. Peter Wollen notes that the Situationist International (SI) "embarked on a number of artistic activities. Artists were to break down the divisions between individual art forms and to create *situations,* constructed encounters and creatively lived moments in specific urban settings, instances of a critically transformed everyday life" (Wollen's emphasis). See Peter Wollen, "Bitter Victory: The Art and Politics of the Situationist International," in *On the Passage of a Few People through a Rather Brief Moment in Time: The Situationist International, 1957–1972,* ed. Elisabeth Sussman (Cambridge, MA: MIT Press, 1991), p. 22. The practice of artistic *détournement* brought forward by the Situationists was a reappropriation, recycling, and deviation of preexisting works, elements, objects into what often looked like a total pirating act, an arbitrary collage of previously foreign elements to an integral piece. As Thomas Crow notes though, this practice of "turning the world upside down" was above all intended to be festive. See Thomas Crow, *The Rise of the Sixties: American and European Art in an Era of Dissent* (New York: Harry Abrams, 1996), p. 52.

37. Baudrillard, *The Perfect Crime,* pp. 132–41.

38. Ibid., pp. 132–33.

39. Apart perhaps from Victor Segalen's work on exoticism. See Marc Guillaume and Jean Baudrillard, *L'altérité radicale* [Radical alterity] (Paris: Descartes & Cie., 1994).

40. An ideal marked by the figure of the always already unmasterable alien perhaps.

41. Jean Baudrillard, "Plastic Surgery for the Other," Trans. François Debrix, *C-Theory: Theory, Technology and Culture* 19 (1995), article 33.

42. Baudrillard, *The Perfect Crime,* p. 112.

43. See Zlatko Dizdarević, *Sarajevo: A War Journal* (New York: Henry Holt, 1994), pp. 151–53.

44. Baudrillard, *The Perfect Crime,* p. 133.

45. Jean Baudrillard, *Le crime parfait* [The perfect crime] (Paris: Galilée, 1995). Despite the fact that Baudrillard's *Perfect Crime* has been translated into English by Chris Turner (I have generally used his translation), I have found it preferable to offer my own translation of this paragraph. The English translation by Chris Turner is very accurate, but, to my mind, it does not render the sharpness of Baudrillard's argument well

enough. This is, however, not a categorical or ontological statement about Turner's otherwise fine translation. It is rather nothing more than a matter of personal (aesthetic?) preference.

46. See Noel Malcolm, *Bosnia: A Short History*, 2nd ed. (New York: New York University Press, 1996), p. 223.

47. See Daniel Plesch, "An Introduction to the Bosnian Conflict," in *The ACCESS Issue Packet on Bosnia-Herzegovina*, ed. Matthew Hingham, Michael Mercurio, and Steven Ghezzi (Washington, DC: ACCESS Publications, 1996), p. 5.

48. Malcolm, *Bosnia: A Short History*, p. 227.

49. Plesch, "An Introduction to the Bosnian Conflict," p. 6.

50. The role of a reunified Germany in such a context was fundamental. Trying to show the rest of Europe that it had recovered a sense of identity/unity, Germany sought to assert its position by becoming more active in foreign affairs. One of its first major international decisions as a newly reunified nation was to recognize the independence of Slovenia, Croatia, and Bosnia.

51. Plesch, "An Introduction to the Bosnian Conflict," p. 6.

52. Malcolm, *Bosnia: A Short History*, p. 230.

53. Christopher Bennett, *Yugoslavia's Bloody Collapse: Causes, Course, and Consequences* (New York: New York University Press, 1995), p. 179.

54. Bennett, *Yugoslavia's Bloody Collapse*, p. 186.

55. Ibid.

56. Malcolm, *Bosnia: A Short History*, p. 231.

57. Bennett, *Yugoslavia's Bloody Collapse*, p. 187.

58. See Charles Lane, "Dateline Sarajevo: Besieged," in *The Black Book of Bosnia*, ed. Nader Mousavizadeh (New York: Harper Collins, 1996), pp. 71–73.

59. Even though, when UNPROFOR was initially deployed in Croatia, its headquarters had already been established in Sarajevo, perhaps as a telling sign of things to come.

60. See Spyros Economides and Paul Taylor, "Former Yugoslavia," in *The New Interventionism, 1991–1994: United Nations Experience in Cambodia, Former Yugoslavia and Somalia*, ed. John Mayall (New York: Cambridge University Press, 1996), p. 67.

61. Ibid.

62. Plesch, "An Introduction to the Bosnian Conflict," p. 7.

63. David Rieff notes that, even though "some of the suffering was being alleviated thanks to the heroic efforts on the part of the United Nations military and UNHCR personnel," the UN's actions were limited and sometimes caused more damage than good. Rieff continues: "[T]he humanitarian disaster was only a symptom of the political disaster. It was a vicious

circle. The UN fed people and allowed them to be shelled; the Security Council declared safe-havens whose safety UNPROFOR was neither disposed nor militarily capable of guaranteeing; and UNHCR sent protection officers into the field knowing that they could not protect. They were, as the bitter Zagreb joke went, 'eunuchs at the orgy.'" See David Rieff, *Slaughterhouse: Bosnia and the Failure of the West* (New York: Simon & Schuster, 1995), p. 120.

64. See Economides and Taylor, "Former Yugoslavia," p. 75.

65. For the text of these resolutions, one may refer to *The ACCESS Issue Packet on Bosnia-Herzegovina,* p. 49.

66. Economides and Taylor, "Former Yugoslavia," p. 85.

67. See Plesch, "An Introduction to the Bosnian Conflict," p. 7.

68. The United Nations's inability to protect the "safe-areas" prompted Sarajevo journalist Zlatko Dizdarević to write that "it is hard to ignore that another illusionary bubble has burst here in Sarajevo and maybe even farther, beyond Sarajevo. This illusion we called the UNPROFOR, or, loosely translated, the United Nations protection and peace-keeping force in the former Yugoslavia." See Dizdarević, *Sarajevo: A War Journal,* p. 48.

69. Plesch, "An Introduction to the Bosnian Conflict," p. 8.

70. See Charles Lane, "Dateline Bihac: Picked Pocket," in *The Black Book of Bosnia,* ed. Nader Mousavizadeh, pp. 108–12.

71. See Tom Hundley, "Defiant Serbs Round up More UN Hostages," *Chicago Tribune,* May 29, 1995.

72. See Charles Lane, "Dateline Zagreb: The Fall of Srebrenica," in *The Black Book of Bosnia,* ed. Nader Mousavizadeh, pp. 116–24.

73. Plesch, "An Introduction to the Bosnian Conflict," p. 8.

74. Ibid.

75. The Bosnian conflict has seen a succession of peace plans that, for different reasons, have been rejected. The Lisbon Agreement of November 1991, prior to the exacerbation of the conflict in Bosnia, already proposed to create three ethnically based cantons under a loose confederate structure (rejected by the Bosnian Muslims). The "Vance-Owen Plan" in August 1992 offered to create ten provinces with a weak decentralized government headed by a tripartite presidency (rejected by Karadžić but accepted by Milošević). The "Contract Group Plan," sponsored by Germany, France, Britain, the United States, and Russia, suggested a territorial division of Bosnia on a 51 percent Muslim-Croat versus 49 percent Serb basis (rejected by the Serbs). Interestingly, the Dayton Peace Agreements were a combination of all these previous plans. In 1995, with the burden of four years of war, the weight of economic sanctions, and the isolation of Belgrade, it became easier for the parties to the conflict, especially the Serbs, to accept the West's conditions. For more on the different peace plans, see Plesch, "An

Introduction to the Bosnian Conflict," pp. 8–9; and Economides and Taylor, "Former Yugoslavia," pp. 74–75.

76. The first elections took place in September 1996. These were general elections in charge of deciding the composition of Bosnia's new "national" institutions. This electoral process created a tripartite executive structure supposedly representative of the three national groups. This election played a symbolic more than a political function (particularly for the West). One year later, on September 13 and 14, 1997, municipal elections took place to elect mayors and municipal councils. As the state was and is still seen by many in Bosnia as an artificial entity, municipal councils have, in effect, a lot of power. The decisions taken by the councils in villages and towns have a more direct effect on the Bosnian population. This is the reason why the municipal elections were the object of intense local rivalries between the various nationalist parties. See Anna Husarska, "Polling Alone," *New Republic*, October 13, 1997, p. 18.

77. In *An Agenda for Peace*, Boutros-Ghali simply defined peacemaking as a strategy of interventionism situated "[b]etween the tasks of seeking to prevent conflict and keeping the peace." Peacemaking appeared to refer to a more active mode of intervention (unlike peacekeeping, perhaps more passive) that would "bring hostile parties to an agreement." Yet, Boutros-Ghali refused to envisage peacemaking outside of peacekeeping. Confusing the issue even further, Boutros-Ghali affirmed that peacemaking, whatever it is, was a logical continuation of peacekeeping and declared that, after all, "there may not be a dividing line between peacemaking and peacekeeping." See Boutros-Ghali, *An Agenda for Peace*, pp. 51–57. As was mentioned in chapter 1, Boutros-Ghali purposefully sought to blur the boundaries between the different UN interventionist strategies. Hoping to give the UN an appearance of power and control in a post–cold war era, Boutros-Ghali introduced vacuous notions (peacekeeping, peacemaking, peacebuilding, etc.), which were meant to simulate force in its absence. A few years later, after the obvious failure of peacekeeping/making in Bosnia, Boutros-Ghali wrote a "Supplement to an Agenda for Peace" in which he introduced yet another deliberately confusing and undefined notion, "multifunctional peacekeeping." Unlike peacekeeping or peacemaking, multifunctional peacekeeping was not so much intended to be a simulation of forceful intervention as it was meant to be an a posteriori justification of the UN's (failed) missions in Somalia and Bosnia. See Boutros-Ghali, *An Agenda for Peace*, 2nd ed., p. 11.

78. This was achieved through Resolution 770, which "authorized UNPROFOR to take 'all measures necessary,' including the use of military forces, to ensure the delivery of humanitarian aid." See Richard Caplan, "Making and Keeping the Peace in the Former Yugoslavia," in *A Global Agenda: Issues before the 49th General Assembly of the United Nations*, ed.

John Tessitore and Susan Woolfson (New York: University Press of America, 1994), p. 9. Caplan also gives another reason for the choice of the term peacemaking (instead of peacekeeping) in Bosnia. Caplan writes that "UNPROFOR's functions [were] many and diverse, but peacekeeping, strictly speaking, [was] not among them, there being no peace to keep" (ibid., p. 17).

79. Such an interpretation is congruent with Economides and Taylor's line of thinking as well. They suggest that, in Bosnia, the term *UN* was used in a very flexible and polysemic fashion. See Economides and Taylor, "Former Yugoslavia," p. 79. If the UN, as Economides and Taylor suggest, may be regarded as a polysemic notion, its peacemaking/keeping strategies can also figure as tropes deliberately put to plural uses.

80. As Caplan notes, the UN's strategy was to try "to deflect world attention from the Bosnian conflict." See Caplan, "Making and Keeping the Peace in the Former Yugoslavia," p. 7. Such a view is congruent with the Žižekian analysis exposed above and, specifically, with the notion that the West cannot face the "actual gaze" of the Bosnian victim.

81. Indeed, as Felice Gaer puts it, the UNPROFOR mission would try to "reply to bombardments and air power could be used, but the Secretary-General could not obtain troops to police and protect the safe areas." See Felice Gaer, "Making and Keeping the Peace in the Former Yugoslavia," in *A Global Agenda: Issues before the 48th General Assembly of the United Nations, 1993–94* ed., ed. John Tessitore and Susan Woolfson (New York: University Press of America, 1993), p. 13.

82. Jean Baudrillard, *Simulations* (New York: Semiotext[e], 1983), p. 38.

83. Zlatko Dizdarević, *Sarajevo: A War Journal,* p. 51.

84. Economides and Taylor, "Former Yugoslavia," p. 72.

85. Felice Gaer, "Making and Keeping the Peace in the Former Yugoslavia," p. 13.

86. Caplan suggests that the February 5, 1994, mortar attack on a Sarajevo market, one of the most mediatically covered events of the Bosnian conflict, was the turning point. Caplan writes that this event "galvanized world leaders into action" ("Making and Keeping the Peace in the Former Yugoslavia," p. 13), and indirectly led to NATO's sudden decision to down Serb airplanes violating the no-fly zone near Banja Luka.

87. As Weiss, Forsythe, and Coate recognize, NATO's creation of a "rapid-reaction force" in the summer of 1995 was the turning point in the conflict and in the Western strategy of interventionism. See Thomas Weiss, David P. Forsythe, and Roger Coate, *The United Nations and Changing World Politics,* 2nd ed. (Boulder, CO: Westview, 1997), pp. 84–85.

88. Although NATO's operations took place within the diplomatic framework established by the UN's Security Council resolutions, NATO was

truly in charge. A de facto transfer of authority had taken place between the UN's Security Council and the North Atlantic Council. This was clearly marked in the spring of 1994 when the North Atlantic Council took the decision to attack Serb positions by means of air strikes, even if, as mentioned above, it took another full year for NATO's air power to have a measurable impact on the actors of the conflict. See North Atlantic Treaty Organization, "NATO's Peacekeeping in the Former Yugoslavia," *NATO Basic Fact Sheet No. 4* (September 1996).

89. Larry George, "The Fair Fame of the Dead: The Precession of War Simulacra and the Reconstitution of Post–Cold War Conservatism," in *Rhetorical Republic: Governing Representations in American Politics,* ed. Frederick Dolan and Thomas Dumm (Amherst: University of Massachusetts Press, 1993), p. 65.

90. Girard argues that, in many societies, scapegoating is an essential component of ritualistic sacrifice. Girard writes that the term scapegoat emerged "in connection with a large number of rituals . . . [that] were based on the belief that 'guilt' or 'sufferings' could be transferred from some community to a ritually designated victim, often an animal but sometimes a human being, the Greek pharmakos, for instance." See René Girard, "Generative Scapegoating," in *Violent Origins: Ritual Killing and Cultural Formation,* ed. Robert Hamerton-Kelly (Stanford, CA: Stanford University Press, 1987), pp. 73–74.

91. Adela Yarbro Collins defines catharsis in a medical context. Catharsis is "the removal from the body of alien matter that is painful and the restoration of the system to its *normal state.*" Adela Yarbro Collins, *Crisis and Catharsis: The Power of the Apocalypse* (Philadelphia: Westminster Press, 1984), p. 153 (my emphasis).

92. René Girard, *Violence and the Sacred* (Baltimore: Johns Hopkins University Press, 1993), p. 286.

93. Ibid., p. 287.

94. Ibid.

95. Ibid., p. 288.

96. Dizdarević, *Sarajevo: A War Journal,* p. 48.

97. See Hundley, "Defiant Serbs Round up More UN Hostages," *Chicago Tribune,* May 29, 1995.

98. A case in point was Bill Clinton's overt opposition to Boutros-Ghali. In the summer of 1996, the State Department repeatedly made clear the U.S. administration's decision to veto Boutros-Ghali's reelection as UN secretary-general. See Lee Michael Katz, "UN Chief Tries to Survive Barrage of US Criticism," *USA Today,* September 30, 1996.

99. Girard, *Violence and the Sacred,* p. 288.

100. Ibid.

101. Since the Dayton Agreements, the focus in Western diplomatic circles has been placed on NATO for questions of international security. Western states, the United States in particular, are now concerned about the financing of NATO's operations in Europe, about its expansion, both in terms of new states desirous of joining the organization, and in terms of possibly extending the geographical domain of NATO's territorial competence. This does not mean, however, that NATO will all of a sudden become a global peacekeeping substitute for the UN. In fact, even if Western diplomats are currently suggesting that NATO's range of action should be extended, NATO's activities, per the North Atlantic Treaty of 1949, are by and large limited to the Europe, North America, and North Atlantic geographic area.

102. U.S. Department of State, *NATO's Role in Bosnia and the Dayton Peace Accords,* Remarks by Warren Christopher and NATO Secretary General Javier Solana (1995), p. 1.

103. Baudrillard, *The Perfect Crime,* p. 137.

104. Ibid., p. 148.

105. Girard, *Violence and the Sacred,* p. 290.

106. See Louis Althusser, "Ideology and Ideological State Apparatuses," (1971).

5. A TASTE OF THEIR OWN MEDICINE

1. It is in this spirit that Bernard Kouchner, former French secretary of state in charge of humanitarian action and one of the founders of the Médecins sans Frontières medical nongovernmental organization, once wrote that "TV news and humanitarian action are remedies for extreme sufferings." See Bernard Kouchner, "Le mouvement humanitaire: Questions à Bernard Kouchner," (The humanitarian movement: Questions to Bernard Kouchner), in *Le débat,* (November–December 1991), p. 35 (my translation).

2. Roland Barthes, *Mythologies,* trans. Annette Lavers (New York: Noonday Press, 1972), p. 18.

3. One of Kouchner's most beloved mottos is "l'ingérence c'est d'abord le regard" (interference is first of all a gaze). See Kouchner, "Le mouvement humanitaire," p. 30 (my translation).

4. Barthes, *Mythologies,* pp. 128–29.

5. Ibid., p. 128.

6. Kouchner, "Le mouvement humanitaire," p. 35 (my translation).

7. Barthes, *Mythologies,* p. 116. I have italicized this quote and the following one on purpose in order to differentiate my use of Barthes's text here from a simple quotation. Indeed, the effect I am searching for here is that of a dialogue between my reading of the humanitarian myth and Barthes's master text/theory on "mythology." Thus, I am inserting Barthes's text, not as a

validation of my myth reading, but as an addition/supplement to the humanitarian myth.

8. Kouchner, "Le mouvement humanitaire," p. 32 (my translation).

9. For a detail of the events that took place in 1994 in Rwanda, see appendix.

10. Alain Destexhe, *Rwanda: Essai sur le génocide* (Bruxelles: Editions Complexe, 1994).

11. Kouchner, "Le Mouvement Humanitaire," p. 32.

12. Kouchner, Ibid., p. 37 (my translation).

13. Barthes, *Mythologies,* pp. 129–31.

14. Ibid., pp. 109–10.

15. Rony Brauman, *Devant le mal: Rwanda, un génocide en direct* (Faced with evil: Rwanda, witnessing live a genocide) (Paris, Arléa, 1994), p. 78–80. Rony Brauman is a former director of Médecins sans Frontières.

16. Myth is for Brauman a reduction of humanitarian action. However, if one reads Barthes and his *Mythologies* closely, one does not have the impression that myth is a reductive practice. On the contrary, myth reworks what Barthes calls the "innocent object" in new and unexpected ways. Such is the work of ideology too. Ideology may seek to reduce an object to a specific meaning or use, but in so doing, it also takes the object beyond the supposedly natural conception people may have of the said object. Ideology is not a dead and inert practice. Through its recodings (and mythical mobilizations), it enhances the object by giving it novel forms (even if that sometimes means abusing the object as well).

17. Brauman, *Devant le mal,* p. 11.

18. Barthes, *Mythologies,* p. 128.

19. Brauman, *Devant le mal,* p. 83.

20. The rivalry between Kouchner and Brauman has often taken, in the French mediatico-politico-cultural landscape of the last five to ten years, the appearance of a struggle for supremacy among two popular public figures who try to convince the public of the veracity of their particular understanding of humanitarianism. This is well exemplified in a debate between Kouchner and Brauman organized by the weekly magazine *Le nouvel observateur* and entitled "Peut-on être ministre et militant humanitaire? Les 'French Doctors' et la politique" (Can one be a cabinet minister and a humanitarian activist at the same time? The 'French Doctors' and politics) (February 20–26, 1992). Among other things, Brauman doubts the fact that, once a humanitarian activist has decided to join a government or political organization, she/he will be able to serve humanitarian causes in an honest and disinterested fashion. The play of power will blind the humanitarian activist turned politician (and here represented by Kouchner). It is true that political aspirations may direct humanitarian action in strategic ways that may have

little to do with the victims. But Brauman is once again (as he was with his reading of the media) blind to the fact that, in his defense of pure humanitarian intervention, he places himself in a position of power and hegemony as well. He affirms himself as the supreme voice of the closed ideology of humanitarian activism that he seeks to represent. Like it or not, he becomes a moral leader, a powerful ideological figure.

21. Roland Barthes, *S/Z,* trans. Richard Miller, (New York: Noonday Press, 1974).

22. Ibid., p. 4.

23. Ibid., p. 5.

24. Augustine, *Political Writings,* trans. Michael W. Tkacz and Douglas Kries (Indianapolis: Hackett Publishing, 1994), p. 97.

25. International humanist and lawyer Jean Pictet traces the origins of humanitarianism to Christianity too. He notes that "Christ had preached love for one's neighbour and had raised this to the level of a universal principle. Human love should be a reflection of divine love—absolute and without motive. It should be extended to *everyone,* even to one's enemies. One should love one's neighbor for himself, without judging his merits and without expecting anything in return." See Jean Pictet, *Development and Principles of International Humanitarian Law* (Boston: Martinus Nijhoff, 1985), p. 12.

26. Which is often the case in the animal world, for example, where a fallen or weak animal is often abandoned by the rest of the herd.

27. Or, alternatively, the transmutation of God into human reason.

28. This decision about what is moral or not is, in practice, sanctioned by the "rule of the majority," as both Locke and Rousseau have stated. As Locke affirms, "[w]hen any number of men have so *consented to make one community or government,* they are thereby presently incorporated, and make *one body politic,* wherein the *majority* have a right to act and conclude the rest." See John Locke, *The Second Treatise of Government,* ed. C. B. Macpherson (Indianapolis: Hackett Publishing, 1980), p. 52.

29. Hobbes, *Leviathan,* p. 185.

30. As Hobbes demonstrated, the state is an "artificial" structure, created by individuals themselves to guarantee protection and defense, and whose sovereignty relies on coercion and codification (or, as Hobbes puts it, on a "right ordering of names").

31. This communitarian principle is summarized by Rousseau in the following statement: "Everyone can see that what unites any form of society is community of interests, and what disintegrates it is their conflict." See Jean-Jacques Rousseau, *A Lasting Peace through the Federation of Europe and the State of War,* trans. C. E. Vaughan (London: Constable and Company, 1917), p. 50.

32. This is, once again, what it means to be "forced to be free" as Rousseau maintains. See Rousseau, *The Social Contract,* p. 195.

33. In the contemporary context, Charles Taylor has reproduced such a rhetoric. Taylor's notion of the community as a "web of interlocution" rests on the premise that "[o]ne is a self only among other selves" and that "[a] self can never be described without reference to those who surround it." See Charles Taylor, *Sources of the Self: The Making of the Modern Identity* (Cambridge, MA: Harvard University Press, 1989), pp. 35 and 40. For Taylor, the "moral space" of a language community is what protects us from individualism and develops a moral behavior in such a linguistically sutured collective.

34. Hugo Grotius, *De jure belli ac pacis,* ed. J. Brown Scott (New York: Oceana Publications, 1964), p. 64.

35. For Grotius, international law must be the expression of the "law of nature," which "is a dictate of right reason, which points out that an act, according as it is or is not in conformity with rational nature, has in it a quality of moral baseness and moral necessity; and that, in consequence, such an act is either forbidden or enjoined by the author of nature, God." See Grotius, Ibid., pp. 38–39. Grotius cannot yet dissociate human nature from the presence of God as creator.

36. Henry Dunant, *A Memory of Solferino* (Washington, DC: American Red Cross Publication, 1939), p. 86. Dunant conceives of the "Red Cross" (the name "Red Cross" is derived from the emblem that the relief workers would wear in order to be easily recognized during a battle) as a "peace machine" in times of war. Its neutrality is mostly medical and its charitable interventions are exclusively limited to this domain.

37. According to Dunant, the slogan "tutti fratelli" was coined by the Italian women in the town of Castiglione who followed Dunant in his effort to bring relief and moral comfort to the dying soldiers. See ibid., p. 54.

38. As Max Huber, former president of the Red Cross, indicated, the Red Cross is a "working collectivity." See Max Huber, *The Good Samaritan: Reflections on the Gospel and the Work of the Red Cross* (London: Gollancz, 1945), p. 73.

39. Jean Lossier, *Les civilisations et le service du prochain* (Civilizations and assistance to one's neighbor) (Paris: Le Vieux Colombier, 1958), p. 218 (my translation).

40. As Jean Pictet recalls, sixteen nations met for a conference in October 1863 that created the Red Cross upon the ideological and ethical foundations exposed by Dunant. The following year, a diplomatic conference adopted the Convention of Geneva for the Amelioration of the Condition of the Wounded in Armies in the Field. This Convention, directly influenced by the Red Cross principles, is, normatively speaking, "the starting point for

the whole of humanitarian law." See Pictet, *Development and Principles of International Humanitarian Law,* p. 26.

41. Dunant, *A Memory of Solferino,* p. 17.

42. Ibid., p. 55.

43. The notion of "humanitarian force" is expressed by Dunant himself when he declares that "the moral sense of the importance of human life . . . [and] the human desire to lighten a little the torments of all [the] poor wretches . . . create a kind of energy which gives one a positive craving." Ibid.

44. As T. O. Elias has shown, much of the UN's work in the domain of humanitarian assistance since its creation has been geared toward incorporating the Red Cross principles into more rigid and controllable structures. See T. O. Elias, *New Horizons in International Law* (Dobbs Ferry, NY: Oceana Publications, 1979), pp. 195–96.

45. See ibid., p. 185. This system of peace is primarily based, as Michael Akehurst has pointed out, on the principle contained in Article 2(4) of the UN Charter which states that UN member states must "refrain in their international relations from the threat or use of force against the territorial integrity or political independence of any State, or in any other manner inconsistent with the purposes of the United Nations." See Michael Akehurst, "Humanitarian Intervention," in *Interventions in World Politics,* ed. Hedley Bull (Oxford: Clarendon Press, 1984), p.104.

46. Elias, *New Horizons in International Law,* p. 186.

47. Akehurst, "Humanitarian Intervention," p. 105 (Akehurst's emphasis).

48. Another major source of UN-sponsored humanitarian law is what is today known as the "Nuremberg Principles." These principles seek to protect the potential victims of genocides and massive racial killings. See Elias, *New Horizons in International Law,* p. 185.

49. James Ingram, "The Future Architecture for International Humanitarian Assistance," in *Humanitarianism across Borders: Sustaining Civilians in Times of War,* ed. Thomas G. Weiss and Larry Minear (Boulder, CO: Lynne Rienner, 1993), p. 172.

50. Michel Veuthey, "Assessing Humanitarian Law," in *Humanitarianism across Borders,* ed. Thomas G. Weiss and Larry Minear, p. 133.

51. The early 1990s also saw the creation of a new humanitarian agency within the UN system, the DHA (Department of Humanitarian Affairs), whose initial mandate was to alleviate the task of the UNHCR. In January 1998, the DHA was renamed the United Nations Office for the Coordination of Humanitarian Affairs (OCHA) with a task of enforcing the "coordination of humanitarian emergency response." See "Bulletin of the UN" online at www.reliefweb.int. For more on the relationship between the UN's

newly created humanitarian agencies and the UN High Commissioner for Refugees, see Thomas Weiss and Amir Pasic, "Reinventing UNHCR: Enterprising Humanitarians in the Former Yugoslavia, 1991–1995," *Global Governance* 3, no. 1 (1997): 41–57.

52. Larry Minear and Thomas G. Weiss, *Humanitarian Politics,* Headline Series, no. 304 (New York: Foreign Policy Association, 1995), p. 23.

53. Political neutrality and ideological independence are claimed by most NGOs. This claim also gives them a special status in the production of knowledge. Because they do not represent anyone's interests, humanitarian NGOs present themselves as the "objective" witnesses and the truthful narrators of the humanitarian situations in which they intervene. This certainly explains the multitude of descriptive accounts of humanitarian crises provided by NGOs' representatives or special envoys. On Rwanda specifically, see, for example, Oxfam's member Guy Vassal-Adams, *Rwanda: An Agenda for International Action* (Oxford: Oxfam Publications, 1994), or former MSF member Alain Destexhe's *Rwanda: Essai sur le génocide,* mentioned earlier. As suggested above, these "expert" testimonies can be read as myths that are just as interesting for the ideologies they display as for the facts they relate.

54. Médecins sans Frontières, *Populations en danger, 1995: Rapport annuel sur les crises majeures et l'action humanitaire* (Populations in danger 1995: Annual report on the major crises and on humanitarian action), (Paris: La Découverte, 1995), p. 174 (my translation).

55. Ibid.

56. Ibid. (my translation).

57. Ibid. (my translation).

58. This is the view specifically expressed by Brauman, who argues that in the case of Rwanda in particular, a lot of the deaths could have been avoided if the members of humanitarian NGOs had clearly stated who the torturers were, that is, that the Hutus were basically responsible for the massacres of the Tutsis. From this fundamentalist perspective, Rwanda certainly inaugurates yet another era of humanitarianism. It is an era in which the rescuers transform themselves into justice-makers and defenders of universal morality. According to this ideology, humanitarianism is not simply a neutral altruistic mission. It is the first step along a course that, ultimately, seeks to impose human morality as a normative and disciplinary construct.

59. Hippocratic medicine emerged as a direct response to early religious (Christian in particular) thinking. Whereas the Christian attitude toward disease and death remained fatalistic and stoic (it was God's will), "Greek" medicine tried to find durable remedies to human suffering. With the Hippocratic turn, it is no longer a question of making suffering more bearable and understandable to the injured/diseased. It is rather a matter of scientifically

developing techniques that can eradicate injury and illness. This philosophy of medical treatment was developed by Hippocrates. Hippocrates then took it upon himself to teach the new approach to his pupils. With his emphasis on teaching and showing, Hippocrates can be taken to be the master of clinical medicine. See D. Runes and T. Kiernan, eds., *Hippocrates: The Theory and Practice of Medicine* (New York: Philosophical Library, 1964).

60. As Hippocrates put it, keeping an oath of professional practice on behalf of the patient is an "art [of medicine], respected by all men, in all times." See Runes and Kiernan, ibid., p. x.

61. See Philippe Pinel, *The Clinical Training of Doctors: An Essay of 1793,* trans. and ed. Dora Weiner (Baltimore: Johns Hopkins University Press, 1980).

62. Ludmilla Jordanova, "Medicine and Genres of Display," in *Visual Display: Culture beyond Appearances,* ed. Lynne Cooke and Peter Wollen, Discussions on Contemporary Culture, no. 10 (Seattle: Bay Press, 1995), p. 203.

63. Ibid., pp. 206–7.

64. In this section, I take Médecins sans Frontières to be representative of the medico-humanitarian field in general. For this reason, I use the terms "medical humanitarianism," "MSF" or "the French Doctors" interchangeably.

65. Michel Foucault, *The Birth of the Clinic: An Archeology of Medical Perception,* trans. A. M. Sheridan Smith (New York: Vintage Books, 1973, p. 20.

66. Mary Ann Doane, *The Desire to Desire: The Woman's Film of the 1940s* (Bloomington, IN: Indiana University Press, 1987), p. 40.

67. Foucault, *The Birth of the Clinic,* pp. 165–66. The clinical symptom is thus perhaps a principle of vision that can be contrasted with the principle of panopticism, also described by Foucault (see chapter 2). Whereas the clinical symptom is a matter of "invisible visibility" (the doctor discovers and interprets signs on the body that are not visible to and understandable by anybody else), panopticism is a principle of visible invisibility.

68. Ibid., p. 166.

69. Witnessing is one of MSF's primordial duties. As Doris Schopper, president of the International Council of MSF, declares, "the responsibility to witness has an essential role to play, not only to inform about people whose very survival may be threatened, but to show how they can be helped to survive and to regain their human dignity." See Doris Schopper, preface to *World in Crisis: The Politics of Survival at the End of the 20th Century,* ed. Médecins sans Frontières (New York: Routledge, 1997), p. x.

70. Another blatant illustration of this phenomenon was offered in the fall of 1997 when one of MSF's members, Dr. Marcel Van Soest, testified in

front of the U.S. House of Representatives to denounce what MSF considered to be the genocide of Hutu refugees by Laurent Kabila's troops in the
former Zaire (soon to be renamed Democratic Republic of Congo) between
September 1996 and July 1997. On behalf of MSF, Van Soest presented to
the U.S. House the results of MSF's "post-mortem investigation" in the former Zaire. In this report, MSF argued that among Hutu refugees from
Rwanda who had found refuge in Zaire and, unfortunately, happened to be
in the path of Kabila's troops, only 17 percent of individuals survived. This
report, in turn, initiated an investigation by other nonmedical NGOs
(Human Rights Watch) and the UNHCR. See Stephen Smith, "Ex-Zaire:
MSF quantifie l'ampleur des massacres" (Former Zaire: MSF measures the
importance of the massacres), *Libération,* November 6, 1997.

71. See Médecins sans Frontières, *Populations in Danger, 1995,*
pp. 35–41; and Destexhe, *Rwanda: Essai sur le génocide,* pp. 45–72. The
United Nations officially spoke of the possibility of genocide through Security Council Resolution 935 on July 1, 1994. For more on this Resolution,
see appendix.

72. Médecins sans Frontières, *Populations in Danger, 1995,* p. 38.

73. Or, to use Foucault's phrasing, their "speaking eye" had become
"the servant of things and the master of truth." See *The Birth of the Clinic,*
pp. 114-15.

74. Brauman, *Devant le mal,* p. 20.

75. I am not suggesting that genocide is a normal situation. I am argu-
ing, rather, that genocide is a normalized sociopolitical concept that can be
measured, assessed, and compared. It has a set of specific variables (total destruction, violence, etc.) that are recognized and accepted by political and
social scientists. It is a standard variable that differs from other comparable
configurations of mass violence (holocaust, pogroms, revolutions, racial
purges, etc.). For more on these different normalized notions of mass violence and destruction, see Robert Melson, *Revolution and Genocide: On the
Origins of the Armenian Genocide and the Holocaust* (Chicago: University
of Chicago Press, 1992).

76. The same can be said about the former Zaire, particularly the eastern region of Goma which, in the summer of 1994, was taken over by
Rwandan refugees and international assistance teams. This part of Zaire became a "new" territory. Overnight, the population of the region was drasti-
cally altered by the influx of Hutu refugees. Furthermore, it became unclear
who held sovereign authority over that region as the international community appeared to assume a de facto jurisdiction in the camps.

77. The French even came up with their own geopolitical remapping
of Rwanda by creating a "security zone" (where Tutsi refugees inside
Rwanda would be temporarily protected), which later was transformed into

a "safe humanitarian zone." See Destexhe, *Rwanda: Essai sur le génocide,* pp. 78–80.

78. Michel Foucault, "Sécurité, territoire, et population," (Security, territory, and population), in *Résumé des cours* (Summary of lectures) (Paris: Juliard, 1989), p. 99 (my translation).

79. Frederick Cuny, "Humanitarian Assistance in a Post–Cold War Era," in *Humanitarianism across Borders,* ed. Thomas G. Weiss and Larry Minear, p. 164.

80. Ibid.

81. Or, as MSF lawyer Ed Schenkenberg van Mierop has put it, trying to explain the difference between MSF and the UN agencies, "the UN can only skim the surface of ponds, rather than drag out the monsters that lurk below." See Schenkenberg van Mierop, "Protection of Civilians in Conflict," in *World in Crisis,* ed. Médecins sans Frontières, p. 15.

82. Cuny, "Humanitarian Assistance in a Post–Cold War Era," p. 165.

83. As was argued in chapter 4, a similar substitute principle was at play in Bosnia. After the United Nations' strategy of deterrence and simulation had failed, NATO intervened and deployed more coercive means, something that the UN, by and large, had been unable to do.

84. Specifically after July 14, 1994, when the Rwandan conflict turned into a refugee problem. The UNHCR started to organize aid distribution and housing for the Hutu refugees in the camps in Zaire and Tanzania. See Destexhe, *Rwanda: Essai sur le génocide,* pp. 77–87.

85. See Thomas G. Weiss, "Overcoming the Somalia Syndrome: Operation Rekindle Hope?" *Global Governance* 1, no. 2 (1995): 171–87.

86. For the detail of these resolutions, see appendix.

87. Fredric Jameson, *The Ideologies of Theory: Essays, 1971–1986,* vol. 2 (Minneapolis: University of Minnesota Press, 1988); see Slavoj Žižek, *For They Know Not What They Do: Enjoyment as a Political Factor* (New York: Verso, 1991); and *Tarrying with the Negative: Kant, Hegel, and the Critique of Ideology* (Durham, NC: Duke University Press, 1993).

88. Both Žižek and Jameson agree that the mission performed by the vanishing mediator is first and foremost an exercise in illusion and make-believe. It does not matter if a change of ideology actually takes place as long as an illusion of change is rendered. Jameson gives a concrete historical example. He argues, on the basis of a reading of Max Weber, that Protestantism figured as a vanishing mediator, as an agent of change, for liberal capitalism. Protestantism is what allowed the passage from feudalism to capitalism. Riding on the back of Protestantism (at least in a German context), the bourgeois class took advantage of the Protestant ethic to criticize feudal modes of production and exploitation and finally take over. The Protestant ethic offered a space of transition/change for the bourgeois class

that, once the feudal system had been abandoned, turned the ethic into another mode of exploitation (Jameson, of course, subscribes to the Marxist reading of capital). See Jameson, *The Ideologies of Theory*, 2:25–26.

89. Žižek, *Tarrying with the Negative*, pp. 227–30.

90. Ibid., p. 231.

91. Žižek, *For They Know Not What They Do*, p. 183.

92. Perhaps the only two regions where its peacekeeping, because it had recourse to panopticism rather than direct enforcement, did not experience blatant failures.

93. John Mearsheimer's essay, "The False Promise of International Institutions," *International Security* 10, no. 3 (winter 1994–95), is emblematic of such a position.

94. Borrowed from the Marquis de Sade, "Philosophy in the Bedroom," in *The Marquis de Sade*, ed. and trans. R. Seaver and A. Wainhouse (New York: Grove Press, 1965), p. 296.

6. THEORIZING THE VISUAL

1. Philippe Quéau uses the distinction between high-fidelity and high-definition to refigure the opposition between representation and simulation. High-fidelity is a mode of visual expression governed by metaphorical representations, whereas high-definition is characterized by the precession of models. Quéau indicates that, with high-definition, "the image finally escapes the metaphorical domain and enters a universe where models prevail." Quéau continues: "We know that metaphors, visual or linguistic, seek to make up for the limitations of representational systems (in natural language or cinematographic discourse, for example) by offering analogies between the normal context of a word or picture and a new context in which the word or the picture is arbitrarily introduced. Such an arbitrary transfer has a heuristic value, but it also causes deplorable deviations and faces intrinsic limits. . . . [By contrast], a model gives a theory a more concrete, more experimental, and more tangible appearance without modifying or falsifying its abstract structure. The model realizes the theory without running the risk of losing its intelligible substance." See Philippe Quéau, *Le virtuel: Vertus et vertiges* (The virtual: Virtue and vertigo) (Paris: Champ Vallon, 1993), p. 32 [my translation].

2. I use the term "invisible visibility" as a way of distinguishing the visual simulation of surveillance from the visual simulation of peacekeeping. Both are techniques of simulation. But, whereas panopticism requires that discipline remain unseen (it cannot leave traces), peacekeeping as simulation requires the referentially invisible (because nonexistent) force of actors, like the UN, to be blatantly displayed. The most direct expression of "invisible visibility" is the practice of clinical witnessing, a substitute form of UN

peacekeeping deployed by the French Doctors in Rwanda. What clinical witnessing achieved was identifying and detailing specific signs of a problem on
a body politic (the Rwandan state, or what was left of it) where signs truly
proliferated and meaning was impossible to ascertain otherwise.

3. This line of argumentation is reminiscent of Avital Ronell's own
analysis of simulation and virtuality. Ronell writes that "in cyburbia [the
world of visually simulated/virtually constructed reality] there is always a
risk of blurring the distinction between simulation and the operational
world. . . . [T]here is still a tendency to retrofit the technological prosthesis
to a metaphysical subject: the sovereign subject of history, destiny's copilot.
In other words, the technological prosthesis would merely be an amplifier
and intensifier borrowed by a centered subject whose fragmentation is, as
they say, a simulation—that is, a device for *disavowing* fragmentation, self-
loss or, on another register, castration." What Ronell indicates is that the recourse to simulation and other virtual prosthetic devices is a way of denying/
disavowing reality (what she calls the "operational world"). In the perspective of post–cold war international relations, disciplinary liberalism is introduced as a prosthetic device of international practice that, through global
peacekeeping, seeks to make up for the ideological fragmentation of the
post–cold war world. See Avital Ronell, "Support Our Tropes II: Or, Why in
Cyburbia There Are a Lot of Cowboys," *Yale Journal of Criticism* 5, no. 2
(1992): 74 (Ronell's emphasis).

4. See Zlatko Dizdarević, *Sarajevo: A War Journal*, p. 48.

5. See James Mayall, *The New Interventionism, 1991–1994: United
Nations Experience in Cambodia, Former Yugoslavia, and Somalia*.

6. One can indeed read NATO and MSF as "virtual UNs." As substitutes for the UN, they strove to mobilize visual peacekeeping in the UN's absence. After the UN's operational accidents in Bosnia and Somalia, NATO
and MSF were, so to speak, the virtual presence of the UN. After all, as
Rony Brauman suggests, humanitarian NGOs like MSF "have been sucked
into a spirit of technicism and moralising conformity which is making them
look more and more like the UN." See Rony Brauman, foreword to *World
in Crisis: The Politics of Survival at the End of the 20th Century*, p. xxvi.

7. This notion is directly borrowed from Timothy Luke and Geróid Ó
Tuathail's essay, "Out of Time, Lost in Space: The Geopolitics of UN Safe
Havens, No Fly Zones, and Expeditionary Forces," *Review of International
Political Economy* (forthcoming).

8. Quéau, *Le virtuel*, p. 28.

9. Baudrillard refers to the architectural design of Early Renaissance
Italian palaces (as described by Machiavelli, for instance) to demonstrate
that power's strength is predicated upon simulation. Baudrillard writes that
"since Machiavelli, politicians have perhaps always known that the mastery

of a *simulated* space is the source of power, that the political is not a *real* activity or space, but a simulation model, whose manifestations are simply achieved effects. *The very secret of appearances* can be found in this blind spot in the palace, this secluded place of architecture and public life, which in a sense governs the whole, not by direct determination, but by a kind of internal reversion or abrogation of the rule secretly performed, as in primitive societies; a hole in reality or an ironic transfiguration, an exact simulacrum hidden at the heart of reality, which reality depends on in all of its operations." See Jean Baudrillard, *Selected Writings*, ed. Mark Poster (Stanford, CA: Stanford University Press, 1988), p. 158 (Baudrillard's emphases). For Baudrillard, power cannot be without its simulated presence (without simulating its presence), without covering the fact that it is perhaps nothing more than "a hole in reality." In *Forget Foucault*, Baudrillard adds that "[p]ower is no more held than a secret is extracted, for the secrecy of power is the same as that of the secret: it does not exist." Baudrillard concludes: "[o]n the other side of the cycle—the side of the decline of the real—only the *mise-en-scène* of the secret, or of power, is operational." See Jean Baudrillard, *Forget Foucault* (New York: Semiotext(e), 1987), p. 51 (Baudrillard's emphasis).

10. These analyses have often taken the form of challenges to the inside/outside, order/anarchy, national/international, North/South types of dichotomies that have long been relied upon by traditional conceptualizations of international politics. In chapter 1, we saw how realism and its vision of anarchy (through Hobbes) was premised on such a mode of thinking.

11. This perhaps echoes Hal Foster's intimation to both modernist and postmodernist scholars to rethink the notion of "critical distance," to refigure the critique that, sometimes in a same movement, re-marks and erases the space between "us" and "them." See Hal Foster, *The Return of the Real: The Avant-Garde at the End of the Century* (Cambridge, MA: MIT Press, 1996), p. 225.

12. I call it "post-postmodern" for lack of a better term. Such a theoretical and critical enterprise is still cognizant of (and faithful to) postmodern modes of thinking. Yet, it also seeks to take postmodernism beyond its safe representational (textual) confines of analysis by introducing the problematics of visuality and ideology. In this effort, the enterprise often chooses to fuse postmodern readings with more critical approaches to ideology.

Index

FRANÇOIS DEBRIX is assistant professor of international relations at Florida International University. He has published several articles on international politics, popular culture, and postmodern political theory in *Alternatives, Philosophy and Social Criticism, Postmodern Culture,* and *Peace Review.* Debrix also translated much of Jean Baudrillard's work for *C-Theory: Theory, Technology, and Culture.*